What is blogging?

Is it, as the estimable blogger's blogger John Band (www.johnband.org) once memorably described it, 'a bunch of midgets fighting over bugger all'? Are bloggers just a sub-culture of pasty-faced middle-aged men sitting in their dressing-gowns frantically typing crap about subjects they know nothing about while waiting for *Countdown* to start? Is a blog, as a thousand bone-dry, bone-headed and bone-idle journalists would have you believe, merely an 'online diary'? Do the citizens of Blogland have anything interesting to say, anyway? The answers are – of course – no, no, no and read on to find out.

For those just coming in, the unique selling-point of blogging – apart from offering free and simple internet publishing for anyone itching to consign their intimate thoughts to posterity – is its interactivity.

Let's imagine you have an interest in big pants. You want to share that interest with others, so you post an article on your newly created Big Pants blog. A little while later, fellow big pants aficionados type 'big pants' into Google and find your article. Maybe they'll link to you from their own blogs. The comment function on your blog allows them to leave messages agreeing or disagreeing with your taste in pants. This creates a dialogue that becomes part of the article. The piece changes constantly and can almost become a collaborative work.

On my own blog, *Chicken Yoghurt* (www.chickyog.net), where I like to moan about how unfair the world is, I find many of the comments are better written and argued than my articles. It's flattering that people take the time to affirm or debunk what I've written. The tone of argument can range from bookish debate to pub ramble, but is rarely uncivil. At the other end of the scale there are blogs that are little more than jungles where the denizens prey on each other without mercy, so it's wise for the newcomer to tread lightly, at least at first.

This cut and thrust, rough and tumble or Punch and Judy (pick your cliché) can be very satisfying and isn't something easily achieved in the newspapers. For newspaper columns the only visible interaction is through the letters page which, for the sake of time and space, does not permit a true dialogue between reader and writer.

This year has been something of a breakthrough year for British blogging. According to a recent report in *The Guardian*, nearly seven million people in the UK – one in nine – keep a blog in some form or other. Brit-blogging has produced its first two superstars in the shapes of Iain Dale (the former Conservative Party parliamentary candidate and now Cameron A-lister) and the pseudonymous Guido Fawkes (political gossip-monger and shameless and scathing watchman of Westminster wrong-doing). Both have garnered newspaper column inches and television interviews.

For the first time blogging has truly shaken the ivory towers of the traditional mainstream media (or 'MSM', as bloggers like to call it) in the UK. Nearly every news outlet, finally realising blogging's potential and that the medium is here to stay, has adopted an 'if we can't beat them, we'll join them' strategy and established their own blogs of varying quality and success. Many newspapers now look to blogs for stories and material (often shamefully lifting and using them without credit), which surely shows that blogging has truly arrived.

So, the more prominent bloggers can challenge and even shape opinion, but there is a larger aspect of the medium that gets overlooked by the mainstream media and even bloggers themselves. In Britain today, we have seven million people writing *for pleasure*. Many may write only for their immediate social circle and have readerships in the dozens, but for all that, they are thinking, learning and ordering their thoughts. And as another blogger's blogger Jamie Kenny (bloodandtreasure. typepad.com) says:

> *What's good about this is that it creates the general feeling that anyone can join in, that anyone can have a go. It's tolerant of difference. It enjoys someone with something new to offer.*

Blogging is inclusive. A blogger, if he or she is to become successful, must reach out to other bloggers. There is, in some corners of Blogland, a very real sense of community. Many people, me included, have made lasting 'real world' friendships with people whose blogs they link to. Blogging, to risk sounding like Tony Blair, is a force for social good.

The Blog Digest 2007

Twelve months of the best writing from the web

Edited by Justin McKeating

FRIDAY BOOKS

First published in Great Britain in 2006 by Friday Books
An imprint of The Friday Project Limited
83 Victoria Street, London SW1H0HW

www.thefridayproject.co.uk

www.fridaybooks.co.uk

ISBN – 10 1-905548-16-8

ISBN – 13 978-1-905548-16-3

British Library Cataloguing in Publication Data

A catalogue record for this book is available from the British Library

Cover design and internal illustrations by Matt Buck
www.mattbuck.com

Internal design by Jason Taylor
www.liquorice-creative.co.uk

Printed by MPG Books Ltd

The Publisher's policy is to use paper manufactured from sustainable sources

CONTENTS

As is customary in these book thingies, I'd like say the odd thank you or two.

First, huge thanks go to all the contributors whose fine, fine writing adorns this volume and to the Friday Project gang – Graham, Heather, Paul, Clare C and Clare W – for giving me this opportunity and guiding me through the production of my first book.

To Tim Worstall, the editor of last year's *2005:Blogged* collection, who graciously passed the baton with sage advice, and to Donald Strachan and J. Clive Matthews for their recommendations and guidance. The drinks are on me.

To my Mum and Dad, Di, David and Marian. This book couldn't have been written without all your love and support. Also, the drinks are on me.

Finally, to my infinitely patient and indulgent partner, Viks, and my monkeys, Maisie and Elsie, without whose loving attentions this book would have been finished weeks ago. Colourful.

JM.

Over the coming pages you'll find around a hundred blog articles written by some of the best bloggers in Britain (and me), ranging across a variety of topics. If you're already a blogger or a reader of blogs, I hope you'll find some new ones to add to your list of favourites. If you're not a blogger, you're about to discover a new medium rich with excellent writing, insight and wit. Who knows, maybe you'll be tempted to give blogging a try yourself. I'll give you some tips on getting started at the end of the book.

Treat this book as you would the real online Blogland. Pick a page at random and see what you find. If you don't like it, don't worry – something you will like is, if not a click of the mouse, then a flick of the page away.

Justin McKeating
Brighton, UK
September 2006

Politics For Pretty People
Culture & Media

'In the future,' Andy Warhol famously said, 'everyone will be famous for 15 minutes'. As it turns out, Warhol, the dear old overrated charlatan, was of course wrong. Wrong. Wrong. Wrong. His 15 minutes was an average figure. The world is seething with infuriating nonentities and spectacular mediocrities who have enjoyed simply hours of unearned fame while far greater talents freeze to death on the streets of Britain every day having had not even a nanosecond of recognition. Add all those times together and divide by the number of people and you get 15 minutes. QED*.

Fortunately, The Blog Digest is seeking to redress this imbalance by featuring in this chapter only articles of culture and refinement. Big Brother and its sub-human denizens, for instance, are afforded the space and respect they deserve (that is, hardly any). Celebrity pin-cushion and alleged popstar Pete Doherty also features but only as the untalented berk he is rightly regarded as being. So pull up a chaise longue, uncork the laudanum and wallow in the best, and a little of the worst, that British culture had to offer this year.

* This theory will be proved if it takes you longer than 15 minutes to read this book.

October last year saw the release of the movie adaptation of C.S. Lewis' *The Lion, the Witch and the Wardrobe*. Philip Challinor takes a literary tour of Lewis' fantasy series, examining their subtexts.

 October 2005 – Lions, Lizards and Gospel

C.S. Lewis was a brilliant writer; no author capable of starting a book *(The Voyage of the 'Dawn Treader'*, I think) with the words 'There was a boy named Eustace Clarence Scrubb, and he almost deserved it' should be entirely dismissed by the discerning reader. But he was also a bigoted, inflexible and, as *Philip Pullman*[1] has pointed out, unforgiving Christian, and this stance permeates the Narnia books. As a child I was intent on the details and the stories, and noticed the propaganda barely if at all; though I do remember looking slightly askance at the characterisation of Eustace Clarence Scrubb, who is fond of mechanical things and also 'beetles, if they were dead and pinned to a card' and whose parents are 'nonsmokers and teetotallers and wore a special kind of underclothes'. I myself was fond of aeroplanes at the time, and saw no particular virtue in smoking and drinking, but I was vaguely conscious that Lewis was holding these little prejudices against me.

At the beginning of *The Silver Chair* something else gave me pause. The heroine, Jill Pole, is being bullied at school; yet worse, she attends what is called a 'mixed' (i.e. a comprehensive) school, something the narration denounces as perhaps 'not nearly so mixed as the minds of those who believed in them'. Bullies are not punished at 'mixed' schools; they are considered 'interesting psychological cases' and, so long as they know 'the right things to say to the Head', they end up rather admired than otherwise. It is a sad spectacle when a writer of Lewis' obvious abilities turns out satire that is too clumsy for a 10-year-old; but it was, after all, only a story.

The most controversial aspect of the Narnia books, and the films to be derived from them, should be the treatment of the Calormenes. The natives of Calormen are dark-skinned and worship a god called Tash, who in the last book turns out to be an evil demon. Since Tash is a three-headed lizard, or something of that kind, Pullman's contention that Lewis is portraying 'a religion that looks a lot like Islam' may not entirely convince; what is certain is that the Calormenes look and behave a lot like Middle Easterners. In *The Voyage of the 'Dawn Treader'*, after the young

[1] observer.guardian.co.uk/uk_news/story/0,6903,1593201,00.html

3

Narnian king Caspian has ended the slave trade in the Lone Islands (and substituted an aristocratic ruler for the bureaucratic governor), the Calormene merchants praise him highly and pay him 'long compliments; but of course all they really wanted was their money back'. Clearly Lewis wants nothing to do with alien, verbose ideas of politeness. In another book, we find that when Calormenes mention their king, the Tisroc, it is the done thing to add 'May he live for ever'; naturally, a straight-talking Narnian exile, who owes unquestioning obedience to a slain and resurrected talking lion, queries this ludicrous custom.

In the final book, *The Last Battle,* Narnia is bloodily invaded by the Calormenes, and the heroes must disguise themselves; only washing with a particular formula, says the king, 'will make us *white* Narnians again' (my emphasis). A young Calormene soldier is eventually admitted to eternal life along with the heroes, presumably by the usual Christian expedient of renouncing his entire culture and previous life; but it is quite clear which of the two races is superior in virtue, independence, thought, courage, faith, etc.

Pullman objects to the books' lack 'of love, of Christian charity'; but I think this misses the point. Like his contemporary and fellow Christian Tolkien, Lewis divides his fantasy world into Good and Evil. The Good, as Ambrose Bierce said in a different context, are the heroes and their friends, and can do no wrong. The Evil are their enemies, and can do little else. Love and Christian charity are for the Good to share among themselves; on the Evil, or the sceptical, they are simply wasted. Near the end of *The Last Battle* a miraculous banquet is set before the heroes; but a band of dwarfs, who lack theological insight, are unable to see more than a few old turnips.

A major theme of *The Last Battle* is an attack on any idea that there might be common ground between religions. A crafty ape drapes a lion-skin over his honest but simple-minded donkey friend and goes about proclaiming that Aslan, the lion-saviour, has come again; it is this swindler who later proclaims that Aslan and Tash are one and the same. Of course, the assertion is ridiculous. A lion may lie down with a lamb, but surely never with a lizard.

Now Disney executives, smitten with the wonder of spiritual things, are 'eagerly anticipating repeating the success last year of Mel Gibson's Jesus biopic [sic] *The Passion of The Christ,* and hoping to heal a rift with Evangelical America that has emerged over such matters as gay-themed days at Disneyland. 'Christian marketing groups', an intriguing alliance between the Temple and the money-changers, have been charged with selling the first Narnia film, *The Lion, the Witch and the Wardrobe.* Eminent theologians at the National Association of Evangelicals and the Billy Graham Centre have praised *The Lion, the Witch and the Wardrobe* as an effective tool for God or his earthly minions to communicate the Gospel message. If *The Observer* has quoted him correctly, Pullman believes that children will be 'corrupted', but I doubt it. *The Lord of the Rings,* which is fundamentally just as simple-minded and reactionary as anything Lewis wrote, does not seem to have caused a massive upsurge in piety. Much of Lewis' satire is too crude or too irrelevant to be more than a slightly distasteful distraction from the plot; if Disney's screenwriters know what is good for them, they will leave it out. If they don't leave it out, their box office will probably suffer. Whether they can handle *The Last Battle* without either emasculating it or alienating half the audience will be an intriguing question to ponder for the next six years or so; I suspect that, whatever the shape or form in which the Lewis gospel comes to the screen, where the soil is not fore-poisoned the seed will quietly choke.

The Curmudgeon
thecurmudgeonly.blogspot.com

Diamond Geezer summarises the major stories from October 2005 while trying to get namechecked on *The Guardian's* daily 'Today on the web' feature, which rounds up what the blogs are saying on any given subject.

 October 2005 – Today on the web

As part of the *Guardian*'s recent redesign and a major internal overhaul, a new blog-fuelled feature called 'Today on the web' now appears in the newspaper at the foot of page two. Some journo called Ben Rooney selects a daily topic of current interest (recently it's been IRA arms, net censorship and Turkish EU entry), then *Googles* for appropriate blog snippets and prints them in the paper. Write something quotable today and your ramblings could appear in the national press tomorrow read by an audience of hundreds of thousands. Alas, I can't provide you with a link to show you what I mean because, somewhat surprisingly, this feature doesn't seem to appear in the online content of the *Guardian*'s website. But as an opportunity to gain wider recognition, it's got to be worth a shot. There now follows a desperate attempt at being both psychic and pithy in an attempt to whore *Diamond Geezer* into Thursday's *Guardian*, whatever tomorrow's topic might be (Hi Ben, hope you're well, and a short version of my URL is *dgeezer.net*, if that shoehorns better into the available space). Let's see if I'm with the zeitgeist...

Conservative Party Leadership: The Tories in their death throes appear completely preoccupied debating their faults openly amongst themselves, whereas they ought instead to be convincing the people who really matter – the bloggerati – that they still have something to offer.

Hurricane Stan: This improbably named storm in the southern Caribbean may have killed far more people than did its big sister Rita, but none of them is American. Global media silence condemns Stan's victims as being worth less and somehow worthless.

Chelsea walkover: It's no coincidence that the Blues' rouble-fuelled dominance comes at a time when Premiership crowds are in decline. This is a savage indictment of the new soccer reality where the balance sheet means more than a clean sheet, where bookkeepers outrank goalkeepers, and where the only goals are corporate.

Asteroid strike: Today's unexpected meteor impact in the Australian outback has acted as a long-overdue wake-up call to humankind. On this occasion only several square miles of sand and a few plants have been vaporised – but next time we might not be so lucky. Our astronomical insignificance should never be underestimated.

Mint sauce crisis: Food lovers up and down the nation will rejoice at the news that Tesco has relaunched its squeezy bottle of this much-loved condiment. It may cost a little more than before, and contain a little less, but it tasted damned good on my pie last night. Good to have the little squirt back.

Government policy criticised/Sudden death of major figure/Social trend emerges/ Celebrity indiscretion/Health scare uncovered/President Bush is a twat: We should not be surprised by latest developments, although the current situation is clearly both undesirable and untenable. The world will judge us tomorrow by our actions today. Let us not be found wanting.

Guardian redesign: Who needs to employ journalists when you can lift up-to-the-minute content direct from the web? Welcome to the new media.

Diamond Geezer
diamondgeezer.blogspot.com

What a year it's been for the nation's favourite moon-faced heroin addict, Pete Doherty. Does anybody know what he's actually famous for? Did someone mention a band? His gruelling tour of the country's courtrooms was documented with admirable restraint by No Rock&Roll Fun.

 February 2006 – Doherty Remains on the Streets

Having pleaded guilty to multiple possession charges, *Pete Doherty has bodyswerved jail and been given a 12-month community order*[1].

Part of it means that Doherty has to go on a drugs rehab programme – although quite where the State feels it can succeed where the combined efforts of some Tibetan monks, Dot Cotton off *Eastenders*, Carl Barat, Kate Moss, the richest doctors in Arizona, stomach implants, Alan McGee and the goodwill of thousands of fans have failed isn't clear.

Doherty's brief threw a successful plea to the magistrates: think of the fans, man:

> *Pete Doherty has asked me to point out another reason he is in the public eye is that people derive enjoyment and are entertained by him. These people are his fans and he is happiest when he's playing his guitar to others. He wants to repay their loyalty and support by coming through this at the other end as a successful and talented musician.*

[1] www.nme.com/news/babyshambles/22166

It's interesting to hear that Pete's happiest when he's playing his guitar. It must have been a bugger all those times he was too gently automonged to even turn up at the gigs; never mind how frustrated he must have felt having to put the set on hold while he went looking for spoons.

If Doherty doesn't stay clean – and he has to have a monthly drug test – he could still end up inside.

No Rock&Roll Fun
xrrf.blogspot.com

The Danish cartoons, needless to say, caused offence, debate and violence. Osama Saeed takes a balanced look at the controversy.

 February 2006 – Those blasted cartoons

HSBC recently had an TV advert boasting their 'world's local bank' credentials by showing things that seemed innocuous in the West but would cause great offence in other parts of the world. Putting your feet on the table is okay here; displaying the soles of your feet in the Far East, not so.

And so we come to the cartoons from Denmark, which have now spread across Europe[1]. The West really needs to understand the love there is for the Prophet, peace be upon him, amongst Muslims. It's an established principle that if you want to make comedy about a group – Asians, gays, Christians – then you get members of that group to rib themselves (e.g. *Goodness Gracious Me*). No longer do you get people from outside poking fun.

Much has been made of the right to ridicule and cause offence. I disagree that there is such a right. I don't remember it being in any UN charter or the Geneva Convention, but I do know of many of these principles being violated in the world without much protest from these newfound upholders of rights in the West. The right to offend doesn't work on the playground and it shouldn't work on the international arena

[1] news.bbc.co.uk/1/hi/world/europe/4670370.stm

either. Even if there is a right to offend, surely there is also a right to be offended? And to complain and even boycott as a result.

However, the cartoons have nothing to do with ridiculing. You just don't do pictures of the Prophet, period. It's a cultural thing, accept it and respect it. And you certainly don't do them with an ugly face and a bomb in his turban. I heard someone on the radio comparing it to having pictures of Jesus throwing Jews into gas ovens. Much work has been done to separate Islam and terrorism, and these pictures take the debate backwards.

It is this that has caused offence and I was interested in the parallel the New York President of the World Jewish Congress, Edgar Bronfman, drew with this and caricatures of Jews over the centuries in *The Times*[2]:

> Over the past 2000 years and until the creation of the state of Israel, Jews have always been a small minority in every country they have settled in. Our ancestors have suffered from pogroms, anti-Semitism and, finally, the Holocaust.
>
> Lies about Jews, the Jewish faith and traditions have never disappeared. In fact, they are staging a comeback, especially in Western democracies which we thought had become immune to anti-Semitism after the horrors of the Holocaust.
>
> Nonetheless, Jewish intellectuals and politicians have always been at the forefront of the fight for human rights, democracy and free speech. But there are limits to free speech that should be respected, and publishing materials considered offensive by a small religious minority is going too far.

Bill Clinton[3] has also linked the cartoons to anti-Semitism.

[2] www.timesonline.co.uk/article/0,,59-2018767,00.html
[3] www.breitbart.com/news/na/060130151546.v8vrasnt.html

At the same time, however, I would advise many in the Muslim world to calm down. Some even seem to have jumped onto the death threats bandwagon. Just as the West needs to get to grips with the psychology of the Muslim world, the Muslim world also needs to understand the mores in the West. Taking entire nations to task over the actions of one newspaper is idiotic, and withdrawing your ambassadors in protest, as Saudi Arabia did from Denmark, says everything you need to know about the state of play in their rancid dictatorships.

Too often we're now seeing people completely misunderstanding what the other is saying. I'm coming to a conclusion that leaders in the Muslim world should simply stop commenting on European and US issues, and leave that to the large Muslim communities that reside here.

Rolled-up Trousers
www.osamasaeed.org/osama

Larry Teabag took a balanced view of a different kind.

 February 2006 – I'm Cartooning Too

I'm so bored of these fucking cartoons. Whoever drew them is a nasty witless shit-stirrer.

The extremists, who angrily respond to the picture of Mohammed with a bomb on his head by threatening to blow people up, are far funnier.

More moderate Muslims who keep appearing on my radio assuring me that these cartoons really are 'offensive to Muslims' can bugger off too. Don't look at them, then. I'm sure they are highly offensive, and I'm sure the twat who drew them intended exactly that. I suggest you rise above it, rather than giving him the satisfaction of letting him know he's got to you.

If, on the other hand, you think you have the right to live in a world where no document exists that is offensive to your religion, then you're either an idiot or a fascist. For fuck's sake, I know a guy who's a Welsh, ginger, homosexual. Imagine if he started trying to rid the world of every book, newspaper, and magazine that offended *him*. There'd barely be anything left.

And the evangelical Christians are now looking on enviously, wondering why they couldn't mobilise similar armies of hypersensitive individuals against *Jerry Springer the Opera*? They are cunts, too.

Tampon Teabag
tamponteabag.blogspot.com

If it's April, it must be time for another court appearance from Pete Doherty. No Rock&Roll Fun files this report.

 April 2006 - Didn't We Have A Lovely Time When Doherty Wasn't Banged-Up?

Because constantly typing 'Pete was told to try and be good this time' quickly gets dull, even for the dedicated sorts at BBC News Online, they came up with a fresh angle for coverage of today's narrow escape for Doherty: watching the fans instead[1]. The Doh-eyed ones had much to exercise them:

> *Fan Michaela Connett, 18, from Barnet, north London, who managed to grab one of the remaining seats along with a friend, said: 'Pete's so softly spoken. He's so sweet. I've never been in a court before, so this is all new for me.'*

> *With the threat of jail hanging over him, fans were left to wonder what was in the brown bag he had with him.*

> *Fan Faye Angeletta said afterwards: 'We hadn't seen him at court with a bag before so we wondered if he thought he was going to jail.'*

> *Students Faye Caldwell and Christopher Youens are fans. 'The thing with Pete is, he doesn't act like a superstar. He's really clumsy so he dropped the bag and everything fell out.'*

[1] **news.bbc.co.uk/1/hi/entertainment/4926972.stm**

See? Mariah Carey wouldn't drop *her* bag. It's nice that selling a few copies of an album hasn't changed Pete Doherty into the kind of person who is capable of carrying a bag. We might go into town tonight and drop our shopping to show that we, too, are down with the street.

Some might suggest that the most ardent of Pete's followers have trouble adjusting their vision to see the world as others do. Some might be right:

> *Rebecca Bourke said: 'You can see Pete is getting better. He looks much healthier.'*

Really?

That is healthy? If his face were any greyer, he'd be in danger from people trying to pull bits off to hold glass in place. We don't know what Ms Bourke's career plans are, but let's hope they're not of a medical nature.

Don't take away the idea that the fans have got up at four in the morning and plodded up to London to see Doherty arrive at court because they're, you know, celebrity-obsessed *Heat* types. For them, it's all about the music:

> *Student Faye Caldwell, 20, said: 'I've been to a lot of Pete's gigs but this is the first time I've been to court for him.*
>
> *'The fans aren't bothered about the tabloid stories about him and Kate Moss, or whatever.*
>
> *'The music is all that matters.'*

Although if the music, and not his tabloid fame as a drug-addled Moss-poker is what's important, why are you outside the court watching him turn up to answer charges about his drug-taking, rather than staying at home to listen to the album?

More to the point, if you don't think that thespecialpeteyoulove has anything to do with the coke-honking Moss-bonker, do you skip over the tracks on 'Down In Albion', which are clearly written by that person? (Which would be, erm, all of them.)

No Rock&Roll Fun
xrrf.blogspot.com

The Sultan's Elephant arriving in London in May was certainly one of the biggest and most exciting spectacles the city has seen. It's one of my biggest regrets this year not to have seen it with my own eyes. Although many bloggers took photos and videos of the Sultan's quest for the time-travelling girl who haunts his dreams (just Google 'sultan's elephant' to find a huge collection), very few attempted to describe it in words. Thank goodness, then, for Diamond Geezer.

 May 2006 – The Sultan's Elephant

The best ideas are often completely bonkers. Let's bring a 16-foot marionette and a 42-ton time-travelling mechanical elephant to the heart of London and then tell a story by walking them round the streets for 3 days. That's exactly what French theatre company *Royal de Luxe* are doing this weekend, and their concept, technical expertise and execution are quite brilliant. The spectacle was premiered in the French cities of Nantes and Amiens last year (to commemorate the centenary of Jules Verne's death) and later in the year you can catch the giant beast in Antwerp, Calais and Le Havre. But right now *the Sultan's Elephant*[1] is touring central London, and it's unmissable.

On Thursday a wooden space capsule[2] appeared overnight in Waterloo Place, just above The Mall. Steam billowed from the (utterly convincing) cracked tarmac throughout the day, and Londoners gathered around to gawp and to take photographs. Then yesterday the metal hatch opened and a small girl emerged. Okay, so she was four times the size of a normal girl, and she was made of wood, and she was being operated by red-suited puppeteers using a big crane and a series of overhead wires, but she was still unmistakably a small girl. She (and her string-pulling entourage) went for a long walk around town, stopping the traffic along the way, before finally ending up at Horse Guards Parade. Here she met and greeted the Sultan and his giant elephant, like you do, before settling down for an afternoon nap in a giant deckchair. The scene was set.

I caught up with the story as Big Ben struck five. An ever-increasing crowd had gathered around the sleeping travellers, most of them families with small children or passing civil servants, fresh from a savage reshuffle. An open-topped red London

[1] www.thesultanselephant.com
[2] www.flickr.com/photos/dgeezer/sets/72057594126333018/

bus entered the arena, and the giant girl slowly awoke. A crane hoisted her carefully onto the top deck of the bus as the elephant rose slowly, majestically to its feet. It roared, shook its head and waved its trunk in an utterly lifelike manner. The crowd were captivated, and struggled to take as many photographs as possible of the stirring beast. And then the performers headed off on a short tour of the St James's area, first the bus and then the elephant. Operators sat precariously beneath the giant head to control the trunk movements, while on the ground one man's job was to lift the elephant's feet forward one at a time to enable it to make progress. Meanwhile *the Sultan and his courtiers* surveyed the crowd from their platform on the elephant's back, or drank tea and made small talk on the balconies to either side.

Where the elephant went, the crowd followed. They watched from the grassy lawns of St James's Park, and massed around the beast in the wider spaces of The Mall. Stewards clutching red tape helped to seal off a movable exclusion zone both in front and to the rear as the elephant passed through. A band of musicians playing loud, magical, Eastern-style jazz followed on a truck behind, adding to the very special atmosphere. Children stood in awe and wonder, while every cameraphone in the vicinity was being pressed into use. And every few minutes the elephant showed off its *party trick*, waving its trunk towards the onlookers and squirting them with a fine spray of water. At least I hope it was water because *I got a soaking*.

And that was just yesterday. The story continues today with further London sightseeing and an official civic reception in Trafalgar Square, then tomorrow there's lunch in Piccadilly and a wander through St James's Park before the over-sized entourage finally departs. Do go and see *the Sultan's Elephant* if you can. If the look on the faces of the crowd yesterday are anything to go by, you'll leave with a big grin on your face and memories to last a lifetime.

[...and, a couple of days later...]

I told you it was brilliant. Throughout the weekend spectators descended on Central London in greater and greater numbers to watch the continuing adventures of the *Sultan*, his *mega-elephant* and a *16-foot toddler*. On Saturday Trafalgar Square was packed with people to see London's Deputy Mayor welcome the Sultan to the capital. Sadly, most of them couldn't hear anything because the loudspeaker system was inadequate, but the grand spectacle made up for it. Yesterday grinning crowds followed the elephant to and from lunch in Piccadilly, while lucky children queued to take a rocking ride on the giant girl's arms in St James's Park. And now they've departed, the girl into her wooden spaceship and the elephant into our imagination. London will miss them all. And next weekend's looking awfully empty already.

Diamond Geezer
diamondgeezer.blogspot.com

And now to philosophy. Clairwil ponders the unanswered and fundamental questions about how we got to be where we are today.

 June 2006 – Whose idea was that?

Hello,

There are those who while away the hours thinking about the meaning of life or working towards important scientific discoveries. I am not one of them. As Mr Clairwil is fond of saying, 'If civilisation had been left to people like us, we'd still be living in caves'. I agree up to a point, although I have my doubts about whether we'd have made it as far as caves. In fact, if civilisation had been left to me and my other half it would consist of a series of half-finished grandiose structures lying about and getting in the way. But on the plus side, we'd all spend about 23 hours a day sleeping.

Anyway, I am pleased to announce that I have been doing some thinking and asking questions. Having a good old ponder, if you will. Here are the results. Who in the name of all that is sacred and holy came up with eating animals? I'm not having a go at people who eat meat or anything. What I'm struggling to imagine is the thought process of the first person to look at a cow and think 'I'm going to eat that'. I like cows, I consider them my friends, but let's be frank: they smell, and they don't smell very appetising. Eating furry animals is even odder. Surely the first person to eat a rabbit must have being doing it for a bet.

Eggs are another puzzle. Who started that peculiar practice? What made someone look at mother hen sitting on her eggs and think, 'I'm going to eat those'? Honey was definitely a bet – it must have been. I wonder if anyone tried to eat a wasps' nest at any point? Actually, I think I'd quite like to see that from a safe distance. I remember a small crowd of us watching one of my neighbours attacking a wasps' nest with a brush. It was hilarious! The wasps were fizzing mad and started chasing us all. My protestations that I hadn't been anywhere near their bloody nest were wasted on the angry swarm but no harm was done, I outran the buggers and remained indoors for several hours waiting for the coast to clear. Clairwil 1, Wasps nil.

To return to eggs for a moment, if I may, how long do you reckon people attempted to eat boiled eggs for before someone invented the egg cup? I don't know if you've ever attempted this feat, but believe me, it is not easy. I once gave all my egg cups to the poor in a fit of extravagance, then promptly forgot that I'd done it. It was only after I'd boiled an egg this evening that I remembered. To say I have suffered agonies is no exaggeration. After chasing the egg across a saucer I tried to balance it on a tea glass, which was a disaster. I then tried to improvise with a strong grip and a tea towel – another failure. In the end I hurled it in the bin and had butterbeans instead. The butterbeans behaved beautifully and did not even make a token attempt to escape. That is how it should be. I will not eat anything that requires chasing – I'm not up to it.

Cheerio,

Clairwil
clairwil.blogspot.com

In June, we were told how much the Royal Family costs the public – 62p each. Chris at qwghlm.co.uk was having none of it.

 June 2006 – The Myth of 62p

> *The Queen and the rest of the Royal Family cost the taxpayer 62p per person, Buckingham Palace has revealed.*

Oh, please stop telling us the Royal Family cost us 'only' 62p a year (even the bloody *Guardian* is in on the act). Why? Because it's a mixture of lies and disingenuous bullshit.

The £37.4m cost (given some, but not very much detail here) covers the Civil List (the Queen's payroll), Grants-In-Aid (maintenance of royal palaces and travel) and expenditure for state visits, but does not cover security or military ceremonies (such as Brenda's *80th birthday bash* the other week). The costs of these are conveniently folded up into domestic security and military budgets; as far as I can tell there is no detailed breakdown of these costs available anywhere, but some indication is given by individual cases (such as the bungled planning of Charles and Camilla's wedding, costing local taxpayers over £1m) that this is no small figure.

Furthermore, trying to reduce it down to a minuscule figure is over-simplistic. The division of the £37.4m cost over the entire population of the UK would only make sense if there were some direct benefit to any sort of sizeable proportion of the population. And no, don't cite the charity work (it's not as if any of them run marathons; if we didn't have a royal family charities would just find some other celebrity for fundraising and patronage) or the tourism argument (if that's your priority, you would support opening up all the royal palaces, art collections and estates to visitors all year round, and charging them top dollar). The only direct beneficiaries are the Royals themselves; even the underestimate of £37.4m, divided by the 20 or so major Royals, is nearly £2m each. 'Royals cost £2m per head' doesn't sound as nice a headline for the Palace, though.

Even more insulting to the intelligence is the grandstanding that money the Royals gouge out of me would only buy me a minute of England v. Portugal, or it's the equivalent of a couple of pints of milk. I'm not in Germany watching England play football because I have better things to do with my money; I don't buy milk either as I don't like the taste. I can and have opted out of both these options, but I have no such chance of doing the same with the Royal Family.

Judging from the diverse comments on the BBC's *'Have Your Say'* there appears to be a good number of people who resent paying a single penny, and an equal proportion who would gladly pay many times that sum to keep the Royals going. Which surely opens it up to a neat solution: privatisation. Well, maybe not actually privatising them fully, but at the very least, decoupling them from state funding altogether. You could set up a charitable foundation, and those who love the Royals enough can set up a direct debit and pay whatever they like per month to keep them going. You could even throw in a few gimmicks – natty wristbands (I'm thinking some sort of jewels and ermine version), 'Royal Aid' gigs (I'm sure Elton and Geldof would sign up like a shot), a letter every month from a Royal of your choice ('Dear Mrs Timpkins, Thank you for the generous £2 you donated last month; it went a long way to paying the £11,555 it cost to fly me to St Andrew's to hob-nob with other golfers. Yours, Prince Andrew').

It's a perfect solution – it would probably raise many times the revenue the Royals currently receive (if only a tenth of the population paid just a quid a month, it would still raise double the '62p a year' figure and probably cover the true cost) while at the same time removing the controversy and giving us whiny republicans less ammunition to aim at the Royal Family. Best of all, it fits in with the shiny vision of twenty-first century Britain which encourages charitable sector over the state for delivering government policy. I'm surprised *Citizen Dave* hasn't made it a central plank of Conservative policy already…

qwghlm.co.uk
www.qwghlm.co.uk

The Flying Rodent says – with élan, economy and accuracy – all that needs to be said about this year's Big Brother.

 June 2006 – Big Brother: Series Seven – Some Thoughts

Please imagine that this space is filled with a shrill rant on the imbecility, worthlessness and pusillanimity of all *Big Brother* viewers, contestants and production crew. I am a little tired, and this will save me having to pull down my thesaurus to look up 40 synonyms for 'moron'.

Between the Hammer and the Anvil
flyingrodent.blogspot.com

Lest we forget, *Top of the Pops* was put out of its misery this year. Paul Rose, AKA Mr Biffo, conducts the autopsy.

 July 2006 – Flop of the Plops

This Sunday, after some sixty score and seven years on air, the powers-that-be are taking a claw-head hammer to *Top of the Pops*.

I'm a big fan of the BBC (said without any degree of irony), but this has to be one of the stupidest decisions in the corporation's history, up there with the little-remembered notion to follow up *Noel's Late Late Breakfast Show* with *Noel's Abattoir and Glue Plant*, before quickly re-naming it *Noel's House Party* when a 'Gotcha Oscar' went horribly wrong, and Jon Pertwee got pulped into a tube of Bostik.

And yet, I sort of don't blame them for axing *Top of the Pops*, because *Top of the Pops* has been rubbish for years. It seemed obvious to me that the only way to counter the threat posed to the brand by dedicated music channels was to offer something you couldn't get on dedicated music channels. And that doesn't mean half-arsed behind-the-scenes interviews, or – whoooh! Radical shake-up, dude! – the album charts.

By dipping into the BBC's music vaults, *Top of the Pops 2* did indeed offer something unavailable to MTV and VH-1 and their ilk, which is probably why it's surviving, whereas its parent show is not.

The thing is, *Top of the Pops* has ceased to be entertaining as a whole. By employing bland pretty boys and vacuous girls, all character has been sucked out of the show. The best edition of *Top of the Pops* I can ever recall watching was fronted by Reeves and Mortimer. After every act they reported that '*Apparently, the lead singer is quite keen on sports*' – and it was funny, and excellent, and if they'd been on every week there wouldn't have been a kid in the country who wouldn't have watched.

And that's what *Top of the Pops* should've been about: the presenters. They needed presenters who were funny, and charismatic, and original, who used the performers purely as props in their own act. They needed a Simon Amstell. Someone who shows no respect to the performers, but doesn't mind making a tit of themselves either. Someone who understood that the music charts aren't remotely important, and that the music industry is inherently ridiculous. A reason to tune in, regardless of whether you liked the line-up of bands that week.

How else do you guarantee that a fan of *Beyoncé* or *The Streets* is going to sit through *Red Hot Chilli Peppers* or *Placebo*?

The last three years – the Andi Peters years, lest we forget – have been particularly depressing. Every attempt to regenerate the show has been more bland than the last. It's been like watching a farmer calling a sheepdog to him, while simultaneously taking pot-shots at it with an air rifle.

And now the dog is dead; shot in the arse by the clueless Andi Peters.

RIP *Top of the Pops*.

Biffovision
biffovision.blogspot.com

Paul Davies visited the Tate Modern and discovered a previously unheralded art form.

 July 2006 – My admiration for modern art

Walking around the Tate Modern, it is impossible to avoid overhearing the disparaging comments made by the exhibition hall's many detractors. It can seem that, other than the parties of art students with their activity sheets, the obligatory oldies and the token bearded woman, everyone is there to mock the works and wish unfriendly things upon the artists.

Well, I disagree. I have only two feelings towards the characters responsible for stocking the rooms of the Tate Modern with their challenging and intriguing creations: envy and admiration.

The talent to sell, often for quite vast sums of money, paintings, sculptures or simply junk that is, quite manifestly, *awful*, that possesses as much artistic merit as my armpit and that would unquestionably fail GCSE art, even under our current levels of grade inflation, is a special thing indeed.

These 'artists' are constantly pushing the boundaries of bad taste – and deceiving many, many misguided luvvies in the process. They are at the forefront of their field.

And for those for whom such a talent is not enough, the quite ridiculous blurbs that accompany each aesthetic monstrosity are nonpareil in their nonsense. For example, Clyfford Still's 1953 untitled *Oil on Canvas*[1] (apparently it's just not cool to have titles) looks like an out-of-focus close-up of a pair of Wimbledon FC football shorts from the mid-1980s. There's really not a lot to it; it's a hazy yellow gash on a dirty blue background. So to come up with a blurb as extravagant as 'He saw the yellow wedge at the top as a reassertion of the human context – a gesture of rejection of any authoritarian rationale or system of politico-dialectical dogma' requires imagination of the very highest and most respectable order. It's gibberish of a truly godlike level.

Now that's art.

The Sharpener
www.thesharpener.net

[1] www.clyffordstill.net/art/1953.html

Time for some literary criticism. Here, Clairwil reappraises a blockbuster.

 August 2006 – Clairwil's Book Club

Hello,

If Richard and Judy can have a book club, I don't see why I can't. No laughing at the back –this week's recommended read is *the* book, the Bible, or to more precise, *the King James version*[1] – accept no substitute. It's been some time since I had a squint at the Bible but I've been unable to put it down all week, which means no one sits beside me on public transport.

I should point out that I haven't got religion or found God. I don't believe a word of the Good Book. It's just that I've only just realised what a cracking read it is. I must stress again that only the King James version will do. The language is beautiful, bloody and brilliant.

I blame schools for the Bible being overlooked as a good read. First of all they palm you off with a sappy 'Good News' Bible. 'Good News' – hahaha! Someone gets offed every second page! Then they ignore some of the best stuff in it. For example, have a peep at my current favourite, *The Book Of Esther*[2]. It's a deranged masterpiece born in the mind of a serial killer. The King is utterly bonkers, which in my mind is how a king should be. He kicks his wife out for refusing to 'do a twirl', acquires Esther as a replacement then lets people run around issuing orders in his name to massacre first the Jews, then the enemies of the Jews. Honestly, I think it's the maddest thing I've ever read.

The Book of Job[3] is just jaw-dropping. I have to say God is the star of the show in this one. Poor Job undergoes awful torture because God and Satan had a bet. Take a moment to absorb this. God allows a perfectly pleasant God-fearing chap, his biggest fan and all-round good egg, to suffer agonies for a bet. If you haven't read it,

[1] www.bartleby.com/108/
[2] www.bartleby.com/108/17/
[3] www.bartleby.com/108/18/#

please do. It's easily as funny as *Justine* by the Marquis de Sade, and about 10 times as cruel.

Leviticus[4] is a sort of *Good Housekeeping* BC. If there is an afterlife I think Kim and Aggie will be fine.

The Book of Samuel 1[5] and *2*[6] are gripping stuff. I can't help but feel all that Goliath business turned young David's head. He appears to have grown up and become a heartless monster. Chilling, but he gets his come-uppance in the end.

I could go on and on. *The Old Testament* in particular is a treasure: it has everything – sex, murder, plague, rape, incest and the many (mad) moods of The Lord. It groans with action, is crowded with incident. Arguably the best read in the world.

Cheerio,

Clairwil
clairwil.blogspot.com

[4] www.bartleby.com/108/03/
[5] www.bartleby.com/108/09/
[6] www.bartleby.com/108/10/

August saw something of a backlash against bloggers and blogging. Blogs 'are the verbal diarrhoea of the under-educated and banal', sneered Janet Street-Porter in her column for *The Independent* on Sunday before rounding off the column with a paean to the joys of porridge (really). 'Where do blog writers and surfers find the time? When do they do the washing, cooking, eating, talking, cuddling, story-reading to the kids? Do they never help with the kids' homework, go to the theatre, make love, read books, talk to friends, entertain?', asked newspaper columnist, media pundit, think-tank researcher and author, Yasmin Alibhai-Brown. There were others.

Sunny Hundal pondered on the origins of the backlash.

 August 2006 – Why do newspapers hate us bloggers?

They call it 'people power'. But most of the media and politicians in America know what it really means. Ned Lamont's win over Joe Lieberman will have repercussions that go beyond the immediate vicinity of Democrats and Republicans; it will be seen as a watershed moment for when political bloggers made their impact felt where it really matters – with voters.

This saga raises some interesting points for British bloggers, some of which are being played out in the national media already. Let me explain.

A day before the Lieberman/Lamont election, *Time* magazine published an interview[1] with Markos Moulitsas of *The Daily Kos*[2], introducing him as 'the man the media has deemed kingmaker'.

The interesting point here isn't whether he is kingmaker – it is the media narrative regarding political blogs. Moulitsas, knowing this, said: 'If Lamont wins, we're [blogger] extremist radicals dooming the Democratic party by pushing it to the left. If Lamont loses, then we're ineffectual, irrelevant and stupid.'

[1] www.time.com/time/nation/article/0,8599,1223869,00.html
[2] www.dailykos.com

This has deeper meaning. As John Dickerson pointed out in *Slate* a few days earlier[3]: 'We're all watching the Lamont race – bloggers, Republicans, Democrats and hacks like me – to see how powerful, sustaining, and relevant the online activists are. Candidates and campaign managers don't like unpredictable events, and bloggers are highly unpredictable.'

It is obvious that the American media was only partially interested in the Lieberman/ Lamont race; it was paying more attention to bloggers because it needs to fit them into a definitive narrative.

Earlier in June, Dickerson said[4]: 'Media infatuations never last. When expectations get too high, the press reverses itself, because one of the laws of journalism is that the story has to change. In this case, political reporters will turn on bloggers if the promised revolution doesn't materialise in the form of a Democratic sweep in the midterms. We are probably just under 5 months away from a wave of coverage positing that bloggers weren't that powerful after all. After we build up the Markos regime, we will help to tear it down'.

Moulitsas knows this, which is why he avoided fitting into that narrative for *Time*. Lamont's victory means the battle has been delayed.

In the UK a similar narrative is being played out. An increasing number of columnists are now found rubbishing blogs after months of hype. The backlash is brewing. Journalists and commentators are itching to destroy bloggers after building them up.

When the John Prescott scandal suddenly thrust Iain Dale[5] and Guido[6] into the limelight, some insinuated that bloggers were somehow less constrained by libel laws and able to write what they wanted. That is of course rubbish, as they repeatedly pointed out.

Other journalists keep repeating that bloggers do not have editorial standards and are not required to be non-partisan. Sure, but the British press is hardly non-partisan. It works like a free market: if your blog is not very exciting then people will go elsewhere.

[3] www.slate.com/id/2147117
[4] www.slate.com/id/2143502
[5] iaindale.blogspot.com
[6] 5thnovember.blogspot.com

The question then arises: why would the national papers be interested in tearing bloggers down? Aren't these people their readers? There are a few theories doing the rounds and I cover them briefly.

1) It could just be the way national papers work; you build something up and then you tear it down. I expect this is somewhat relevant here. Stories that change attract more attention than ones that remain the same.

2) It could be that the press see bloggers as competition and want to neutralise the medium before it gets too powerful. I don't doubt some journalists retain this view given the partisan and usually rabid way many bloggers want to criticise the mainstream media (MSM). Some, like Michelle Malkin, keep referring to it as 'dinosaur media' while continually using it for stories and TV appearances.

3) The vociferous abuse that many commentators get underneath their articles or in the blogosphere may be another reason they abhor the medium. They are exposed to having their beautifully constructed prose taken apart savagely. As Francis Sedgemore points out[7], this is partly because many of them take provocative positions and play to readers' prejudices.

I see constructive abuse as a good development. Truly getting to grips with bloggers requires that they confront their readers (provided that they want to be balanced) before the article is even finished. You anticipate the counter-arguments before someone writes them. This forces you to be balanced and become a better commentator. I have a feeling our current generation would prefer to avoid this, hence making this a plausible reason.

4) Bloggers such as Clive[8] and Tim Worstall[9] say that as the number of commentators expands the market value of the elite will fall. Or to put it another way, the sudden glut of political commentary will make it harder for those at the top to justify their six-figure salaries.

It sounds logical but I disagree. The vast majority of the public will continue to want to passively consume informed commentary rather than actively search around for

[7] www.skysong.eu/2006/07/on-the-feeding-of-trolls
[8] discuss.pressgazette.co.uk/journalism-article.aspx?id_Content=5141
[9] timworstall.typepad.com/

the best blogs that will offer them what they want. While there will be increased competition for those coveted commentator spots, the supply remains constricted for the vast majority of the population.

In the spirit of blogging I'd like to hear other possible reasons why the commentariat may turn against bloggers. Or could it be I'm blowing this out of proportion and the newspapers are just playing hard-to-get?

On the other hand, is it a matter of us political bloggers simply saying: 'Let the games begin…'?

Sunny Hundal
commentisfree.guardian.co.uk/sunny_hundal/

You probably won't be surprised to hear that a lot of bloggers are passionate about freedom of speech. In August a Muslim group offended by a blog post on Tory überblog Conservativehome.com campaigned to have its author sacked from his job (such campaigns are not unheard of). Robert Sharp sounds off.

 August 2006 – Why are we wasting our time with this shit?

> *Islamophobic – anyone who objects to having their transport blown up on the way to work.*

I know bloggers like to think that they occasionally have an impact on politics and the mainstream media, but tonight, please God, what happens in the blogosphere must stay in the blogosophere.

I don't know what annoys me more: Inigo Wilson's ill-advised *Lefty Lexicon*[1] at Conservative Home, or the ill-advised attempt by MPAC[2] to have the man lose his job at Orange.

[1] conservativehome.blogs.com/platform/2006/08/inigo_wilson_a_.html
[2] Muslim Public Affairs Committee: www.mpacuk.org

For the majority who remain blissfully aware of the 'controversy', the aforementioned lexicon was posted by Mr Wilson a couple of weeks ago. Its unfunniness is mildly annoying, but the lack of any depth to the apparent satire renders it totally harmless to actual debate. At no point does the ridicule actually change someone's mind – those who are fed up with political correctness will applaud; and those of us who believe that, say, 'institutional racism' exists, will continue to do so.

As an aside, I find the piece has added annoyance, due to the fact that any criticism that one might possibly level at it would automatically be met with gleeful cries of either 'Lefties can't take a joke!' or 'Looks like I've hit a nerve' – or some such retort. 'If I've annoyed a Lefty, I must be doing something right!'

Whatever. The piece isn't meant to be debated. The impossibility of engaging with it, on any level, is built into its very construction. It's just a line in the sand for people to dance about, a midweek distraction for the lazy. Why ridicule actual government policies when you can attack a straw-man wrapped in a cliché?

More annoying, however, is that a week later, someone began *agitating* for Wilson to be sacked from his job in the communications department at Orange. Via Pickled Politics we hear that he has now been suspended[3].

How ridiculous. Provided the guy does not allow his political viewpoint to prejudice a customer or employee, it's nothing to do with Orange! There is no suggestion that when Wilson writes on a Conservative blog, that he is doing so in a professional capacity. He should be allowed to write what he wants, even if he is *'a rancid, braying little tick'*[4]. By lobbying Orange, MPAC are either misunderstanding the nature of free, political speech... or they are engaging in a cynical publicity stunt. Foolish or opportunistic? Personally, I suspect the latter. If they succeed, Inigo Wilson could become a martyr to political correctness. And no one wants that.

Instead, it is Conservative Home that should do the 'sacking', because it is only there that his political views count. Such crass humour reflects badly on a site that seeks to become influential in Cameron circles, and a wise editor would not have allowed the article to be published. As it is, the entire site loses some credibility for carrying

[3] www.pickledpolitics.com/archives/715

[4] www.chickyog.net/2006/08/16/but-i-will-defend-to-the-death-your-right-to-be-a-smug-humourless-little-cockstain/

the lexicon in the first place. It then loses some more, due to the lack of contrition at publishing something so tired. Bizarrely, they show no embarrassment at their mistake.

Whichever way you look at this issue, all actors look ridiculous. Worse still, both sides have acted to polarise the debate. Their words have only served to reinforce the prejudices of those with the opposite viewpoint. What a waste of time.

Robert Sharp
www.robertsharp.co.uk

I know what you're thinking: we need an update on Pete Doherty's progress. After another court appearance for drug offences, at which the judge praised Pete's music (true!), Pete found himself in The Priory clinic. Here, for the final time in this volume at least, is No Rock&Roll Fun.

 August 2006 – Pete Doherty: Class Warrior

Pete Doherty? He's so street, it's a wonder he's not been paved over. He's going to lead us into rebellion[1] of all sorts:

> *'I've got a fierce passion for politics but I can't stand the smarmy, hypocritical upper-middle-class dictator nation that prevails and has always prevailed in this country.*
>
> *'I'm up for petrol bombers, mate, and fighting in the streets.'*

Pete made these comments from luxury private hospital The Priory. Pete's family are British Army through and through. At the age of 16, the British Council paid for him to go and do poetry in Russia; last year he shared a stage with Elton John at Live8. He hangs out with the likes of Kate Moss and Sadie Frost and much of his free time seems to be spent scoring or doing drugs – and you don't have to be too smart

[1] www.gigwise.com/news.asp?contentid=21488

to know that cocaine production is pretty much directed at supporting a dictator elite, albeit overseas. The casual observer might notice that when he's not living the life of the elite, he's too far gone to be tipping it over.

Indeed, in most well-run revolutions of the people, Doherty's self-obsessed louche lifestyle would place him near the top of any list being drawn up to order when people might be given a blindfold and last cigarette.

No Rock&Roll Fun
xrrf.blogspot.com

Chris Dillow on the ultimate test of a politician's integrity – do they watch Coronation Street?

 September 2006 – Corrie's truths, Campbell's cretinism

Iain Dale proves[1] that Ming Campbell is an utterly contemptible figure – because he doesn't watch *Coronation Street*.

In this *great* piece[2], Johann Hari said that he could never love anyone who didn't love *Corrie*. I can't even respect someone who doesn't – especially if they're a politician. *Corrie* demonstrates the greatest political wisdom of all – that the poorest he that is in England hath a life to live, as the greatest he.

In *Corrie*, people are not simple ciphers, to be boxed, stamped, labelled and managed as managerialists think. They are real, multi-dimensional people. Take Roy Cropper, the mocked and bullied geeky, autistic loner, with his Christ-like humility. Or his wife Hayley, who has done more than almost anyone to show that trans-sexuals are not freaks. Or Eileen, showing that single parents aren't feckless scroungers, but battlers against adversity. Or the sadly departed Sunita, showing that the mousy Asian shopgirl has an intelligence and sensuality beyond the cultural stereotype. Or Steve MacDonald, showing that ex-cons can come good.

[1] iaindale.blogspot.com/2006/09/ming-fails-coronation-street-test.html
[2] www.johannhari.com/archive/article.php?id=844

What's more, *Corrie*, more than any TV programme, embodies a tradition. It's hinted at by that prominent but never discussed poster in the Rovers advertising Wilfred Pickles[3], the homage to Donald McGill[4] within Jack and Vera and Les and Cilla, and the distinctively Northern character types represented in different ways by Emily, Ken, Norris and Blanche. In all this we see an embodiment of a part of English – Northern – history, a history we are in danger of losing.

Being non-political, *Corrie* also contains an important political message – that politics, or at least managerialist party politics, isn't that important. People try, and often fail, to control their own lives – and no one, not even Les and Cilla, looks to the state very much. And then, of course, there is the peerless writing. Here's an exchange from a few months ago:

> Sally: 'Sophie – eat your breakfast. There are children starving in Africa.'
> Sophie: 'Name one.'

Was ever such truth spoken in Westminster?

All of this should reveal just how contemptible Campbell and his like are. They think the petty manoevrings of the Westminster village – a soap with all the characters, wisdom and dignity removed – are more interesting than *Corrie*.

Stumbling and Mumbling
stumblingandmumbling.typepad.com

[3] **en.wikipedia.org/wiki/Wilfred_Pickles**
[4] **www.bbc.co.uk/bbcfour/documentaries/features/photogallery/saucy_postcards1.shtml**

The Honourable Member
Sex

The beast with two backs. The mattress mambo. Touching the Void. Posting Yul Brynner first class. Where would the British be without euphemisms for the sexual act? In possession of a much more mature attitude towards sex, no doubt, but having fewer laughs along the way.

This year's rash of political sex scandals (is that the appropriate collective noun?) heaped yet more ridicule on politics and politicians. The avid interest and disapproval aimed at those affairs by the media and the public showed us to be simultaneously – and paradoxically – both prudish and prurient.

Sex still sells big. It's to be wondered how much envy plays a part in the voyeuristic intrusions we make into other people's sex lives; is it that we would quite like to be doing those kind of things with our own John Thomases and Lady Janes?

If you ask me, the story of Mark Oaten and his predilection for male prostitutes brought out the very best and the very worst in British bloggers. The now famous Guido Fawkes (by 'famous' I mean that his blog receives more visits than any other in the country – many bloggers set store by such things, much like comparing manhoods) and his associate Recess Monkey, another political gossip-monger, tried to claim a role in Oaten's outing. Many bloggers were pretty disgusted.

Tim Ireland takes up the tale with a round-up of how the blogs saw the affair. The following pieces contain many links but they're worth following to gain the full flavour of how the story played out in Blogland.

 January 2006 – 'Our legal advice is that Mark Oaten is not a paedophile.'

> Guido – it's the Pod what did it[1]: *Wednesday night, a few drinks, a digital recorder, Guido and a drunken Monkey. A podcast for a select few emailed on Thursday. Those of you who heard the podcast will know why Guido is smirking. Did it hint enough? We posted the feedback responses over at GuidoandtheMonkey.Com Thursday and Friday.* Popbitch *(the home of webmongs, gayers and unemployed freelance journos) referred to the libellous nature of the podcast. Anyway, it was in the public domain Thursday, 'bloggers are making jokes about it', and coincidentally the News of the Screws swoops...*

> Recess Monkey – a good job he likes a bit of humiliation[2]: *To all those that counselled me a few days ago that I would be sued by Mark Oaten: please feel free to eat your hats.*

> Europhobia – Oaten outing follow-up[3]: *Still can't quite get my*

[1] 5thnovember.blogspot.com/2006/01/its-pod-what-did-it.html
[2] www.recessmonkey.com/2005/02/14/a_good_job_he_like_a_bit_of_humiliation
[3] europhobia.blogspot.com/2006/01/oaten-outing-follow-up.html

head around what the point of this whole outing thing was... Guido claims the scoop, anyway. Not much to be proud of, I'd have thought, destroying the life of a minor politician and doubtless his family to boot... Still, Guido's commenter seems to be having fun – latent homophobia or just the repression of wishing they had the guts to hire some arse themselves?

Curious Hamster – joining the dots[4]: Oaten's role in Blair's blackest day might have already been forgotten by most people in the country. That he was once high on the Sun's list of traitors may also be forgotten. I tell you what though. I bet I can name at least two other people in this country who do remember. Can you guess? OK, here's a clue. Their initials are TB and RW.

Chicken Yoghurt – Oaten[5]: What a bloody disgrace. Does this kind of thing really still sell newspapers? In the twenty-first century? Are people really that lacking in their own lives? What the hell has this got to do with anyone except Oaten and his family (including two daughters who have to go to school tomorrow)? What Oaten did was wrong, yes. But within the confines of his marriage. To say he's been politically naive is an understatement but that's not a hanging offence yet either. It seems Oaten has enough problems without the moral adjudicators of a Murdoch newspaper stirring the pot... None other than Guido Fawkes himself is claiming Oaten's corpse. He says he outed Oaten in a drunken podcast that made its way as far as that august journal of public morality, Popbitch. He also gives some self-serving, arse-covering excuse about Oaten having been hypocritical over the Government's plans for prostitution. If this is the kind of thing bloggers need to do to get noticed then I for one want no part of it. And if this turns out to be the first stripe British bloggers earn ('British bloggers claim first scalp'), it will have been scrawled with a turd.

[4] bsscworld.blogspot.com/2006/01/joining-dots.html
[5] www.chickyog.net/2006/01/22/oaten/
[6] doctorvee.co.uk/2006/01/22/who-said-blogging-was-an-antidote-to-the-msm/
[7] fairvotewatch.blogspot.com/2006/01/piggy-backing-on-oaten-but-he-was.html

DoctorVee – who said blogging was an antidote to the MSM?[6]: *I like Guido's and Recess Monkey's blogs. But I wish they would stick with the jokes and jibes rather than this privacy-invading sub-tabloid tittle-tattle.*

Jarndyce – piggy-backing on Oaten, but he was drunk, mind [7]: *Look, look at me everybody. Go on, look. LOOK. It's another one of my scoops that I break fucking ages after it's broken somewhere else. And look, mummy, I caught one of those nasty bummers this time. Yes, mummy, a horrid, sordid little homo. But I nailed him. I really gave it to him. Roasted the little bastard. Skewered him. His daughters, too. So, pleeeease look. Pleeease. Puh-leeeease.*

I'm equally depressed and disappointed by this... and I agree that Guido and Recess Monkey don't have a lot to be proud of.

Topical as they may have been, the paedo jokes in the podcast that formed the bulk of the 'obvious' hints send an insidious message. You should also note that Guido and Recess Monkey make a point of revisiting the same joke/message twice:

GUIDO & MONKEY[8] –19 JAN PODCAST (02:33):

'Can you imagine if you were sitting at home watching Big Brother or something and Mark Oaten rings you up, saying 'Please, can I have your support?'. It's like... 'Yeah, just fuck off, and stay away from my kids.''

'Is he the creepiest Lib-Dem candidate?'

'Yeah, I think he is. Yeah, he's definitely gay*.'

'Wouldn't want him near a school playground.'

[jokes about pallid complexions and comb-overs, then a change of subject]

[8] guidoandthemonkey.blogspot.com
[9] www.bloggerheads.com/snippet.wma

'*Anyway... Leo.*'

'*I don't think Mark Oaten has touched Leo.*'

[*This word is talked over... but it was formed of one syllable, began with a strong 'g' and rhymed with 'hey'. Perhaps they said he was definitely 'grey'? As in pallid? Works for me Your Honour.]

UPDATE: *Here you go:* judge for yourself (23kb WMA)[9]. *Back to the show... seven minutes later... same gag all over again.*

GUIDO & MONKEY – 19 JAN PODCAST (09:08):

'*Do you know what? I would be quite concerned if I saw him hanging around outside a playground.*'

'*He does have the look of a paedo about him.*'

[laughter, then, in a put-on voice...]

'*Our legal advice is that Mark Oaten is not a paedophile.*'

[change of subject]

'*Ah, Leo Blair...*'

'*No, I don't think Mark Oaten's ever been touching Leo...*'

Message: If you are a homosexual, you are a pervert. Therefore, no perversion is beneath you. Ipso facto (conspectus procto) if you are a homosexual, you are also a kiddie-fiddler. (Also, there is no such thing as a bisexual. A bisexual is simply a homosexual who hasn't made his or her mind up yet... between men, women and children, that is.)

It's a compelling argument (made even more compelling by use of the word 'rent-boy' to describe a 23-year-old man), and it's one echoed by many of those who claim to be our moral guardians, but Guido and Recess Monkey should be warned that it is unlikely to stand up in court.

UPDATE: Before making the script for the podcast, this view was aired by Guido on 9 January: 'Oaten? A slaphead who most mothers would feel uneasy seeing near a playground.'

Bloggerheads
www.bloggerheads.com

Shortly after Mark Oaten's downfall, Lib Dem leadership candidate Simon Hughes was outed as gay by *The Sun*. Surely only a homophobe could have failed to be disgusted at the 'Another One Bites The Pillow' tagline and sniggering that went with it.

Here, Iain Dale, former Conservative parliamentary candidate and current Cameron 'A-lister' speaks of his own experiences while sympathising with Hughes' predicament.

 January 2006 – Simon Hughes deserves both our condemnation and understanding

And then there were two. Only Chris Huhne and Ming Campbell remain as serious contenders in the Lib Dem leadership race following Simon Hughes' outing in today's *Sun*. It's not the fact that he's gay that's the problem. It's the fact that like Mark Oaten and Charles Kennedy he has lied. Although you wouldn't know it from his comments on the media today. Let's be clear, when questioned by *The Independent* he didn't hedge around the question, he said quite categorically he was not gay, not once but twice. He repeated the answer in another newspaper. That, in my book, is a lie. I was on *Radio 5 Live* this morning talking about this with gay Lib Dem MP Stephen Williams. He seemed outraged that Simon Hughes could be accused of lying. Indeed, he said that Charles Kennedy hadn't lied over his drinking. He must be living on a parallel planet. To people out in the real world the fact that politicians don't tell the truth is far more serious than what they get up to in the bedroom. As I said on *5 Live* this morning, the most damaging aspect of the Oaten and Hughes sagas is that young men all round the country who are firmly in the closet will probably remain there for that bit longer because Simon Hughes' behaviour indicates a feeling of shame. The other aspect to this is Hughes' behaviour during his by-election campaign against Peter Tatchell in 1983. I heard Tatchell on *5 Live Drive* this evening and he was quietly impressive in his protection of Simon Hughes. He accepted his apology and praised him for his voting record on gay rights and human rights issues. Hughes was a young man at that time and probably didn't control the direction of his campaign, which included the infamous SIMON HUGHES – THE STRAIGHT CANDIDATE poster.

There's no question that Hughes is a man of courage. At great personal risk to himself he appeared in court to give evidence against a gang of thugs and contributed to them being put away for a long time. He received threats of physical violence and, I am told, death threats. Despite this he persevered and justice prevailed.

We must also remember that he is 54 years old and for him to come out now will have been psychologically trying for him to say the least. I know myself the traumas one goes through when one 'comes out', particularly with regard to the reaction of one's family and friends. When I decided to go into politics I came out before being selected as a candidate. I remember having to tell friends of 20 years' standing something they may have suspected but we had never talked about. Without exception their reaction was amazing and it made me think I should have done it years earlier. But I had regarded it as no one's business but my own. But if you go into politics you know what can happen. You know that journalists are always looking out for a saucy story, and being gay still provides them with the salacious headlines they love. I made up my mind that the only way to avoid the 7pm phone call on a Saturday night from the *News of the World* was to be open. If people couldn't cope with it, well that was their problem. But Simon Hughes couldn't have done that in 1983. Since then he has been circumspect and avoided the issue. Many people in Parliament suspected he was gay and he had been seen in gay bars and night clubs. Apparently in his constituency it was an open secret. And that's how he would have preferred it to stay. He didn't want to worry his ageing mother with it and his Christian activities mitigated against making any form of public statement. I totally understand that. Where he went wrong was to give interviews to two newspapers where he told an untruth. Or perhaps where he went wrong was to stand for the Lib Dem leadership in the first place, if he wasn't willing to be open. But we also have to face the fact that if Mark Oaten hadn't been outed on Sunday, Simon Hughes probably wouldn't have been today. My great fear now is that the media smell blood. I wouldn't be at all surprised if there were further revelations between now and Sunday. If I were an MP with a personal secret I don't think I'd look forward to answering my phone on Saturday.

So is Simon Hughes finished as a leadership candidate? I think it's difficult to tell, but if I had to fall off the fence, I'd say yes. I am not familiar enough with the grassroots Lib Dem members who have the vote to make a judgement on whether being gay will lose him any votes. I suspect it may cost him a few in rural areas but the issue of having told a lie will cost him more. Alternatively, depending on how he copes with the next few weeks, he made get quite a decent sympathy vote. Time will tell.

But just spare a thought for two other men tonight: first, Charles Kennedy – he can be forgiven if he has a slight feeling of 'serves 'em all right' – and second, Mark Oaten, who has reportedly been told by his wife that their marriage is over. No one can derive any pleasure from seeing a man's life fall apart in the space of 5 days, no matter what he has done. I just hope he has some good friends to count on.

Iain Dale's Diary
iaindale.blogspot.com

Bookdrunk has a suggestion for those God-bothering types looking to interfere in the bedroom (so to speak).

 March 2006 – The best idea I ever had (this evening)

I think the most appropriate response to 'no sex before marriage' is 'no religion before sex'. If people are going to try to regulate other people's sexuality, they should at least have some vague idea what they're talking about.

Rhetorically Speaking
rhetoricallyspeaking.blogspot.com

Finding evidence of a youth being currently misspent reminds Mr Biffo of another youth previously misspent.

 May 2006 – Porn-Oh!

In the process of building a giant funeral pyre (bonfire) on Saturday afternoon, we found a load of hardcore porno mags at the bottom of our garden. After I spent 5 minutes furiously denying ownership, we concluded that they probably belong to the teenage boy who lives in the house at the bottom of our garden (that's not, like, literally a little wendy house at the bottom of our garden – rather, a house whose garden backs onto ours).

Presumably, he sneaks out of the house and has a little tug behind our shed. This is not really something I want to be thinking about. I had wanted to paste photos of Noel Edmonds' face all over the pages, and leave them where they were, but that would've meant touching them, rather than just kicking them onto the bonfire.

It reminded me of a holiday to Great Yarmouth, when I was 15. A friend – who shall remain, for now, anonymous – came with us. It was a good holiday, not least because we met a couple of nice girls, who were staying in the caravan opposite.

However, that aside, for inexplicable reasons said friend had brought with him a large carrier-bag full of a year's worth of a soft-core sex-education partwork. Apparently, he'd borrowed them off a friend at school at the end of term, but had since become paranoid that his oh-so-strict parents would discover them while he was away. Rather than risk a beating (so to speak) upon returning home, he thought it safer to bring them with him.

At the end of the week he was in quite a state. I knew his parents were pretty strict, but he was beside himself at the thought of having them going through his suitcase, and finding a year's worth of a sex-education partwork. For reasons I'll never understand, I let him pressure me into taking them home, and keeping them safe until the start of the new term.

The magazines were in a carrier bag, sealed with a very tight knot. Even if I'd wanted to read them, I would have had to tear the bag in order to do so, and then he'd have known that I'd been... using them. Aside from anything, he'd probably been doing just that, and I didn't really want to use them with that thought in my head. Because of this, and because the bag wasn't see-through, I figured it would be safe enough to hide the bag under my bed. Which I did, not accounting for my mother's inability to respect anyone's privacy.

The first time she cleaned my room after returning from Great Yarmouth she found the bag, and tore it open, but the first I knew of it was overhearing her discussing the contents with my sister and dad. Naturally, I walked downstairs and attempted to protest my innocence, but the more I protested the more awful it sounded.

'*I was looking after them for a friend*' never rings true, even when it is.

To make matters worse, my dad called me a '*mucky bugger*', at which point my mother leapt on him, and said – I remember this very clearly – '*At least the ones he's got are educational... don't think I haven't heard you rummaging around in your briefcase after I've gone to bed.*'

That was the last time I ever offered to look after someone's sex-education partworks.

Biffovision
biffovision.blogspot.com

Birds do it, bees do it, even Deputy PMs do it. In May, the story broke of John Prescott, his cocktail sausage and his diary secretary, Tracey Temple. Cue much hilarity. Harry Hutton reckoned a Deputy Prime Minister on the job was much less dangerous than one doing his job.

 May 2006 – In defence of John Prescott

'Scotland Yard has confirmed it is looking into a complaint that Mr Prescott broke the law by allegedly having sex in his Whitehall office.'

If I were his lawyer, I would point out that using a government office for having sex with his secretary was far less ruinous for Britain than how he might otherwise have been using it. While Prescott was harmlessly fucking his secretary, the rest of the cabinet were probably hatching schemes to make us all line up and be fingerprinted. Put it this way: would you rather he was shafting his secretary, or the nation? We got off lightly.

I would go further: I would say that screwing his secretary is his main achievement since taking office, and one of the things that sets him apart from monomaniacs and cyborgs like Blair, Brown and Straw. Blair would no more fuck his secretary than he would read a novel. Why? Because he's a lunatic and a freak, with no more sense of proportion than a Saudi cleric. Brute that he is, Prescott is one of the few members of the establishment who is still recognisably earthling.

'I'm the one who acted stupidly,' he said. What was stupid about it? It was normal and human, and one of the few things he has done recently of which sane people might approve. You vote to abolish Habeas Corpus and the Magna Carta, then you apologise for screwing your secretary? Seriously, what's wrong with everyone on that island? Besides which, to describe it as 'stupid' is insulting to the woman, you great oaf.

Incidentally, trivia question: how many jags does 'two-jags' own? He owns one jag (second hand). If he were French or Italian he could use his ministerial car to buy milk, visit his whippets, or whatever else he does with his wretched life. But because he was scrupulous, on that occasion, about the difference between government property and private property, he got jumped on.* And the same people who call him two-jags now bitch about him getting his end away in Whitehall.

I think he comes out of these scandals rather well. I still hope to see him hang, however.

*And to carjack or hotwire his jags would be another assault on the Magna Carta[1]: 'No sheriff, royal official, or other person shall take horses or carts for transport from any free man, without his consent'. This often gets overlooked.

Chase me, ladies, I'm in the cavalry
chasemeladies.blogspot.com

[1] www.fordham.edu/halsall/source/magnacarta.html

Shortly after the Tracey Temple scandal broke, Tony Blair held a webcast on the Number 10 website answering questions from the public put to him by two journalists. Being the cynic, I thought the searching question would be weeded out and the chances of one being put to the Prime Minister were slim. So, I held a little competition on my blog. Anyone managing to have their question asked would win a prize. As it turns out I was the winner. My question was about a largely overlooked aspect of John Prescott's conduct. But as you'll see, asking the Prime Minister a question is one thing. His answering it is quite another.

 June 2006 – Ask Tony and win: the winner is...

...nobody. Although I was fortunate enough to have my question put to the Prime Minister in his recent webcast, it just became part of the expected unedifying spectacle. I imagine everybody involved had far more important things to do and I'll generously include the Prime Minister in that. You can read the transcript, watch the video or download the MP3 here[1].

The piece of cake that is having your question addressed to the Prime Minister himself looks fabulous. A huge slab of light, golden sponge, stuffed with fresh cream and jam, and a thick layer of succulent marzipan on the top. Needless to say, in his refusal to answer my question to any satisfactory degree, the Prime Minister denied me the pleasure of eating said delight. Ah, the giddy whirl of speaking truth to power. It's a real privilege to finally get a sniff of how soul-destroyingly frustrating and pointless life as a political journalist must actually be.

If you'll indulge me, here was the question I sent to Michael White and Sarah Sands:

> There have been several allegations of sexual harassment made against the Deputy Prime Minister, notably from Linda McDougall, the wife of MP Austin Mitchell who alleges, in 1978, that he 'pushed me quite forcefully against the wall and put his hand up my skirt'.

[1] www.number10.gov.uk/output/Page9565.asp

> *Were these allegations to be made against a teacher, social worker, a doctor or anyone else, do you think they should be treated as 'a private matter', as you regard the Deputy Prime Minister's conduct, or do you think that person should face disciplinary proceedings?*

As was stated from the outset by Number 10, '[t]he questions chosen to go to the PM will not be selected by his office'. To test this assertion I emailed Sarah Sands, not to ask her to put my question to the Prime Minister, but merely for confirmation that she had laid eyes on my question and that it hadn't been weeded out by the myrmidons overseeing the *questions@pmo.gov.uk* inbox. She emailed back to say she had seen the question and had shortlisted it.

In answer to my question, Blair said:

> *I think the simple answer, Sarah, is if someone has done something wrong they should face disciplinary proceedings. But I am not going to accuse someone of doing something wrong on the basis of, well I don't know actually, I haven't heard about this thing, but presumably a report in the paper. And I think, how can I put this, I think the problem that we have is that of course politicians should be accountable for their behaviour, and actually if you look back over the years politicians are regularly held to account. But I think the most important thing is that if we do something wrong, fair enough, but I think like everybody else we shouldn't be assumed to have done certain things just because people make allegations about us. And I try to, when allegations are made of particular behaviour, I try and investigate it and there are ministers that have left government as a result of doing things that are either wrong or contrary to the interests of the government. But I think sometimes you can get into a situation where you are expected just to follow every single story that is written about someone, and my experience is that when something happens and someone does something wrong, there may be truth in the original allegation, but then virtually anything can be then added in the mix to say that they have done half a dozen other things that when you actually investigate them turn out not quite to be right.*

For someone acclaimed as one of the finest politicians of his generation, he really doesn't come across as good at thinking on his feet, without a briefing or autocue. His answer is just yet another demonstration of how divorced from reality the poor sod is. (It's also eerily similar to the excuses he's made over extraordinary rendition – the line to take is one of ignorance and then a refusal to order inquiries based on perceived tittle tattle.) This is what you get when the Prime Minister is the final arbiter of ministerial conduct: there's no separation of Church and State. It's the Catholic Church hierarchy hushing up priests' abuse of children. It's the football manager claiming he didn't see the crunching foul that got his winger booked. Where's the Prime Minister's interest in investigating allegations made against his own cabinet ministers by (nice, disparaging, touch this) '*presumably a report in the paper*'?

> *I try and investigate it and there are ministers that have left government as a result of doing things that are either wrong or contrary to the interests of the government.*

Is he saying here that Prescott has done nothing wrong or anything 'contrary to the interests of the government'? How would he know if he'd only just heard this particular allegation and shows no sign of pursuing it? If '*there may be truth in the original allegation*' why not apply sanction on the basis of that truth once it's uncovered? You have to hope that the police don't back away from allegations in their investigations just because allegations made in previous cases turned '*out not quite to be right*'? Here's an idea. Why not carpet Prescott and ask him if he assaulted, groped, pinched the arse of (or however you want to paint it) Linda McDougall in 1978? And then move down the list from there.

I know I harp on about it, and maybe I just have an over-inflated sensitivity to sexual violence and harassment towards women, but this kind of behaviour is not tolerated anywhere else in our society. It's like Prescott punching people who throw things at him. Oh, how we laughed (and continue to laugh) at the be-mulleted fool the Deputy Prime Minister pluckily took at swing at. 'John is John', grinned the Prime Minister at the time. I wonder if he'd be so kind as to say 'Justin is Justin' on TV if I were to sock one of the idiots chucking popcorn about the next time I go to the pictures. Do you think he'd prevaricate and obfuscate for me if I were to go next door and put my hand up my neighbour's skirt?

Chivalry and feminism are dead, at least inside New Labour. Maybe I'm old-fashioned, maybe it's what comes of having daughters or being mindful of the memory-scorching stories my partner would bring home when she worked in women's refuges, but I thought there might have been a little more anger over this. If I was Austin Mitchell I'd be planning an ostentatious political shanking, not going on Newsnight to defend the man who'd assaulted my wife (I notice there's been no denial, writ or complaint to the Press Complaints Commission forthcoming from Prescott over the allegations). It's clear I've failed to understand just how things work at the top of the tree in this country.

Which probably explains why I'm running an obscure blog from my bedroom, and not shagging, groping and pushing women quite forcefully against the wall in the corridors of power.

Chicken Yoghurt
www.chickyog.net

Acerbia is the archive of the many and fabulous adventures of D. Like a hard-bitten son of Michael Moorcock's Jerry Cornelius taught to write by William S. Burroughs, D has led many lives; continually reincarnated, he's a boxer fuelled by sexual frustration one day, a patient at the doctor's with a case of sentient ringworm the next. Here he explores the eternal triangle by way of a cinematic classic.

 May 2006 – Bit player

The conversation dries up at the table and everyone takes a drink from their beer. Kathy is first to finish, though, and between sips has thought of one of those questions intended to kick-start the conversation again.

'If you could re-enact any scene from a movie, which would it be?'

This one is easy – I've practically got it memorised already.

'I'd be Pacino in the scene where he sits across from De Niro in Heat, talking about his dreams and telling him to his face that he's going down,' I say.

Kathy looks to her new boyfriend, who doesn't seem to have understood the question.

'I'd be...' He hesitates. 'I dunno, some guy who doesn't have to act much or do much work but gets paid lots,' he finally says, completely missing the point.

She's had enough time to think about it and decides upon her answer.

'I'd be Ingrid Bergman in the end scene of Casablanca, when Rick tells her to get on the plane'.

'Haven't seen it', grunts her squeeze, who is eyeing up the waitress as she walks past.

'Its brilliant, she's had an affair with Bogart but then her husband turns up alive, having escaped from a concentration camp and they all reunite in Casablanca trying to escape to the U.S. and although she loves Bogart he does the honorable thing and puts her on the plane, sending her off with her husband... Christ... what's the husband's name?'

I try to help: 'Well Bogart plays Rick of Rick's Café Americain and you've got Claude Raines as the French cop, Bergman plays Ilsa... Ilsa... can't remember her married name'.

Kathy and I sit almost nose to nose, extolling over the plot and intricacies of Casablanca as her boyfriend yawns and watches the crowd. We talk of the letters of transit and Ferrari at the Blue Parrot bar and neither of us can remember the name of Ilsa's husband. I do my Peter Lorre impression and she quotes Sacha the barman 'Yvonne I love you, but he pays me', and for a moment we both forget that her boyfriend is right there, revelling in this connection.

'I'm going for a piss', he says and heads off to the bathroom.

I lean in close to Kathy and tell her that I've remembered the name of Ilsa's husband and I'll tell her in exchange for a kiss. Her face flushes red and she looks away guiltily. She can't. It's not that she doesn't want to, she does, but she can't. And yet she desperately needs to remember, needs to fill that mental void. She can picture him but she can't name him, and the longer she waits the greater the chance that she could be caught kissing another man.

She finally makes a decision but before she can act on it he's back at the table, standing over it expectantly.

'Shall we go?' he says, bored of the scene and more than a little threatened by me.

We do the round of goodbyes and as I kiss Kathy on the cheek I whisper to her that she's got herself a Victor Lazlo.

Acerbia
www.acerbia.com

Lucy is on A Spinster's Quest. She's attempting to find 50 ways to find a lover – an anti-Paul Simon. She's determined to try online dating, lonely hearts columns, singles' nights and wherever else love may linger. Here, she tries speed-dating.

 June 2006 – Speed-dating

Speed-dating. The very idea is repulsive. 'Would they do that in Italy?', I ask myself. 'No, they bloody wouldn't'. Two things that really shouldn't be rushed are food and love. Even Diana Ross' mum knows you can't hurry love. Still best not knock it.

I book to go to a place in Soho. It's £20, 20 people, £1 a person. I'm torn between thinking 'What good value', and 'Aren't I worth more than a quid?' I'm nearly 30 and at the Pound Land of dating.

I'm scared. Speed-dating in Soho will be full of stubbly men in post-production wearing nicely-battered expensive trainers. I feel exposed. I don't want to put myself on the conveyer belt. I don't think I'm much of a catch. I just want to watch *Casualty*.

I find myself dwelling on negatives. I've got a heat rash. Also there's a spot at the side of my mouth. It's out of control. I didn't use toothpaste. I used surgical spirit. It is catatonic now. I wouldn't want to kiss it. I can't dwell on negatives. I must be positive and confident for this to work. Anyway, *Loaded* is always full of pictures of skin afflictions.

Slightly worried that it's been a long time since I had a 'more than platonic moment'. Also we're having a heat wave. I will be using alcohol for courage. I must realise that my standards plummet when under the influence and remember that I am too old for drunken snogging.

I vow to:

1) Talk to them as though they're ugly (it's always much easier to talk to ugly people).

2) Ask them if they know any good jokes (then at least I will learn something).

Oscar Wilde once said that a woman needs '*a tiny streak of a harlot in her*'.

I remember this when dressing.

I show breast.

The look is 'prim secretary with underlying filth'.

I arrive. It is ghastly. It is just not sexy. In fact it is the antithesis of sex. It is unsex. It is like sex with the sex taken out of it. It is about as sexy as a smear test. I spy just one interesting man. It is name badges and numbers and a nervous 'Have you ever done this before?'. It is the sort of environment that makes you want to rebel. I want to say cunt a lot. The only answer is strong lager followed by white wine and then gin.

Ladies sit at tables and the men rotate. The girl they all meet before me is a petite Spanish-looking girl, making me the minger afterwards. It's not ideal. The whistle blows. The battle commences. It's... really loud. But, above the cacophony of militant pleasantries, the turgid drone of the old *Keane* album can be heard. Any woman knows that *Keane* should only be listened to when driving away from your cheating boyfriend's house in the early hours. After the old *Keane* album we listen to the old *Keane* album again. Unbelievable.

The motley crew of men are all very nice. Except one who is a bit scary. Sometimes I am unable to ask for jokes because of the male militia's banal barrage of questions. I get on really well with one bloke. I'd like to see him again but not with any rudeness in mind. I'm not sure how that works in the world of twenty-first century dating.

There is one, though. He is funny and easy to talk to and I like the look of him. He tells me an old joke about Shakespeare being bard from a bar. I let him off. He has a something about him. I mark my notes with 'I like him!!'

The bugger about speed-dating, however, is that – true to life – there are many more attractive women than men. Also a man will excuse most personality flaws (except maybe a murderous streak) if a woman is beautiful. Sadly, women don't or can't do this. The man I liked the look of at first is eerily earnest to speak to and fills his minutes lambasting the speed-dating process. I nearly laugh a one point. I think he's researching a character for a new Steve Coogan sketch. However handsome I think he his I wouldn't touch him with a pair of sterile gloves and a pipette. My male friend sums up the difference between men and women when I ask him about the petite Spanish girl. 'Mad as a brush... but I'd still shag her.'

The dating entrepreneurs blow the final whistle. The loveless drink and mingle. The women get on well. We all like each other's bags and shoes. My favourite guy has barricaded himself in at the bar with a pretty blonde. Luckily for me my male friend fancies the pretty blonde. With tactics learnt at Youth Club we approach. My male friend takes the blonde away. I chat white wine nonsense to my favourite guy. We get on. I tell him he was the only one I enjoyed speaking to. I get out my comments sheet. He gets out his. I show him mine. He shows me his.

Under 'Comments' he wrote: 'Says cunt a lot'

My mum would be proud.

I will add that I said it twice, for shock value and comedic effect and I pronounced it beautifully.

Oh well. Let's be positive,

Why are pirates called pirates?

They just 'AAARRRRGGGGGGHHHHHHHHHHHH'

A Spinster's Quest
www.spinstersquest.com

**Here's a piece from Emerald Bile's Noreen about her gynaecologist.
Don't say you weren't warned.**

 July 2006 – Achilles' cunt

A long time ago, I had a very inappropriate gynaecologist. He insisted on a really
long chat before getting his speculum out, like a creepy sort of foreplay; the type of
conversation one would have with a man in a bar. He would talk about his marriage
going to pieces and how his children hated him to death. When he examined me, the
inappropriate gynaecologist would always close his eyes as he rummaged around,
and make little peeping sounds in his throat. It was weird. All his patients (because
I knew a few of them) used to bitch about his weirdness and how slimy he was, but
I always thought to myself that I would keep going to him because he was a good
gynaecologist, but with an unfortunate bedside manner.

Anyway, one day, there were two women outside his office – also patients –
discussing his unusual medical practices and how he had told one of them that
she had the most elastic vagina he had ever seen. In response to that, the other one
pulled herself up in her chair, all the grand woman, and said, 'Well, he told me I had
the most beautiful vagina he had ever seen!' So then I was interested to see what the
gynaecologist would have to say about my vag., and do you know what? He said
nothing at all except 'peep, peep, peep'. I felt ignored.

I had almost forgotten about having a mediocre vagina until I saw my friend who
has a foot fetish recently, and he was telling me about the time he bought a perfect
stranger a pair of shoes in order to see her bare feet before she tried the new shoes
on. I asked him if he thought my feet were the type you could have a fetish about.
He shivered his shoulders slightly, pasted on a kind look and said, 'I've seen your feet
already.' Fucking thanks a million. I was all hurt about having a mediocre minge and
feet a fetishist won't touch, so I took myself to the shoe shop and the woman said:
'Buy these, these are fuck-me shoes,' and I did, thinking that the shoes would distract
from the mediocrity of the other two parts, but fuck me, they were fucking high, and
fucking tight and all they did was make me need corn plasters.

Emerald Bile
emeraldbile.blogspot.com

Donald from the blogging collective The Sharpener performs a stylish high-wire act over the most divisive of issues.

 October 2006 – Talk amongst yourselves, we couldn't possibly comment

One word absolutely not on the lips of political hacks, not even Tory political hacks, is… abortion. Not party conference week, not any week. It's impolite conversation inside the beltway.

But a post here at The Sharpener[1] last year attracted over 250 comments. Just publishing the word is pure Google-juice. Everyone in the real world has an opinion, so why does nobody in political Britain want to discuss abortion in public? It can't be that 186,274 (2001 data[2]) annual terminations don't warrant justification or inquiry.

My own theory on the silence is this: nobody talks in public because it's too easy to get drawn into dark places, or to find yourself with idiotic allies. You could play the God card; but there's no debating with faith, and polite society considers the faithful ever so slightly simple.

Religion aside, 'pro-lifers' (who isn't?) offer other weak arguments. One claims the foetus has rights because of its potential for humanity (fully realised in a way that an egg isn't). This is nonsense: nobody has the rights of what they might become, only for what they are. Neither I, nor the inhabitants of Guatemala City, have the rights of a US citizen, though we have the potential to become one. (I suspect that some Americans making arguments based in potential wouldn't fancy us having those rights, either. Not the Guatemalans, anyway.)

A second argument claims a right to life for the foetus as soon as it's 'viable' – able to survive outside the body. Owen replies[3]:

> *Whether or not a foetus has moral worth cannot possibly depend on whether scientists have yet developed an effective artificial incubator. Whether or not a foetus is a bearer of rights does not change over*

[1] www.thesharpener.net/2005/08/25/abortion/
[2] www.statistics.gov.uk/downloads/theme_health/AB28_2001/AB28_2001.pdf
[3] www.owen.org/blog/528

*time with scientific progress, nor does it vary between countries
according to the state of the health-care system.*

Quite. It's often a dishonest, spineless[4] line of reasoning, rightly skewered.

But 'pro-choicers' aren't short of poor arguments themselves. One goes a bit like this: 'Male control over birth rights, over women's bodies, has been a tool of patriarchal oppression for centuries'. True, but any reasonable ethics only allow remedial action against the oppressor. Most of them are long dead, none of them are foetal – so what's the relevance to an abortion in 2006? Even if the medicalisation of terminations in America involved (male) doctors claiming power[5] over (female) midwives, this is irrelevant. History should only carefully be a guide to justice – and only if it suggests a just remedy. Thin-end-of-the-wedge arguments are usually weak, and this is no exception.

There's an instrumental pro-choice argument, too: 'I couldn't give the child a good life. Why bring it into the world if it will never be fulfilled?' It's a version of the Freakonomics guide to abortion[6]. For this to be valid, two things need to be true: that there is a shortage of couples willing to adopt newborns, and that death is preferable to a sub-optimal life. The first is demonstrably false; the second is repellent to (most of) the living, just a short hop from eugenics.

Yet another solution was proposed by a commenter[7]:

> *...you don't have to be an out-and-out libertarian to think that there
> should be some boundaries to the state, and the cervix seems like as
> good a start as any.*

Which is fine, and perfectly consistent if you permit abortions right up to birth. This might appear a 'liberal' position, but only if you assign no rights at all to a fully developed foetus, only physically distinguishable from a 'baby' by its home address. This is a position most people would reject as tyrannical (which doesn't mean it's wrong).

[4] news.bbc.co.uk/1/hi/health/5099362.stm

[5] mollysavestheday.blogspot.com/2006/01/finishing-what-roe-started.html

[6] www.isteve.com/abortion.htm

[7] www.thesharpener.net/2005/08/25/abortion#comment-2762

So, what's left? It's messy. Both a foetus and the mother must have rights. The mother has the right to bodily autonomy, and the foetus, from some point in pregnancy, a right to life. If we're going to have time restrictions on abortion, then a foetal right to life somehow trumps a woman's right to autonomy. (But this argument has its own dark place: we're allowing the right to use another's organs against their will. So, could we force someone to give up a kidney against their will, if they were the only person able to help? Perhaps, if kidney donation was as safe as normal pregnancy, which it isn't. (Giving blood is, though: see Cecile Fabre's great book, *Whose Body Is It Anyway?*[8], for more along these lines.)

The question is: when does this right to foetal life trump a human being's right to autonomy? Not from when it can survive outside the womb ('viability'). Not surely at the point of 'independence': that would permit post-birth, involuntary euthanasia. And not at full self-awareness; some children never get there. Perhaps when it can feel pain? When it becomes conscious? When it develops the capacity for abstract thought or experience[9], and therefore humanity? All these are coherent positions, intuitively ethical, based in science, subject to change as knowledge progresses, explicit in limiting female abortion rights. None seems to suggest moving the current 24-week limit very far in either direction, as far as I can tell.

The corollary to a policy of forced childbirth (for that's what abortion time limits are) is that legal terminations should never be interrogated. If we base our laws on the undeveloped foetus lacking (before acquiring) rights, then the only medical concern is the woman's physical and mental health. Access to early abortion should be free and easy. Pragmatism also suggests that sex education (like maths and English) should be compulsory, and contraception (through schemes like the c:card[10]) accessible. Prevention is better than cure, sure; it's also cheaper.

[8] www.amazon.co.uk/Whose-Body-Anyway-Justice-Integrity/dp/0199289999/sr=8-1/qid=1159876202/ref=sr_1_1/026-2538156-9309247?ie=UTF8&s=books
[9] dreamflesh.com/archives/2006/06/news-from-the-womb/
[10] www.ccard.org.uk/

None of this is simple for politicians to discuss. Arguments have to be clear and careful. None readily tabloidise. But if party hacks are wondering about electoral disaffection, they could start by interrogating their own eagerness to abdicate. While they're happy to confine health debates to PCTs and the small print of dentistry contracts, the politics of abortion is happening[11] without them.

The Sharpener
www.thesharpener.net

[11] philobiblon.co.uk/?p=1602

We've Had A Bit Of A Falling Out
War

From the smallest playground spat to intercontinental nuclear exchanges, fighting in all its ugly forms is regarded by all right-thinking people as A Very Bad Thing. Unfortunately, these days, right-thinking people aren't allowed within 500 yards of the apparatus of power and this is where it's got us. The last one to come close was probably Mahatma Ghandi, and look what happened to him. Somebody shot him.

Conflict is a subject with many contradictions. Glass someone in the pub and you're a common thug; push the button on half a million* Iraqis and you're a statesman. As the soldier says in Monty Python's Meaning of Life: 'I killed 15 of those buggers. Now, at home they'd hang me; here they'll give me a fucking medal, sir.'

Here, some of Blogland's foremost thinkers attempt to traverse the moral minefield that is Fighting Each Other, whether it be in Iraq, on the home front of the War Against Terror in London, or raking over the coals of World War II.

* At the last estimate, according to research published in *The Lancet.*

Iraq may have been on a slow slide down the news agenda this year but it still refused to disappear. Away from the ongoing carnage it remained a highly divisive issue in Blogland with arguments usually degenerating into insults and vitriol pretty quickly. Jarndyce wrote a thoughtful and thought-provoking piece about where we were in Iraq and how we got there.

 November 2005 – Bloody Iraq, for the last time

I don't really write much here about Iraq. I certainly don't have a book on it in me. In fact, I might never write about it again, partly because it's a bit boring being branded a warmonger or an accomplice of Islamism, and partly because it doesn't actually matter what my opinion is, either way; or yours.

I'm only writing about it now because I've had a bit of mud slung my way recently. Not especially intelligent mud, but then intelligent mud on this issue is rarer than a morel in autumn. So, I supported the war, and still do. To justify this, I'll revert to a bit of hack philosophy. Bear with me: it's just one paragraph, then I'll get my hands dirty with the specifics…

You're walking past a duck pond. In the pond, a child is drowning. You have the power to save him. There are 20 people sitting on the bank doing nothing about it, and you fail to swim in and save him. If he drowns, you've done a bad thing. But so have they – it wasn't your responsibility alone. Perhaps you're blameless: maybe you can't swim, or at least can't be sure you'll be able to save him without serious risk to yourself. At worst, you can swim, but they all can too, so there's blame to be shared around.

But what about this: there's nobody else around who can save him, and you obviously can. It's either you or he drowns. You are obligated to save his life under any sensible moral code. Failure to do so marks a serious ethical breach. And it's here I think the 'West' sat in relation to Iraq, *circa* 2002. We were obligated to do something – something to replace 'Let's starve them of medical supplies and food for the another decade'. To do nothing at all while they laboured under totalitarianism (worse: part-created by us) would have been reprehensible. File under Spain, 1930s.

Of course, that something didn't have to be invasion, and there are myriad objections to my simplistic logic and the conduct (especially the aftermath) of the war:

1. We're robbing them blind. This seems perfectly possible, knowing the narrow, greedy agenda of the global megacorp. But if in the process of saving the child, we pinch his wallet, on balance is it better that we should have let him drown? Obviously not. I'm not naive enough to think our motives in Iraq were primarily or even secondarily noble. So what?

2. It's an imperialist project. Heh, so was Japan in 1945. Now, instead of militaristic fascists invading their neighbours and peasants begging for rice, they're selling us Gameboys and cheap cars, and employing half of Sunderland. It's not utopia, but it sure beats the Meiji Restoration. Next.

3. We've committed war crimes along the way. There has never been a war where victor and vanquished didn't. 'Young man with gun abuses position of power'. In other news: the sun rose this morning. Prosecute them, and move on. Next.

4. We've killed a lot of innocent people. The alternative to invading Iraq wasn't that nobody died, just that different people did. A non-decision may be easier, but it's still a decision. Does it matter if there have been more or fewer deaths than the counterfactual? Is that number knowable? Do you construct moral cases for or against war on the basis of crude numerical analyses?

5. It was illegal. I guess that should read 'probably illegal', but it doesn't matter. The Bush administration's attitude to international law has been dangerous. But, in this case, if you've already decided this war is moral (or immoral), is legality much more than window dressing? Can anyone construct a decent argument to change their attitude to killing tens of thousands on the basis of bought-and-paid-for UNSC abstentions from Putin and Chirac?

6. It was bound to increase the terrorist threat to the West. Also a fair point, but it didn't create that threat. Non-action wouldn't have eliminated it, perhaps not even have reduced it significantly. Even the genesis of London 7 July stretches back as far as 2001, if recent intelligence leaks are accurate. Should we take care not to do the jihadists' recruitment for them? Absolutely. Should the existence of this rival imperial project deflect us from a policy we've already decided is right? Not unless you're happy for al-Zarqawi to be given a job in Whitehall. This objection is trivially true but irrelevant, a rehashed version of 4.

7. It's shown the world the true nature of American hegemonic power. Which is a bad thing? Next.

8. It can't possibly work. This is where most intelligent objectors come from, the Kissingerian conservatives and the anti-imperialists. They may be right. But, looked at from a distance of a decade or two, they might also be wrong. World War II looked a mess in Dunkirk. This is ultimately a judgement call, a realpolitik puzzle, one to which nobody alive knows the answer for sure. There are good reasons why it will never work: no basic liberal culture to sew democracy onto, nothing granted rather than earned ever sticks, little interest from the occupying powers in creating real democracy. There are good ones why it might: decent electoral turnout in dire circumstances so far, the innate human desire for autonomy realised through democracy, the tendency for democracy to grow organically over time, no matter how limited its initial seed. Political scientists call it a 'fuzzy gamble', which is a nifty bit of jargon.

I'm not arrogant or deluded enough to expect this piece to change anyone's opinion. I'm merely justifying my deeply irrelevant, pragmatic support for invading another sovereign country. (Now, if you want to misrepresent me, you can do so accurately.) We owed the people of Iraq a shot at liberty and democracy, and there was no viable alternative way to pay the debt. By 2003, there was the first opportunity since 1991 to cough up. The result will obviously be flawed, imperfect. But we were right to invade.

I'm glad I didn't have to fight, though a sort-of cousin did. I'm relieved I didn't have to make the decision: non-decisions are much easier, and I changed my mind several times along the way. I do, though, think that how you call this says little about your political stripe. It does make you an idiot to pronounce on with certainty. However much you pose and preen, your best guess at a known unknown doesn't make you a virtuous or evil person. See you in hell, perhaps.

The Jarndyce Blog
fairvotewatch.blogspot.com

It wasn't just a case of soldiers engaging in battle this year – a certain tabloid editor has been in the wars as well. 'Gotcha!' said the soaraway Curmudgeon.

 November 2005 – At least she isn't a gipsy

Redhead Rebekah Wade[1] has been released to terrorise the community after an alleged assault on her soap-star husband.

Passionate Rebekah, 37, is understood to have met saucy ex-minister David Blunkett last night after his resignation.

The couple's commiserations seem to have led to domestic troubles. Rebekah returned home some time before 4 a.m. and split her husband's lip.

Rebekah is known for her hard-hitting style. As editor of *The News of the World* she raised sales and eyebrows with a policy of 'naming and shaming' convicted paedophiles.

The campaign was only stopped because some paediatricians[2] were too polysyllabic for the moral force of sexy Rebekah's readers.

As editor of *The Sun*, the wavy-tressed stunna has overseen a campaign for action against domestic violence, but she is thought to be fairly tolerant of hypocrisy.

Although she originally worked in France, Rebekah lives in Battersea, south London, where residents are thought to be wondering why the government does not do more to control violent evildoers.

The Curmudgeon
thecurmudgeonly.blogspot.com

[1] news.independent.co.uk/media/article324382.ece
[2] www.bbc.co.uk/bbcfour/documentaries/profile/rebekah-wade.shtml

Garry Smith, the Curious Hamster, makes a pre-emptive strike…

 December 2005 – What's your problem?

Some of my friends and I were in Aberdeen town centre the other night. We were walking down a back lane, on our way to the cinema, as it happens, when we spotted a suspicious-looking fellow walking towards us. All of us seemed to sense that he'd be trouble.

As he got closer, I began to get the feeling that he had a knife. Some quick, whispered questions confirmed that my friends all had similar fears. He got a bit closer. Further whispering centred on the possibility of avoiding him altogether, but that would have been exceedingly difficult by this stage. He was only 10 paces away and we'd have had to basically turn and run. We walked on silently.

He'd got to within five paces when he started reaching for an inside pocket. I was absolutely convinced that he had a knife. So I shot him. In the head, as it happens. He became an ex-knife murderer in a very short space of time. Surprisingly fragile thing, a human head.

We searched him, of course, and it turns out he didn't have a knife after all (not much in his wallet either, which just added to the sense of anti-climax). But he did have in his possession a fishing magazine, and in this fishing magazine were several advertisements for knives. It is clear to me that this man had been saving up for a knife. It was only my timely intervention that prevented him from acquiring enough money to buy a knife, ordering that knife, waiting 28 days for delivery of the knife, getting a little card through the door from the postman saying 'I called today to deliver your knife but you weren't in', getting up early on a Saturday morning to collect the knife from the Post Office, unwrapping the knife, taking the knife out with him, walking down a back lane with the knife in an inside pocket, and using that same knife to stab an innocent bystander. Viciously.

As you can see, it's just as well I intervened the way I did. I take full responsibility and am absolutely confident that I made the right decision. I really was sure he had a knife. And he definitely was a nasty piece of work.

Some of my friends have fallen out with me over this. They say I should not have shot the suspected knife-wielding maniac as I couldn't 'be sure' he had a knife.

Ludicrous. Some of them have even suggested that I manipulated their fear of a knife-wielding maniac in order to gain access to the chap's wallet. Outrageous. You had been notably short of money in the weeks before the incident, they say. Barking moonbats. Some have even suggested that I may have committed a crime. Absolutely ridiculous (and a moot point. As I'm Grand Master of Aberdeen Lodge, I very much doubt I'll be facing a police investigation any time soon*). It's people like these, these defeatists, these apologists for knife-wielding maniacs, who've made knife-wielding maniacism the threat it is today. These people would sit by and watch their own family being brutally slaughtered by knife-wielding maniacs and then try to 'open a dialogue' with the killers. Cowards, every one of them.

Would you believe that quite a few of the guys' friends are trying to kill me now? Unbelievable, the way some people behave. Bring it on, that's what I say, bring it on. Now, are you, yes you, with me, or are you against me? Think hard before you answer.

(Do I need to point out the obvious? Legal notice: this is a made-up story.)

*Apologies to any Masons reading this. I'm sure Freemasonry has moved on a great deal since Monty Python.

Curious Hamster
bsscworld.blogspot.com

With Iran looking to become one of the world's hottest destinations in the coming months, the Curious Hamster provided this handy and rather good cut-out-and-keep rough guide to the country and its recent history. Lots of links, well worth following.

 January 2006 – Iran

Iran is the new black, apparently. Here are some facts about Iran which might come in handy this year. I've written this mostly for my own benefit, to be honest.

66

Basics

So, Iran is predominantly populated by Shiite Persians (not Arabs). Their Shia fundamentalist Islam is not the same as the Sunni Wahhabism[1] of the Taliban or bin Laden. In fact, Wahhabis believe that the Shia are not 'proper' Muslims at all (the Taliban viciously oppressed[2] Shiites in Afghanistan). The idea that bin Laden would form an alliance with Iranian fundamentalists is a bit like believing that Ian Paisley would form one with the Pope. Not hugely likely, in other words. The Iranian government does have strong connections to the Shiites[3] in the new Iraqi government, though. The Iranian government are also strongly linked to Hezbollah[4], a Shia group. The spiritual leader of Hezbollah, Sheikh Fadlallah, has said that the September 11 attacks on the US were un-Islamic and 'barbaric'. Hezbollah does, however, support suicide bombings directed against Israel.

That Coup

In 1953, the Shah was reinstalled after the sort of successful conclusion of Operation Ajax[5]. The operation involved the CIA, with British support, orchestrating a coup against the nationalist Prime Minister of Iran (who had nationalised the British-owned Anglo-Iranian Oil Company). This CIA article[6] analyses the after-effects of that operation.

> *TPAJAX got the CIA into the regime-change business for good – similar efforts would soon follow in Guatemala, Indonesia, and Cuba – but [...] the Agency has had little success at that enterprise, while bringing itself and the United States more political ill will, and breeding more untoward results, than any other of its activities. Most of the CIA's acknowledged efforts of this sort have shown that Washington has been more interested in strongman rule in the Middle East and elsewhere than in encouraging democracy. The result is a credibility problem that accompanied American troops into Iraq and continues to plague them...*

[1] en.wikipedia.org/wiki/Wahhabism
[2] en.wikipedia.org/wiki/Taleban#Shia_under_the_Taliban
[3] www.southcoasttoday.com/daily/01-06/01-29-06/07world-nation.htm
[4] en.wikipedia.org/wiki/Hezbollah
[5] en.wikipedia.org/wiki/Operation_Ajax
[6] www.cia.gov/csi/studies/vol48no2/article10.html

The question is, has anyone told *President Bush?*[7]

> *They hate what we see right here in this chamber – a democratically elected government. Their leaders are self-appointed. They hate our freedoms...*

Perhaps, in the case of Iran, they hate the fact that the US government took away that very freedom and reappointed and supported a Western-friendly government while disregarding the sovereignty of Iran. Bush can't be blamed for that, it happened in 1953. But it did happen. This led to the first use of the term 'blowback'[8].

That Revolution

The regime of the Shah was highly corrupt and used brutal methods to maintain power. Nevertheless, the government continued to be supported by the West, particularly by the US, as it was thought to provide an effective barrier to Soviet entry into the strategically important Middle East region. Growing discontentment with the Shah created the conditions that led to the revolution and brought the Shiite Islamists to power. The United States government had assured the Shah that they would 'back him to the hilt', but in the end they decided not to. The revolution, after the twists and turns common to many revolutions, brought Ayatollah Khomeini to power in 1979.

That Mad President

Today, President Ahmadinejad is in charge. Sort of. The Supreme Leader, Ali Khamenei, is Comander in Chief of Iran's armed forces, including the Revolutionary Guard, and has the exclusive power to declare war. Last year, Khamenei issued a fatwa against production, stockpiling and use of nuclear weapons (although I doubt that's very reassuring to most people). He is a staunch religious conservative and strongly opposed to reform. The Guardian Council further complicates the issue, as does the Assembly of Experts. How this all fits together is demonstrated by a handy BBC graphic[9]. Sort of.

[7] www.whitehouse.gov/news/releases/2001/09/20010920-8.html
[8] en.wikipedia.org/wiki/Blowback_(intelligence)
[9] news.bbc.co.uk/1/shared/spl/hi/middle_east/03/iran_power/html/default.stm

Anyway, the point is that Ahmadinejad does not have the same powers as President Bush for example. Ahmadinejad cannot simply impose his will on foreign policy issues.

That Nuclear Issue

This is the big issue and, of course, the reason why Iran is the new black. The latest news is that there has been *no progress*[10] in talks between the EU and the Iranians. There'll be much more on this in the coming months, no doubt.

And Finally

From that BBC report:

> Many Western powers and also Israel distrust Iran, partly because it had kept its nuclear research secret for 18 years before it was revealed in 2002.

I wonder what Mordechai Vanunu[11] would say to that?

Curious Hamster
bsscworld.blogspot.com

[10] news.bbc.co.uk/1/hi/world/middle_east/4662702.stm
[11] www.indymedia.org.uk/en/2006/01/330754.html

The terrorist threat was still ever-present. And we weren't allowed to forget it.

 December 2005 – Reassurance GLA-style

Jenny Jones, member of the London Assembly and the Metropolitan Police Authority, was briefed recently on the terror threat to the capital. Yesterday she told a conference:

> *'If you knew what we knew, you would really be scared'.*

Whereas, of course, now that we know that she knows something deeply alarming, but still don't know what it is, we are completely reassured.

Try this technique if your children won't sleep.

Child: Mummy/Daddy, I'm scared there's a monster under my bed.

Parent (looks under bed, screams): just be grateful you haven't seen how big and scary that monster is.

For the record, I believe there is a serious terror threat. I just don't like the policy of be-afraidism.

Rafael Behr
rafaelbehr.typepad.com

The arrest and conviction in Austria of the historian David Irving brought debates about World War II and the Holocaust to the fore once again and managed to divide and unite bloggers simultaneously. While some welcomed with his conviction and some didn't, nearly all agreed that it couldn't have happened to a nicer man. Mr Eugenides put it best.

 December 2005 – David Irving and Holocaust denial

The 'revisionist' [sic] historian, David Irving, was arrested in Austria last month and now faces charges relating to his controversial, and oft-repeated, views about the Holocaust (including the claim that there were no gas chambers), that country having some of the strictest laws against Holocaust denial of any in Europe. (Incidentally, I think the Austrian justice minister missed a trick. When asked by the press, I would have denied that Irving was being held, and claimed that there was no evidence he had ever even existed.)

[As an aside, it turns out, brilliantly, that while banged up in jail near Graz Irving found two of his books in the prison library. He autographed them and returned them to the guards.]

At the time of Irving's libel trial against Deborah Lipstadt[1], the writer D.D. Guttenplan wrote this piece[2] for the Guardian, which neatly crystallises some of the issues surrounding Holocaust denial. In essence, there are two main questions here:

1. Should the denial of the historical fact of the Holocaust, whatever the motivation, be a criminal offence?

2. More generally, is there really such a thing as objective historical 'truth'?

Let's take the second issue first. As Christopher Hitchens has pointed out (more of him in a moment or two), and Guttenplan confirms in the Guardian article cited, quite a lot of what we think we know about the Holocaust is untrue. For example:

[1] www.holocaustdenialontrial.org/ieindex.html
[2] www.guardian.co.uk/irving/article/0,2763,194413,00.html

Jewish prisoners were turned into soap

Jews were gassed in Belsen and Dachau

are both untrue statements.

The first was a contemporary urban myth which has now largely been debunked; as for the second, Belsen and Dachau were concentration camps, not death camps (perhaps a rather academic distinction to the thousands that died there) but Belsen never had a gas chamber, and Dachau's was never used. The gas chambers were in other death camps, most notably Auschwitz, but also Treblinka and Sobibor.

None of this is to deny or in any way challenge the historical fact of the murder of up to 6 million Jews by the Nazis. Yet the fact that I even feel compelled to insert that disclaimer is a measure of how dangerous it is felt to be to question the accepted narrative of history.

In so many areas of our past there is a commonly understood consensus, within reason, on what happened, and why. Sometimes this consensus is broadly correct; sometimes not. Into the latter category fall those stories from history which have attained almost mythological status. Thus American schoolkids are taught that George Washington never told a lie, British schoolchildren that King Canute sat on the beach and tried to turn back the tide (although they probably won't be taught that for much longer[3]), and everyone believes Catherine the Great died shagging a horse.

By and large, we recognise these types of stories for what they are, or rather what they represent. But sometimes the inaccuracies, the inevitable elisions and omissions, are more subtle. Thus, despite the recent reinstatement, thanks to the forces of PC, of the place of 'native Americans' in that country's history, the American concept of 'manifest destiny' is still taught to every schoolchild – as if it were really any country's divine right to expand its borders by purchases, landgrabs and (let us not shy away from the word) genocide.

Thus we are all told that Winston Churchill was the greatest Prime Minister that Britain ever had. There's little mention now of his authorship of the Gallipoli tragedy, his changes in position during the 'locust years' between the wars, his

[3] **news.bbc.co.uk/1/hi/scotland/4415418.stm**

mistakes in the conduct of the war, his cold-blooded agreement with Stalin – done, according to legend, on the back of an envelope – to carve up Eastern and Southern Europe, and his frequent bouts of drunkenness and depression – because the history has been written already, and we don't like our assumptions of the old Dresden-crusher challenged.

What these 'accepted narratives' have in common is not that they are untrue – I believe WSC was indeed the greatest non-female politician these islands have produced – but rather that they are [relatively] rarely revised or challenged, and so take on the status of shibboleths, any questioning of which immediately marks the enquiring mind as (at best) an iconoclast but, in the worst-case scenario – when the totem in question is something as serious, as deadly serious, as the Holocaust – as a crypto-fascist, a denier and an outcast.

And so to Hitchens. On a number of occasions prior to Irving's libel trial, Christopher Hitchens defended him in print, both on the grounds of free speech and, perhaps more tendentiously, as an important and serious historian, even if a morally dubious one – 'not just a Fascist historian, but also a great historian of Fascism' (a quote he probably now regrets). Following his defeat in that libel case, Hitchens was moved to comment that he had been wrong about Irving, writing that, in reading a detailed account of the many falsifications and distortions in his work, 'I mentally closed the book [against Irving] when I reached this stage'.

Yet this has still been sufficient for Hitchens to be labelled a 'Holocaust denier' by the more easily excitable elements in the US.

Many intelligent thinkers consider the Holocaust to be a historically unique event, different not merely in scale but also in kind from other historical genocides, such as the Armenian genocide of 1915 or the ruthless 'Year Zero' purges of the Khmer Rouge (both of which killed a larger proportion of their target populations, incidentally).

This cult of exceptionalism can sometimes have distasteful corollaries. Thus, for example, the fate of the homosexuals, gypsies, even Jehovah's Witnesses murdered by the Nazis seem to fade into the background (in the context of such a horror, I suppose, how could it not?). Thus Armenian attempts to gain recognition of their own holocaust fall, all too often, on stony ground – it is to Israel's everlasting shame that it is unwilling to upset its cosy relationship with Turkey by recognising the crime that served as Hitler's template for the Final Solution. And to watch

Europe imprisoning Holocaust deniers whilst simultaneously extending the hand of partnership to Turkey, which denies the existence of that genocide, is to watch doublethink made reality.

The dispute about whether it is better to take on Fascism and its apologists in open debate, or to try and suppress such dangerous lies before they can gain widespread currency, is a well-trodden one, and will not be rehashed here. But to elevate the grotesquery of Holocaust denial to the status of a 'crime' is, I suggest, to turn it into a thought crime almost unique in kind.

Is it right to deny the Holocaust, or the existence of the gas chambers? No. Is it historically correct to do so? In as far as we can ever be certain of these things, no. Is it a crime to believe it? Surely not. And yet, apparently, it is. As Rod Liddle puts it in today's *Spectator*:

> *David Irving and people like him call themselves 'revisionists', of course. But the study of history itself is nothing more than a painstaking and sometimes painful act of revisionism; A.J.P. Taylor, you might argue, was a revisionist. So, too, Trevelyan. Banging up David Irving intellectually dignifies his repulsive opinions and makes sopping liberals like me squirm with anger at the injustice of it all; that one could face the wrath of the state for contradicting the officially sanctioned view.*

I couldn't agree more. We face enough challenges over laws to outlaw the 'glorifying of terrorism' and 'religious hate speech' without turning pathetic apologists for Hitler like David Irving into test cases for free speech. Like an Iron Cross once worn with pride by one of his heroes of old, Irving's reputation has slowly been tarnished by the steady oxidisation that time, and constant exposure, brings. Lock it away, by contrast, and it remains brilliant and gleaming, the more so in the mind's eye for being out of sight.

Let him go; let him publish; let him be damned.

Mr Eugenides
mreugenides.blogspot.com

Another battle: Evolutionists versus Creationists (or IDers, as they have recently rebranded themselves). The Ministry of Truth takes sides.

 January 2006 – Irreducible stupidity

Nice of the Torygraph to *give a platform to Stephen C. Meyer*[1], one of the leading proponents of the supposed 'theory' of 'intelligent design', as his article nicely illustrates everything that is wrong with this unscientific piece of crap and its supporters.

That life evolves is a matter of fact. More than that, it an observable fact as anyone working in the field of virology or bacteriology will happily explain. Viruses mutate and evolve, which is where we get everything from nasty new strains of bird flu to hospital superbugs to rats that are immune to warfarin.

Evolution by natural selection is a scientific theory inasmuch as it explains how things evolve in response to environmental pressures. Again this can be observed and tested in the real world, and has so far stood up to every test put to it. It's not difficult to understand; if we take the humble rat and alter its environment by laying poison for it, then it dies; and rats will keep on dying until a minor genetic variation results in a rat that survives the poison through having developed a resistance or immunity to its effects. That rat breeds with other rats, passing on its genetic code and, hey presto, we have a whole bunch of evolved rats who don't die when we try to poison them.

The same process applied to bacteria and antibiotics and to viruses and anti-viral agents.

Frankly, were I a doctor and there really was such a thing as an intelligent designer, then I'd be wanting to know who they are, where they are and, most important of all, what it would take to get them to piss off and stop fucking designing all the nasty, shitty illnesses that keep making people sick and messing up my nice orderly hospital.

[1] www.telegraph.co.uk/opinion/main.jhtml?xml=/opinion/2006/01/28/do2803.xml&sSheet=/opinion/2006/01/28/ixop.html

Alternatively, I suppose the drug companies would be paying them to keep right on designing away, as this whole new illness thing gives them a nice steady stream of profits.

But all that it by the by – there is no intelligent designer, it's all a bullshit hoax anyway.

There are many things I could pick on to show why ID is a pile of crap, but the one thing I want to pick up on here is its proponents' claim that it is evidence-based.

Scientific methodology is based on a very simple principle – you take a question to which the answer is unknown or incomplete, you examine the evidence, derive a hypothesis from that evidence and then use more evidence, derived from experiment and observation to test that hypothesis – and you keep right on testing against new and more detailed evidence over and over again. If you then fail to find evidence to contradict your hypothesis, your theory stands up – at least until the next test and the next batch of evidence.

Darwin's theory of evolution by natural selection has been tested in this way for more than 100 years and has stood up to every test; hence it is treated and taught as science.

ID, on the other hand, commits one of the cardinal sins of scientific enquiry inasmuch as it is selective in its use of evidence – it doesn't test the theory against evidence, it mere chooses evidence to fit the theory and ignores everything else. Meyer actually does this right from the outset of his article by citing the apparent 'conversion' of philosopher Anthony Flew[2] to deism:

> In 2004, the distinguished philosopher Anthony Flew of the University of Reading made worldwide news when he repudiated a lifelong commitment to atheism and affirmed the reality of some kind of a creator. Flew cited evidence of intelligent design in DNA and the arguments of 'American [intelligent] design theorists' as important reasons for this shift.

[2] en.wikipedia.org/wiki/Anthony_Flew

Of course what Meyer neglects to mention is that Flew, in 2005, went on to reject both the fine-tuning[3] argument and his earlier claims that DNA could not be explained by naturalistic theories, both of which are essential to the workings of intelligent design – Flew remains a deist, so far as I know, but one whose conception of a supreme being is strictly non-interventionist after the point of creation (the Big Bang), a view that rules out a belief in intelligent design or an intelligent designer in the form supported by Meyer and others.

I'll pass over the matter of 'irreducible complexity', which used to relate to the eye until it was debunked[4], and now rests on the flagellum bacteria, which has also been solidly debunked as well[5], much as Meyer and others desperately cling to this idea, and move on to this statement:

> *DNA functions like a software programme. We know from experience that software comes from programmers. We know that information – whether, say, in hieroglyphics or radio signals – always arises from an intelligent source. As the pioneering information theorist Henry Quastler observed: 'Information habitually arises from conscious activity.' So the discovery of digital information in DNA provides strong grounds for inferring that intelligence played a causal role in its origin.*

Information may well habitually arise from conscious activity but as any physicist worth their research grant can tell you, the universe is full of information that does not rely on conscious thought: information does not always arise from an intelligent source – that is mere anthropic conceit on Meyer's part. It is perhaps no great surprise that Meyer avoids this topic and merely makes his unsupportable and entirely false claim about information. The physics of information derives primarily from quantum theory, which the ID lobby tend to studiously avoid, due in no small measure to their inability to take on and refute Heisenberg's Uncertainty Principle – there being no room for a designer in a universe that is intrinsically random at the sub-atomic level.

In short, Meyer's contention here is utter nonsense.

[3] en.wikipedia.org/wiki/Fine-tuned_universe
[4] www.resonancepub.com/remstatocys.htm
[5] www.millerandlevine.com/km/evol/design2/article.html

Not much more to say really, other than to note that Meyer's PhD is in the philosophy of science and it's to philosophy that one must turn to refute his contention that ID is not based on religion.

Let us take, for a moment, the hypothesis that there is such a thing as an intelligent designer. Now ask yourself this – where did this designer come from? Who designed the designer?

There are only two possible answers to this question. Either that it is no one, that the supposed designer has always existed or came into being by a process of spontaneous self-creation and, therefore, exists outside of the confines space–time – in which case the designer is God and ID is based on religion; or that there must be an infinite series of designers, all of whom are out there in an infinite universe designing new designers – in which case you have a *reductio ad absurdum*[6].

As far as I can see Meyer has yet, as a philosopher, to attempt to tackle this question – perhaps he should before continuing to claim that intelligent design is based on scientific evidence.

Ministry of Truth
www.ministryoftruth.org.uk

[6] en.wikipedia.org/wiki/Reductio_ad_absurdum

Ever the voice of reason, Harry Hutton spotted an even bigger danger than Holocaust deniers such as….

 February 2006 – David Irving

David Irving jailed[1] for Holocaust denial.

Seriously, have you ever met a Holocaust denier? Can you, off the top of your head, name three Holocaust deniers? They don't scare me. In the UK I would say they are about 900th on the list of dangers, behind escaped zoo animals and clumsy people with hot drinks.

People who don't look where they are going are a genuine menace, but once again our political class buries its head in the sand.

Chase me, ladies, I'm in the cavalry
chasemeladies.blogspot.com

[1] news.bbc.co.uk/2/hi/europe/4734648.stm

One of the more tedious aspects of the debate about the War Against Terror is the accusation levelled at critics of US foreign policy that they are 'anti-American'. Jim Bliss mounts a defence far more nuanced than that of those doing the name-calling.

 March 2006 – The madness of anti-Americanism

Tony Blair has just called me 'mad'[1]. What a bastid. And talk about your pots and kettles!

Also, I notice he flew all the way to Australia to do it. Clearly decided to put some distance between us before unleashing the insults. Probably afraid I'd lamp him. And lamp him I would if I were ever within arm's length of the freakin' psycho.

Many moons ago, on a blog not unlike this one, I wrote a piece entitled 'Why I'm anti-American'. I shall reiterate the main points of that, as I feel they bear repeating on a day Tony Blair dismisses those who disagree with him as clinically insane (and presumably in need of sedation) rather than worthy of engaging in debate.

First, let's make it clear what being anti-American is not about. It isn't about disliking Americans. There's already a word for that… 'bigotry'. Disliking or discriminating against someone because of their nationality or skin colour just means you're an obnoxious tosser. It doesn't make you 'anti-American' in the sense I'm using the phrase.

And because anti-Americanism isn't about disliking people, there's thankfully no danger of it ever manifesting as a desire to murder a whole bunch of Americans indiscriminately. So I utterly reject the idea that anti-Americanism of itself has a logical extension in what happened on September 11, 2001. What you had there was anti-Americanism mixed up with a whole bunch of other stuff. The anti-Americanism chose the target, but it was the other stuff that chose the tactics.

Needless to say, I favour different tactics, and I'm just as opposed to the other stuff – the stuff that justified thousands of murders in the eyes of extremists (as Dubya Bush and Tony Blair are). But that 'with us or agin us' crap? It doesn't wash with me. My enemy's enemy is not always my friend.

[1] politics.guardian.co.uk/iraq/story/0,,1740613,00.html

Anti-American'ism / Anti-'Americanism

Most people would agree that there is a genuine difference between being anti-Islam and being anti-Islamist. No such distinction currently exists in our language between anti-American and anti-Americanism. Though perhaps one should.

Whatever the intentions of the Founding Fathers and a succession of constitutional scholars may have been, in the eyes of much of the world the United States no longer stands for what most Americans are taught it stands for in school. Schoolchildren throughout the days of Empire in Britain were taught that colonialism was all about bringing 'civilisation' to the savages. The savages saw it as rape, murder and the theft of their land and resources. These days it's America and not Britain, and it's 'democracy' and not civilisation. The savages still use the same words, though.

And that's very much part of the problem. The whole 'we confer upon you lesser people the right to rule yourselves' thing. It's so much bullshit. And it's transparently bullshit. There's no moral high ground here.

The Iraqi people know that for half of Saddam Hussein's rule he was supported by exactly the people who ousted him. And the Iraqi people, more than anyone, know just how brutal he was during that time. The Iraqi people also know that when – after the first Gulf War – they were urged to rise up against the regime, those who did were left dangling by US forces ordered not to help. And finally, after more than a decade of crippling economic sanctions causing poverty, misery and death, reducing a once-functioning nation to a 'failed state', these same erstwhile friends of Hussein decided that 'Shock And Awe', followed by a 3-year occupation – launched from corrupt and compliant dictatorships next door – was the best way to help the poor Iraqi people who can't run their own affairs… and shepherd them towards democracy.

If I were Iraqi, I'd probably mutter something about how if you'd only left us alone 100 years ago, then maybe we wouldn't be in this mess. And how being carpet-bombed and subjected to a further period of occupation is probably NOT WHAT WE NEED RIGHT NOW! Although that said, the average Iraqi is probably too busy trying to track down enough fresh drinking water without being blown up or having his head chopped off to be thinking very much about historical context. Life in Baghdad is probably focused very much on the next few minutes, rather than the last 100 years.

What Tony Blair is unwilling to admit or too thick to understand is that the vast majority of people whom he'd describe as anti-American are actually anti-Americanist. They may have American friends and love a lot about America but they are against what America has come to stand for. Not what it says it stands for, but what its actions demonstrate.

Americanism is a kind of rapacious, aggressive capitalism willing to ignore all ethical concerns in the desire for global dominance. Americanism is a willingness to unilaterally use a military machine unrivalled in all of human history to reduce to rubble entire nations that it designates, falsely, to be a threat. Americanism is the arrogance of power... 'freedom is occupation'... 'democracy is compliance'. It's all a bit *You Know Who*[2].

And speaking of Orwell, can I just cite a short passage from *Politics and The English Language* better to illustrate this point...

> *The words democracy, socialism, freedom, patriotic, realistic, justice, have each of them several different meanings which cannot be reconciled with one another. In the case of a word like democracy, not only is there no agreed definition, but also the attempt to make one is resisted from all sides. It is almost universally felt that when we call a country democratic we are praising it: consequently the defenders of every kind of régime claim that it is a democracy, and fear that they might have to stop using the word if it were tied down to any one meaning. Words of this kind are often used in a consciously dishonest way. That is, the person who uses them has his own private definition, but allows his hearer to think he means something quite different.*

I wonder if Tony Blair has ever read that essay. I don't imagine Dubya Bush has, but you'd think someone might have sent a copy to Blair by now. After all, it was written in 1946.

[2] www.levity.com/corduroy/orwell.htm
[3] news.bbc.co.uk/2/hi/middle_east/4855210.stm

The point being that when Blair calls anti-Americanism 'mad', he's essentially saying that anti-Americanism translates as anti-freedom and anti-democracy. But the freedom being exported by America is the freedom to have US corporations make billions off the back of Iraqi misery. And the democracy is limited to electing those approved by America[3].

It's Abu Ghraib and Guantanamo Bay for crying-out-loud. It's secret 'rendition flights' shipping suspects to central Asia for torture. And because these are not 'blips on the radar' or 'a few bad apples', but instead clearly represent the policies of modern America, then it is necessary for all those who believe in a world without state torture, secret police and 'the military option' to label themselves anti-American.

In our time, political speech and writing are largely the defence of the indefensible. Things [... that] can indeed be defended, but only by arguments which are too brutal for most people to face, and which do not square with the professed aims of political parties. Thus political language has to consist largely of euphemism, question-begging and sheer cloudy vagueness. Defenceless villages are bombarded from the air, the inhabitants driven out into the countryside, the cattle machine-gunned, the huts set on fire with incendiary bullets: this is called pacification. Millions of peasants are robbed of their farms and sent trudging along the roads with no more than they can carry: this is called transfer of population or rectification of frontiers. People are imprisoned for years without trial, or shot in the back of the neck or sent to die of scurvy in Arctic lumber camps: this is called elimination of unreliable elements. Such phraseology is needed if one wants to name things without calling up mental pictures of them. Consider for instance some comfortable English professor defending Russian totalitarianism. He cannot say outright, 'I believe in killing off your opponents when you can get good results by doing so.' Probably, therefore, he will say something like this:

While freely conceding that the Soviet regime exhibits certain features which the humanitarian may be inclined to deplore, we must, I think, agree that a certain curtailment of the right to political opposition is an unavoidable concomitant of transitional periods, and that the rigours which the Russian people have been called upon to undergo have been amply justified in the sphere of concrete achievement.

The inflated style is itself a kind of euphemism. A mass of Latin words falls upon the facts like soft snow, blurring the outlines and covering up all the details. The great enemy of clear language is insincerity. When there is a gap between one's real and one's declared aims, one turns, as it were instinctively, to long words and exhausted idioms, like a cuttlefish squirting out ink. In our age there is no such thing as 'keeping out of politics.' All issues are political issues, and politics itself is a mass of lies, evasions, folly, hatred and schizophrenia.

George Orwell, *Politics and The English Language*

The Quiet Road
numero57.net

Here's Dave of Acerbia again, reincarnated this time as a roboticist, fighting in the eternal battle that is Man vs Machine.

 March 2006 – Telemachiavelli

Monday: I took Unit 4 offline today to see what internal modifications it had made to itself. To my surprise Unit 4 scuttled away as I approached it, although it couldn't possibly suspect my intentions. When I finally did manage to corner it there was a scuffle and I was scratched by one of Unit 4's manipulation mandibles. Whether this was intentional or not on the part of Unit 4 I was unable to determine as I pulled the connector cable to its portable generator and carried it to the work bench.

Tuesday: My investigation into Unit 4 deepened today when I discovered that by using its own existing parts Unit 4 has managed to upgrade most of its internal workings – increasing data storage, motor functions, processing ability and overall performance. The majority of the improvements are unconventional hacks and mechanical upgrades bordering on insane genius.

The core has yet to be cracked open and investigated as Units 3 and 7 today somehow managed to topple themselves and I spent some time observing them after I had righted them. None of the units has toppled over since the first week of the experiment so I am at a loss to explain why they would do so now when they have such a superior grasp on balance and all their gyros should be pitch-perfect.

Wednesday: A worrying discovery today; inside Unit 4's core was a wireless short-range transmitter that I had most definitely not put there. Unit 4 has been transmitting large amounts of data and telemetry right up to the point where I actually cracked the core. I do not yet understand who/what could have put the transmitter there or to whom the data was being transmitted but I have initiated a trace on the signal.

Thursday: My signal trace has narrowed down the receivers to be within the building. As I waited for the trace to complete I spent some time with the other Units, watching them congregate and collaborate. They appear to be gathering pieces of scrap and taking apart an old computer case I left in their enclosure; it was very enjoyable to watch them, my greatest creations.

Friday: Watched the security camera feeds three times before I could actually accept what had happened. Units 5 and 7 tore Unit 2 into pieces, stripping every usable component from the chassis. Their Asimov routines should have come into effect and somehow didn't. Unit 2's self preservation drive also seems to have failed. A worrying development indeed, as hostile tendencies have never before been displayed by any of the Units. My investigation is on hold while I check through their code.

Saturday: Still checking code.

Sunday: I'm trapped in my laboratory. Units 1 and 3 are using some sort of pulse cannon they created from the power supply of Unit 2 and the remains of the PC case. They've already given me some pretty nasty burns from some near misses, so I have no doubt the damn thing is lethal if they can just aim it properly. Investigation into the signal shows that Unit 4 was transmitting his own autopsy to all the other Units right up to the last moment. I've smashed Units 5 and 6 into pieces with a chair, but so far no sign of Unit 7, he could be anywh

Acerbia
www.acerbia.com

Iran and its nuclear ambitions were also in the sights of the Western Powers this year. In a nice piece of reportage (still quite rare amongst British blogs, I think) and analysis, Kitty Killer found some Labour MPs willing to support armed Iranian resistance groups.

 April 2006 – No to war, yes to proxy war. Labour hacks support armed Iranian resistance

No one wants to go to war with the Iranians. But why not support someone else to save us the trouble? That's the message from loyal Labour MPs and peers, who attended a demo in Brum on Saturday in support of an armed Iranian resistance group.

The demo, which took place in Chamberlain Square and attracted around 100 protesters, was billed in an email sent out to Birmingham activists as a 'gathering in Chamberlain square… to support human rights, peace and democracy in Iran,' under the further banner of 'No to war and No to Appeasement'. It turned out to be a rally in support of the People's Mujahedin of Iran (PMoI)[1], otherwise known as the MKO. Supporters could be seen waving old Iranian flags, flags of the MKO and blue and yellow flags which were unrecognisable. Speakers called for the MKO to be removed from official terrorist lists – the organisation had been added during the previous reformist government – and for greater sanctions against the Iranian regime.

Among the speakers were several members of the Labour party. I couldn't stay for the whole protest but I did catch Lord Corbett and Steven McCabe MP for Birmingham Hodge Hill. Also due to attend, according to an organiser, was Roger Godsiff, Labour MP for Sparkhill and Small Heath. Both spoke to the assembled crowd of 'democracy', 'human rights' and the terror of the current Islamist government in Iran. Corbett highlighted that it was the Iranian resistance who 'warned' the world of the country's alleged nuclear weapons programme, seemingly oblivious to the vested interests a group such as the MKO could have in making such a claim.

It is interesting to note the voting record of the British politicos who attended the rally. Steven McCabe MP is rated by Theyworkforyou as a strong Labour loyalist, voting for the Iraq war, ID cards and the Anti-Parliament bill. Public Whip puts Corbett in favour of ID cards and notes that he very rarely rebels. Godsiff was himself moderately for the Iraq war through votes in Parliament. None of those who attended can be claimed to

[1] en.wikipedia.org/wiki/PMOI

be anti-war activists of any colour, and they are certainly not rebels.

One thing that was particularly striking was the vague detail given from some speakers about the organisation itself. They called for the return of Maryan Rajavi, the MKO's figurehead, to lead a 'democratic' government in the country. One speaker noted her as 'president elect', implying without clarification that she was an exiled leader of the country. This is bollocks. Ms Rajavi was elected president by nobody except the National Council of Resistance of Iran, of which the MKO is part.

For all the talk of taking the PMoI/MKO off the terrorist watch list, there was little explanation of what the organisation actually stands for. A quick check of Wikipedia and the BBC clarifies that the MKO was thought to have had support from Baghdad before Saddam was toppled, although the organisation denies this. It has also been allowed to operate freely in the country during the most recent conflict. Indeed, CS Monitor reported in 2004 that the group was granted 'protected status' under the Geneva Convention by the US, despite remaining on the terrorist watch list. It is unclear how much support the organisation has in Iran itself, especially in light of the former Baghdad link. The MKO has an armed wing, and has been blamed for a number of attacks on Iranian government figures since the revolution. [Since writing this article, I learned from several sources that the organisation has in fact little or no support in Iran, with one Persian friend of mine describing the MKO as a 'cult'.]

The rally's presentation of the MKO as whiter-than-white is also up for debate. Despite condemning Iran's human rights record in street theatre surrounding the event, the MKO's own reputation on the subject is murky. Human Rights Watch reported that MKO dissenters were imprisoned in Iraq for long periods of time, either within MKO camps or Iraqi prisons. One individual, Mohammad Hussein Sobhani, said the organisation subjected him to 8 years of solitary confinement. While the Islamic republic is no Switzerland, the MKO are not velvet revolutionaries.

So what could be the implication of loyal Labour parliamentarians putting their name publicly behind an organisation that has been known to use armed resistance against the Iranian regime, and may have even been previously supported by Saddam Hussein? While they called for no war against the country, they are happy to support other groups who desire achieve the same aims through armed conflict. During cold war times, this is what many would call a war by proxy.

The fact that the figures are relative to ardent Labour loyalists also begs the question on the government's official policy. Will Blair and Bush, when they get bored of playing phony diplomacy, back up a resistance to save British and American troops from another embarrassing deployment? Even if, if Wikipedians are correct, the MKO is Marxist in its outlook? If so, then the groundwork for building support for such help is already in place, thanks to Corbett and McCabe, within the governing Labour party. Whether they have had authorisation from party heads to attend the event, we'll never know – the show of support for an organisation that does have an armed wing by pro-war Labour figures could be indicative of something wider.

And as a side note, one wonders what Charles Clarke the Safety Elephant's proposed law against glorifying terrorism would have to say about Labour's own ardent members…

Kitty Killer
kittykittykillkill.blogspot.com

Peter Gasston spots a double standard with regard to the treatment of two countries that both have uranium enrichment programmes.

 April 2006 – The same, but different

Despite signing the Nuclear Non-Proliferation Treaty, this country is opening a uranium-enrichment centre capable of developing the raw fuel for nuclear weapons. It claims that it cannot and never will use its nuclear programme for non-peaceful activities, but key elements of its enrichment facility have been kept hidden from international inspectors.

This country is Brazil[1].

And, curiously, despite the parallels with Iran[2], no threats of military action have been made against it.

The Inside Of My Head
www.petergasston.co.uk

[1] seattlepi.nwsource.com/national/267515_brazil21.html
[2] news.bbc.co.uk/1/hi/world/middle_east/4031603.stm

July brought the first anniversary of the London suicide bomb attacks. Steve Lovegrove, a survivor of the Piccadilly Line bombing, gives his account of 7/7 one year on.

 July 2006 – 07/07/06

Only a few days after the 7th last year I knew I would feel the need to be back in London to mark the anniversary; I just wasn't sure how. However, on the evening of the 6th I felt I should make my way to King's Cross the following morning. So three of us who left our hostel the same morning a year ago made our way to King's Cross; however, this time we went from Angel as opposed to Barbican, to avoid making an exact repeat journey. We decided to use the tube; perhaps it was a show of resolve, but it was probably most likely out of laziness. We had already conjectured that the Underground was bound to have undercover officers all over the network, so I actually felt quite safe and was impressed and pleased that everyone seemed to be commuting as normal.

There was a large police presence underneath King's Cross, and I made my way up to the station the same way we were evacuated. We met other fellow passengers who also felt they should be here on this day, and at 8.50 we said a few words to remember those who never completed their journey, and had a quiet moment of reflection. After spending a short time at St Pancras church where some of the other passengers laid flowers we broke away and continued with our day.

We then spent the day on Oxford, Regent and Carnaby streets, only stopping to mark the 2 minutes' silence by standing at Oxford Circus. My phone was going off all day as I received texts from friends wishing me well. Bad things bring out kindness in people.

In the evening we met up with others in Islington and headed over to Soho. Obviously I knew the way, so I led everyone to Piccadilly Circus via King's Cross. We had to run for the Piccadilly Line connection, which meant I had no choice of carriage or position (avoiding someone with a stupidly massive rucksack), and we ended up in the middle of the first carriage. Once on the train I pointed at the floor and gestured that it was here where it happened, and I pointed out the eastbound tunnel junction out the window on the right-hand side (you see the wall disappear), the exact point where it happened.

I was okay until 11.30 p.m. when I completely broke down in a bar in Soho – the day had finally caught up with me. All the pretending that it was 'just another day' and trying to distract myself was futile. I have been the same all weekend; before, I was able to speak about it without feeling anything, now every time I do so I want to cry. It is the sheer violence and senseless waste of life that is hitting me.

I came home to find many kind messages left for me on here. Thank you for your kind words and thoughts. Once again, this has shown me that bad things bring out kindness in people.

Steve Lovegrove
stevelovegrove.blogspot.com

It's a fact of political blogging that if you're going to make any kind of point about the Israel–Palestine issue, you should be prepared to get flak from both sides of the argument, even if you write an even-handed piece. Comment threads degenerate quickly into insults, hyperbole and expletives. The pro-Israeli camp will call you anti-Semitic. The pro-Palestine camp will call you a supporter of tyranny. Eventually someone will mention the Nazis, at which point you have to invoke Godwin's Law ('As an online discussion grows longer, the probability of a comparison involving Nazis or Hitler approaches one') and call the whole thing off.

With the kidnapping of Israeli troops by Hezbollah and the retaliatory bombardment of Lebanon, an already complex situation was complicated exponentially ('What they need to do is get Syria to get Hezbollah to stop doing this shit and it's over,' was George Bush's now famous appraisal of the situation). Rochenko at Smokewriting wrote what many thought was one of the best pieces about the unfolding carnage. Thoughtfully and sympathetically argued, it's written more in sorrow than in anger.

July 2006 – The Powerlessness of Israel

The temptation when faced with an escalation of aggression as utterly unwarranted as this[1] is to turn moral.

Because yes, a nation's right to defend itself brings with it responsibilities also. Not to seek war beyond the requirements of self-defence, not to harm non-combatants – whether directly or by cynically exploiting the doctrine of double effect, USAF or RAF-style, in dropping 200lb bombs on residential areas of Beirut, which the BBC now routinely refers to as 'Hezbollah strongholds'. Not to pursue collective punishment, and to avoid targeting entirely non-military objectives. The advantage of moral rhetoric is that it brings into play the power of the charge of inconsistency, or rather, hypocrisy. Yes, in Israel soldiers with their M16s ride everyday on buses with civilians – in a country whose government routinely condemns its opponents for hiding among non-combatants. Yes, Israel acts as if its sovereignty, in grand *realpolitische* style, gives it the right to overturn the sovereignty of other countries if it so wishes. But the weakness of moral rhetoric, in aiming to establish the requirements of justice, is that it is promiscuously reversible. Once in use, it spreads like brushfire, and almost immediately all sides are employing body-counts to establish who is at fault, accusing their opponents of being poisoned by a unique evil, and *tu quoque*-ing sententiously in the service of their indignation.

In the midst of this kind of horror, morality is an easy resort. And the language of right, in such an atmosphere, is easily reduced to the language of the playground: he started it, no you did. And from there it's a short distance to the language of annihilation, of crying for an end to 'evil' even if it involved the extermination of every man, woman and child of the group that you imagine your opponent represents.

So instead, ask, with Ilan Pappe[2]: what does Israel want? But not strategically speaking – let's leave aside the cynicism of its leaders, and of its *foreign backers*, as another invitation to morality. What does it want as a collective? What does it desire? Peace and security? But those universals, in this particular context, what do they mean? Behind them is a pathology of ceaselessly maintained tension, one that is at

[1] www.guardian.co.uk/israel/Story/0,,1824039,00.html
[2] electronicintifada.net/v2/article5003.shtml

odds with the interests of the nation and its people, but one that nonetheless makes its presence felt every time an Israeli politician employs the rhetoric of the decisive blow and of the iron wall of security and military deterrence, which is always about to be completed. And every time too that the final victory is deferred again – the fighting lessens, the troops withdraw across the border, returning people to the everyday dread so well described by David Grossman, writing in 2001[3]:

> *Israel has plunged into a kind of apathy. Seemingly, life goes on as usual. Everyday affairs are conducted with the characteristic Israeli mixture of vigour and edginess. But as anyone who has lived here all his life knows, everything has a strange and disheartening kind of impassivity. Life in slow motion. Israel is now slipping back into the psychological stance that is most dangerous for itself – the stance of the victim, of the persecuted Jew. Almost every threat to it – even from the Palestinians [or Hezbollah – R.] who can never defeat Israel on the battlefield – is perceived as an absolute peril requiring the harshest response.*

The idea, anathema to its supporters, that Israeli military action produces aggressive responses, receives an affirmation from within this everyday fear, the repression of which is a necessary condition of life continuing at all. Following the IDF's latest incursion in Gaza or the West Bank, the expectation of bombs on buses or in cafés mounts. In such an atmosphere, more military action is, if anything, a relief – and the grander in scale the better. And each time, the violence is anchored to weariness, to a once-more gathered desire to have done with violence, by way of the final victory, the perfect iron wall.

This time the Palestinians will understand that we mean business: they didn't get it in 1989, or in 1997, or in 2002, but they will now.

The Lebanese failed to comprehend in 1982, 1993 and 1996 – but they will now.

The history this desire feeds on is one of repeated failures by the 'Arab world' to knuckle under to the acceptance of the security of Israel. It is a history that affirms, on the one hand, the military power of Israel, its ingenuity, its independence, and on the other its weakness, its incapacity to use its power to protect its citizens. And

[3] **Death as a Way of Life, 2001**

it always returns to the desire for the decisive gesture, generating a pathology that is a hugely dangerous one to fall prey to in politics, and indeed in war. History always continues: slights, real or imagined, are suffered and remembered. The parents of dead children and the children of dead parents nurse their grief, their rage and their shame. No single gesture settles all accounts. But a pathology of desire wants to repeat, above all.

The history that forms the backdrop to the rhetoric of decisive gestures is also, never forget, the history of Israel's failures – under Shamir, Netanyahu, Sharon – to cease provocations in the name of security, to avoid adding to existing tensions, to escape the temptation to return to open war from out of a state of hidden war. The reliance on the idea of the final strike, the ultimate defeat of all the enemies, is a fantasy that gives birth to the strangest efflorescences: an underground wall to keep out the tunnellers of Hamas; an invasion of Lebanon to destroy 'terrorist infrastructure' and 'remodel' the politics of the country.

That particular stab at the 'decisive gesture' was tried before in 1982, when the enemy was the PLO rather than Hezbollah. Following Israel's decision to annex the Golan Heights in 1981 and the resulting increase in tension, in 1982 the Israeli ambassador to London was shot and wounded by terrorists led by Abu Nidal, an enemy of the PLO leadership. Blaming this attack on the PLO gave the Israeli government the perfect opportunity to seek to 'destroy' the PLO and install a friendly government in Lebanon. This particular 'release of tension' took in, amongst other things, Lebanon reduced to political chaos, 600 Israeli troops killed, the massacres at the refugee camps of Sabra and Shatila, and the birth of Hezbollah – a movement founded to drive out the Israeli invasion. Another intervention that produced only further chaos, more hatred, more injustice, and more insecurity for Israel.

The conclusion is inescapable. Behind the ceaselessly failing logic of the decisive gesture, there is the desire to maintain that state of tension, of enervating deadlock that Grossman describes. A militarised society, secure in its bomb shelters, suffused with the constant fear of being blown apart in a bar, a nightclub, on a bus.

What Israel wants is to repeat.

Smokewriting
www.smokewriting.co.uk

On the subject of the Israel vs Hezbollah war, Devil's Kitchen gave us a thought-provoking and debate-catalysing call to arms after Tony Blair had made a speech in America about the future direction of the War Against Terror. There was, he said, much criticism from bloggers of how the war was being conducted but little suggestion of how to bring it to an end. Why not play along too? Solving the Middle East crisis is a game for all the family.

(This is an unusual post from Devil's Kitchen, since he is famous across Blogland for his liberal peppering of articles with the kind of inventive swearing that would make Dennis Hopper whistle with admiration. DK's imaginative use of Anglo-Saxon was even quoted by Environment Minister David Miliband at a recent awards ceremony.)

 August 2006 – Tony and his detractors

Our Dear Leader has made a 'landmark' speech[1] which is, indeed, well worth fisking; I, alas, cannot be bothered at present but Chicken Yoghurt[2] and Curious Hamster[3], to name but two, have looked at it.

Go and read them if you wish – although, in my opinion, were you not to then you might find something more constructive to do. For instance, instead of reading a load of people saying that Tony is an idiot and quite possibly delusional to boot (which, elegantly though those named two do it, is hardly news), you might try considering what you might do to solve the crisis.

[1] news.bbc.co.uk/1/hi/uk_politics/5236896.stm

[2] www.chickyog.net/2006/08/04/arc-of-the-convenient

[3] bsscworld.blogspot.com/2006/08/few-minor-corrections.html

It is very easy to criticise and, as regular readers will know, I'm happy to do so. But, and however wrong you think that my conclusions may be, I do try to suggest some ideas, some prospect of how I would try to solve a particular question. And there seems to be a number of pertinent questions that could be asked about this whole 'War on Terror' thing.

Do you, for instance, think that there are a bunch of people out there who are implacably opposed to our way of life? Do you think that there are a bunch of people out there whose promises to destroy Israel are a little more than rhetoric? And do you support these people against the Israelis (and if your answer to that question is, 'yes', I really hope that you can justify that response)?

Let me make this entirely clear: I am well aware that there are a lot of people out there who think that Israel has over-reacted (indeed, I am one of them). However, I live in a country in which 50 people having the shit blown out of them by a bunch of suicide bombers is a rarity; I live in a country that has not been threatened with invasion in 60 years. And I am certain that if I lived in Israel, I would be pretty paranoid and prone to over-reacting too.

So, let me ask you, what would you do to solve this crisis? Would you perhaps pour money into strengthening the Lebanese army so that they could obey UN Resolution 1559 and disarm Hezbollah? Would you look to the UN to help, as it did so effectively in the Balkans and Rwanda? Or perhaps we should invade Israel and 'force' this ceasefire that everyone talks about?

Anyone? Bueller?

Devil's Kitchen
devilskitchen.blogspot.com

This year heralded the fifth year of the War Against Terror. The announcement that the security services had foiled a terrorist plot which, as the Home Secretary John Reid described it, would have caused death and destruction on 'unprecedented scale' was met with a degree of scepticism. Nosemonkey, AKA J. Clive Matthews, spoke for many.

 August 2006 – Oh, come on…

Yesterday: Major terrorism policy announcement by Home Secretary John Reid[1]

Today: A 'plot to blow up planes' is apparently foiled[2], and Heathrow airport shut down.

And my first reaction? Utter disbelief and a sigh of resignation.

They've simply cried wolf too many times before[3] – until I see the smoke I won't believe them, and even then I'll have my suspicions. Remember the tanks at Heathrow[4] just before the Iraq war?

Update: For the record, I reckon that this plot probably was real – but my first reaction was still 'that's bollocks'. Desensitising people to this extent through the constant 'ooh! Be scared!' announcements is utterly counterproductive.

It does, however, mean that I can carry on with my life utterly unphased by the fact that lots of people want to blow me to shit.

More coherent thoughts: We used to be told that we will not give in to terrorism. We used to be told that we will not change our way of life in the face of this new threat. Now we are told that we MUST change our way of life.

[1] news.bbc.co.uk/1/hi/uk_politics/5257518.stm
[2] news.bbc.co.uk/1/hi/uk/4778575.stm
[3] europhobia.blogspot.com/2006/08/terror-threat-tackiness.html
[4] news.bbc.co.uk/1/hi/uk/2749659.stm

The threat of terrorism is very, very real – you'd have to be a fool to deny it. But the clue is in the name – the point of terrorism is to cause terror.

The terrorists themselves have been remarkably inefficient at scaring the bejeezus out of us, which is their prime modus operandi. They have successfully struck in the West remarkably few times – 9/11, Madrid, 7/7. With the exception of 9/11, the death toll caused by these psychotic maniacs has been, in the grand scheme of things, insignificant, and even the property damage and disruption caused have been relatively minimal.

Instead, it has been our own governments who are terrifying the populace with their constant warnings and announcements of foiled plots; it is our own governments who are causing disruption through airport and railway closures.

Terrorism thrives on the oxygen of publicity. 'Martyrs' look forward to being remembered and noticed. So why do we constantly do their PR work for them? Why do our governments keep using their publicity machines to propagate the terror that the terrorists want to cause?

Yes, we obviously need to act quickly and effectively to prevent more attacks. I don't want our governments to sit back and do nothing to prove the point, and I'd far rather we have a few more Forest Gate raids, non-existent ricin plots 'uncovered', and a few more people arrested for allegedly trying to buy radioactive substances that don't even exist than see one single other person killed for the twisted beliefs of a tiny, rabid minority. But I do dispute the effectiveness and sense of the current tactics, which appear to be little more than to ensure that we all have a good scare every few months, supposedly to keep us on our toes.

One thing I do agree with Home Secretary John Reid about is that we can't afford to get complacent. But the more often you get scared, the less impact those scares start to have, and complacency begins to set in.

Europhobia
europhobia.blogspot.com

Confusing Power With Greatness
Politics

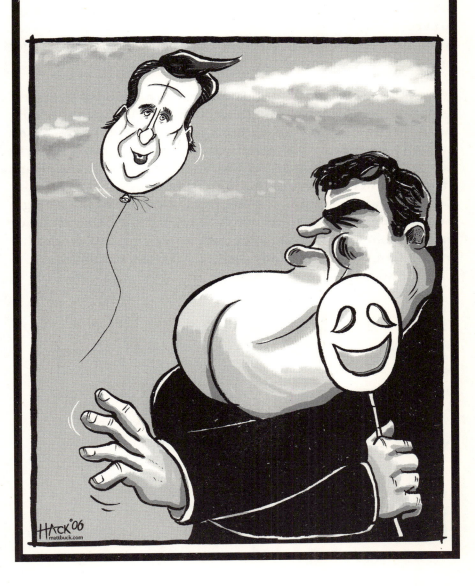

Those readers who aren't fans of drama, democracy, or tales of dirty deeds done dirt cheap, should skip to the next chapter. Whoever says politics is boring deserves a wet slap, this year more than ever. To try to chronicle everything that has gone on in British politics this year would fill this volume and beyond. And being a political blogger myself, I was very tempted to try.

We've had the resignation of Charles Kennedy as Liberal Democrat leader and the election of Ming Campbell as his less than sparkling successor; Tessa Jowell's moody mortgages; David Blunkett resigning (again); John Prescott visiting a billionaire businessman's ranch to talk about cowboys but not casinos (Prescott's sexual shenanigans are dealt with elsewhere in this book); the passing of the Identity Card legislation (I think it's safe to say that there isn't a single British blogger who's in favour of that); the Tories' ascendancy in the opinion polls despite their lack of policies; and continuing speculation about when Tony Blair might retire to the US lecture circuit. And more…

December saw the election of David Cameron as Conservative Party leader. Alex Harrowell, the Yorkshire Ranter, attempted to burst Cameron's bubble from the outset.

 December 2005 – David Cameron: not just more right-wing than you think...

...more right-wing than you can imagine. Think about it – here we have a character who has paffled through the election campaign saying that Tory foreign policy has to be about more than Zimbabwe and Gibraltar, but has just made William Hague his shadow foreign secretary. Hague's brief is apparently to 'target Jacques Chirac'.

How insane is this? Target him with what precisely? To what end? Wouldn't it be better to target the Labour Party? Seriously, he seems to think that he is campaigning in a French election. Now, I remember Hague babbling about Britain being 'a foreign land', but I didn't realise Hague's response to this would be to inner-emigrate to France. Does he think Jacques Chirac knows who he is? Given the state of the EU budget talks, a fit of anti-French ranting backed (no doubt) by the tabloids would do more to strengthen Tony Blair's bargaining position than anything else, a curious aim for an Opposition.

Billy Hague's judgement has never been great (something conventional wisdom tends to overlook in favour of assuming it was all to do with his looks). He never got over the impression that his party thought a Labour government was a bizarre workplace accident and didn't take it seriously, except for a sub-set of madmen who were convinced the sky was about to fall in. His initial centre-ground strategy failed, due to a serious lack of commitment and policy ideas; except for donning a baseball cap, who remembers any policies of his that went in that direction? He then swung over to the hard right, chiefly I think because it was easy, forgetting that Blair was quite happy to see the Conservative Party celebrating its tribal hard-rightness. He lined up with some very odd people, drank too much dotcom koolaid (he was still going on about funding universities from radio spectrum licensing after the 3G auctions were over and it was abundantly clear no one would ever pay those sums again), and went ape by falling in love with fascist killer Tony Martin.

Now he is convinced that, far from being in opposition, he is actually the real foreign secretary. Chirac, if asked, would probably think you were talking about the nuclear reprocessing plant at La Hague in Normandy. Which is quite accurate: Cameron's cabinet looks like an industrial facility for the reprocessing of spent political fuel rods. Here we have Francis Maude, a man whose record of continuous failure since 1997 does not seem to be any bar to his continuous promotion. Here David Davis, slowly twisting in the wind. Here Dr Death, Liam Fox, whose continued failure since 1997 awards him the defence portfolio and the title of Maximum Leader of the Tory Right. Cazart! Is that Oliver Letwin? Even Iain Duncan Smith has the chairmanship of a committee. For a Young! Modernising! influence, they all seem terribly familiar figures.

But the real problem is Cameron himself. He quit politics in 1994 to become Director of Corporate Affairs at Carlton Communications, a TV channel remembered in the joke that 'we are entering the age of narrowcasting, of hundreds of specialised channels instead of a few general ones like BBC1 that everyone watches. For example, there's Sky Sports for sport, the History Channel for documentaries about Nazis, and then there's Carlton for utter shit'. The joke points out a deeper truth. Remember 'narrowcasting'? Remember hundreds of TV channels? Remember when that was the future? Yup, that's right – 1994. Next year the Web happened as a mass phenomenon and the tellycrats have been feebly trying to keep up in terms of ideas ever since. Well, David Cameron did something similar. He spent the years 1994–2001 as a glorified PR man for a fourth-rate TV channel, then returned to politics... and he hasn't changed a bit.

He is quite evidently convinced that PR, earnest and slightly posh public speaking, looks out of Lisa Simpson's favourite magazine *Non-Threatening Boys*, and utter intellectual blankness is still the New New Thing. Tony Blair is still the Modern Age for Cameron, not a tired pre-internet model one step from the scrapheap and two steps from the ultimate cultural death, nostalgia. It took time, but it became clear with Blair that, when the veneer of telly wore through, there was something ugly, writhing and dripping from its leathery fangs. It won't take 5 minutes with Cameron; the antibodies have been produced.

His failure, by the way, began at his first PMQs when he turned on Hilary Armstrong. Apparently those present thought it was a good performance. I disagree. He came across as even more arrogant than Tony Blair (some feat), and more of a bully. 'Has she finished? HEV YOU FINISHED?' Christ, it's a stretch to imagine Boris Johnson gaining votes anywhere but Henley, but this was 40 times worse. He sounded and looked like the most obnoxious and boorish pub poshster you've ever met. Most people have had this experience at least once, and it's not a good association to trigger.

The Yorkshire Ranter
yorkshire-ranter.blogspot.com

Upsetting his own party, policy U-turns, making things up on the hoof: with the election of David Cameron, there was more than a whiff of 1994 in the air. Blair and his supporters accused Cameron of the same tricks that Blair had been guilty of 12 years earlier. Being the father of two small children, I thought I had spotted just why New Labour were so jealous of the new arrival.

 January 2006 – In understanding be men

> *'It remains to be seen whether he can develop substance alongside style…'*

That's Alan Milburn, taking a break from hurling rocks from his conservatory, *writing about David Cameron* in the Observer.

> *'… or whether the Tories are so hungry for power they will digest an unpalatable diet of policy U-turns.'*

Don't mention the (Clause) Four. Milburn is spectacularly lacking in self-awareness, principle, shame and, it would seem, long-term memory. That's how he can say what he does and why he can be safely ignored, except for the purposes of sport, as the political equivalent of John Mills' character in *Ryan's Daughter*.

You have to feel a little sorry for Tony Blair, though, since Cameron's arrival. The new Tory leader sheds his principles like, well, a power-starved politician shedding his principles, and sets about systematically alienating his party while U-turning on a sixpence. The media are all like, 'Wow, look at him go!', forgetting that Blair did it all before 12 years ago.

Tony must feel like the older sibling of a toddler. Sure, Tony can walk and talk but the little fella's so much cuter, just finding his feet and saying the funniest things. It makes you wonder if all the fussin' and a'feudin'[1] over the education reform bill isn't Tony making some kind of jealous cry for attention.

'Look at me everybody,' he trills as everyone coos over the antics of the youngster, 'I can still piss off the activists and tear up what little of my party's heritage hasn't been incinerated by my blowtorch vanity.' But those who do pay him any attention just tell him to stop being so silly. Maybe one or two people looking at Cameron say, 'Aw, remember when Tony used to do that, wasn't he cute?'

But Tony's not cute any more. Talking like a baby isn't that endearing when you're not a baby. People expect a little maturity and get cross when you don't show it. David on the other hand can say he wants to be like Tony when he grows up and everybody laughs encouragingly as he shuffles round in his big brother's boots. Just as we did when Tony tottered around in his mum's[2] high heels back in 1994. When he does that now people just thinks it's creepy, like Norman Bates in his mother's dress.

Chicken Yoghurt
www.chickyog.net

[1] **Politics.co.uk: Blair defiant over education reform**
[2] **www.margaretthatcher.org**

In January Charles Kennedy resigned as Liberal Democrat leader after revealing a drink problem. Most people were sympathetic – 'This battle with the bottle is nothing so novel,' as _Elvis Costello_ once sang. Here's Jamie Kenny with a couple of observations.

 January 2006 – My name is Charles Kennedy

and I am...[1]

> _In a personal statement at Lib Dem HQ in Westminster, Mr Kennedy said: 'Over the past 18 months I've been coming to terms with and seeking to cope with a drink problem, and I've come to learn through that process that a drink problem is a serious problem indeed._
>
> _'It's serious for yourself and it's serious for those around you. I've sought professional help and I believe today that this issue is essentially resolved.'_

In the great tradition of Asquith[2].

> _'You would have been amused at the Prime Minister last night. He did himself fairly well – not more than most gentlemen used to drink when I was a boy, but in this abstemious age it is noticeable if an extra glass or two is taken by anyone! The PM seemed to like our old brandy. He had a couple of glasses (big sherry glass size!) before I left the table at 9.30, and apparently he had several more before I saw him again. By that time his legs were unsteady, but his head was quite clear, and he was able to read a map and discuss the situation with me. Indeed he was most charming and quite alert in mind.'_

Personally, I could hack a drunk as Prime Minister. Let the mellow fumes of single malt billow forth from Number 10 and cover the land in an amber glow. It would make diplomacy interesting as well. 'George... George... yer fuck... yer fuck... yer me best fuckin' mate, y'bastard...'

[1] news.bbc.co.uk/1/hi/uk_politics/4582930.stm
[2] politics.guardian.co.uk/print/0,3858,5151832-107971,00.html

On the other hand, the thought of someone indoctrinated by Alcoholics Anonymous as PM gives me the creeps. Christ on a bike, it'll be action stations for the therapy crowd over the next few days. They'll be storming the TV stations, waving their ten-step utopias and detox demarches, each with something to sell…

Blood & Treasure
bloodandtreasure.typepad.com

 January 2006 – A new job for Charlie

Literary critic[1]:

> His romance with the literary agent Georgina Capel during the late 1990s is said to have come to an abrupt end after she woke in the flat they shared to discover her soon-to-be-ex urinating over the only manuscript copy of Brian Keenan's An Evil Cradling.

Well, maybe he had to go. But if you're staging a coup, isn't it customary to get the successor lined up first? Given that they knew about Kennedy's drinking – pretty much, anyway – it looks to me like Cameron stampeded them.

Now they keep wittering on about dynamic leadership, etc. What's the point of that? No one's going to pay any attention to a Lib Dem leader jumping around the place patting the little people on the head. Third party politics is about battlefield medicine. You just go about picking up the casualties, which Charlie did pretty successfully. Otherwise, you might as well get pissed.

Fools. Cameron invited them in a completely unsubtle way to tear themselves to pieces, and that's exactly what they did.

Blood & Treasure
bloodandtreasure.typepad.com

[1] news.independent.co.uk/uk/politics/article337237.ece

Writing in The Observer in February, the Prime Minister attempted to rebut accusations made against him of authoritarianism and the destruction of our civil liberties. Charlie Whitaker, along with a lot of others, didn't believe a word of it.

 February 2006 – Liberty? You have no idea how lucky you are

There is a concern, echoed across the political spectrum, that New Labour has lost sight of what democracy is: in particular, that Tony Blair doesn't understand it.

New Labour's regal response:

> *I have given away more prime ministerial power than any predecessor for more than 100 years.*

> *'I don't destroy liberties, I protect them'*[1], *Tony Blair, The Observer, 25 Feb 2006*

But democracy is not, in itself, about the extent of the Prime Minister's powers. It is about accountability. A free society can choose to grant its leadership extensive power – as long as it retains the right of informed democratic oversight. The powers the Prime Minister describes are not his to take or to give away. They belong to the nation.

The Prime Minister cites devolution as an example of his 'generosity'. There's certainly a case to be made regarding the Scottish and Welsh parliaments: John Major's government ran a *de facto* Scottish parliament – an elevated form of the so-called Scottish Grand Committee, in which decisions concerning Scotland were made by the 72 Scots MPs alone, sitting in Scotland – but the creation of fully-fledged legislatures for Scotland and Wales, with separate elections, is a dignified acknowledgment that both are nations within a union. But where is the English parliament? What about the West Lothian question? You don't have to be much of a sceptic to see that New Labour devolves power when it's confident about retaining party control of the new devolved assemblies. London, which might conceivably go Tory, has the fewest powers of any devolved assembly. Last week its Mayor was removed from office for a month by an unelected quango created by, uh, New

[1] observer.guardian.co.uk/comment/story/0,,1718133,00.html

Labour. The Lord giveth with one hand: but what is he doing with the other? We don't see until our new 'freedoms' are removed with a sudden swipe.

The Prime Minister says nothing – nothing at all – about the Legislative and Regulatory Reform Bill[2], which has just received its second reading in Westminster. In a comment piece on liberty this omission is a surprise, to say the least. New Labour intends to grant ministers the power to rewrite existing laws and create new laws, bypassing the elected representatives in parliament. This is profoundly undemocratic. What's worse is the evident cynicism. The new law isn't getting much press coverage and New Labour is content to lay low and ride its luck all the way to royal assent. The hidden hand.

The Prime Minister also seems to believe that liberty is a zero-sum game: you can't have more of it, you can only shift it around. In his view, it's all about achieving the right 'balance'. His rhetoric is, likewise, 'balanced', although also – in this case – bizarre:

> What about the charge that ID cards and anti-terrorism legislation transgress basic liberties and are, as David Cameron put it, 'unBritish'? Here, we must put a new case about liberty in the modern world. I am from the generation that I would characterise, crudely, as hard on behaviour, but soft on lifestyle, i.e. I support tough measures on crime but am totally pro gay rights. I believe in live and let live, except where your behaviour harms the freedom of others. A society with rules but without prejudices is how I might sum it up.

But since when did gay rights 'balance' tough measures on crime? How, exactly, is behaviour opposed to lifestyle? And just how do ID cards and anti-terror legislation help with any of this? The prime minister says:

> … the 'rules' are becoming harder to enforce.

He has no evidence for this. Actually, the crime rate is falling[3]. If Tony Blair wished, he could claim this as an achievement. He doesn't. It's true that behaviour that limits the freedoms of others tends to attract sanctions but this principle is not modern; it is centuries old. Our legal system is well developed and, assessed by the total of

[2] www.perfect.co.uk/2006/02/the-tipping-point
[3] www.crimestatistics.org.uk/output/Page54.asp

crimes brought to justice, which is rising[4], continues to do its job.

> *In theory, traditional court processes and attitudes to civil liberties could work. But the modern world is different from the world for which these court processes were designed. It is a world of vast migration, most of it beneficial but with dangerous threats. We have unparalleled prosperity, but also the break-up of traditional community and family ties and the emergence of behaviour that was rare 50 years ago.*

Perhaps the world is different because it is becoming better. The crime rate is falling. If you want make an honest argument, you have to acknowledge the facts. You also have to acknowledge that the risk of punishing the innocent is also a threat, and one very important reason why our legal system is designed as it is. Instead we find that New Labour has legislated to limit the use of jury trial[5]. Tony Blair speaks[6] of the 8 years he has 'battered the criminal justice system to get it to change'. But if there is a balance to be struck, it is perhaps in the difficult task of securing convictions without sending the wrong people to jail.

Finally, ID cards:

> *On ID cards, there is a host of arguments, irrespective of security, why their time has come. Most people already have a range of different cards, for workplace, bank or leisure. And, contrary to what is said, it will not be an offence not to carry one.*

The cards we already have are cards we choose to have. We can choose not to have any one of them without losing much. The national ID card won't be compulsory? Untrue. The sanction for not owning one may not be jail, or even a fine, but it looks likely that it will be: no leaving the country, no state benefits, no mortgage, no consumer credit, no bank account, no job.

[4] lcjb.cjsonline.gov.uk/ncjb/perfStats/obtj.html
[5] www.parliament.the-stationery-office.co.uk/pa/cm200203/cmbills/008/03008.22-25.html#j527
[6] news.bbc.co.uk/1/hi/uk_politics/4287370.stm

You can't fool all of the people all of the time. The starting-point for a debate on liberty is – unsurprisingly – honesty. We all need reliable information to make decisions about the issues that face our society. If deception, dissimulation and manipulation are your aims, you don't know what liberty is. You don't know what democracy is.

Charlie Whitaker
www.perfect.co.uk

In a year when Labour went nuclear and the Conservatives went green, Tony Blair wanted to hound hoodies and David Cameron wanted to hug them, quite a few political bloggers came to the conclusion that the terms 'Left' and 'Right' were losing their usefulness in determining someone's political standpoint. Here, Phil Edwards suggests a new system for finding just where we stand.

 April 2006 – Living in the thick of it

Chris[1] and Rob[2] have been finding different kinds of fault in the classic Left/Right political spectrum: Chris prefers two criteria that (he argues) are more or less orthogonal (pro- and anti-state, pro- and anti-poor people), while Rob opts for 'conservative' and 'liberal' as fundamental alternatives.

The trouble with all these discussions is that so many different oppositions end up being overlaid. In comments on Chris's post, for example, Tim Worstall makes a pretty good fist of locating himself on the Left. Speaking as a Marxist, I'm not fooled for a minute – but I have to admit that I often feel closer to the Worstall Right than to the Euston Manifesto Left.

I gave some thought to this stuff some time ago, in an attempt to work out why I counted at least one Tory among my trusted friends while finding many genuine socialists hard to be around. I dismissed the thought that I was moving Right

[1] stumblingandmumbling.typepad.com/stumbling_and_mumbling/2006/04/against_left_an.html
[2] considerphlebas.blogspot.com/2006/04/whose-is-invisible-hand.html

with age, partly because it was uncomfortable and partly because I knew that my position on Chris's rich-or-poor scale hadn't budged; I don't think there are many right-wingers who enjoy singing along to '*The Blackleg Miner*', put it that way. I also dismissed the thought that the difference between my Tory friend and my irritating socialist acquaintances was that the former was a thoughtful and intelligent bloke; there was no a priori reason for this exclusion, you understand, it was just a bit too obvious.

Anyway, what I came up with was a two-part scale, covering both your views on human nature and your views on political change (the greatest flaw of Robert's liberal/conservative scale, in my view, is that it tends to conflate these). Each of these two breaks down into two elements, giving a total of 16 distinct positions. Where human nature is concerned, we look at whether people should be controlled or liberated and at who should be doing the controlling or liberating. As for political change, we ask both whether we believe change should be welcomed or resisted and how we relate this change to the present.

Human nature first. The most fundamental question: are people good or bad? In other words, if left to themselves would people destroy social order or create a new and better society? For this part of the scale I'll borrow from Church history.

An **Augustinian** believes that, ultimately, people are sinful; politics is, or should be, concerned with establishing laws and institutions that enable sinful people to coexist without tearing one another apart.

A **Pelagian** believes that, ultimately, people are good; politics is, or should be, concerned with enabling people to work together, play together and generally enjoy life in ways which have hitherto not been possible.

Now for the location of control or liberation: central or local? government or community? ruler or family?

A **Jacobin** believes that all politics worthy of the name happens in government; left to their own devices, communities tend to stagnate or run wild.

A **Digger** believes that politics happens in affective communities and in everyday life; left to government, politics becomes managerial and sterile.

An **A**ugustinian **J**acobin is an **Authoritarian**: people need to be governed, and who better to govern than the government?

An **A**ugustinian **D**igger is a **Communitarian**: what we want isn't law abiding individuals but communities of respect.

A **P**elagian **J**acobin is a **Liberal**: the government can help people realise their potential, either by freeing them from oppressive conditions or simply by getting out of the way.

A **P**elagian **D**igger is a **Hippie**: isn't it great when people get together and do stuff, without waiting for politicians to tell them what to do?

A Liberal is the opposite of a Communitarian; an Authoritarian is the opposite of a Hippie.

Now for attitudes to political change.

A **W**hig believes that change should, all things being equal, be embraced: that the risk of regression and lost opportunities is greater than the risk that change will destroy something worth preserving.

A **T**ory believes that change should, all things being equal, be resisted: that the risk of losing valuable cultural and political resources outweighs the risk of failing to grasp opportunities for progress.

Finally, let's look at how change relates to the present. For this part of the act I'll need a volunteer from the history of Western philosophy; specifically, G.W.F. Hegel. Hegel believed that historical change had an immanent meliorist teleology – in other words, that things were getting better and better, and would eventually reach a point where they couldn't get any better. He also believed that this point had in fact been reached (cf. Francis Fukuyama,[3] who rather amusingly trotted out precisely the same argument the best part of two centuries down the line). Marx adopted the Hegelian framework, but with the crucial modification of placing the end of history the far side of a future revolution. We can call these two positions Right-Hegelianism

[3] The American philosopher who declared 'the end of history' after the fall of Communism in 1989.

and Left-Hegelianism.

A **Right**-Hegelian believes that, to the extent that it makes sense to talk of a good society, the good society is an extension of trends that have a visible and increasingly dominant influence on society as it is now.

A **Left**-Hegelian believes that it emphatically does make sense to talk of a good society, and that such a society will in important senses require the reversal or overthrow of society as it is now.

A **Right**-Hegelian Whig is a **Reformer**: things have changed, things will continue to change; there has been progress and there will be more progress.

A **Right**-Hegelian Tory is a **Conservative**: our existing institutions are valuable and should not be put at risk for the sake of speculative benefits.

A **Left**-Hegelian Whig is a **Revolutionary**: things could be much better, and things can be much better if we push a bit harder.

A **Left**-Hegelian Tory is a **Historian**: things could be much better, but our main task is to keep alive the resources of that hope.

The opposite of a Revolutionary is a Conservative. The opposite of a Reformer is a Historian.

Liberal, Authoritarian, Communitarian, Hippie; Conservative, Reformer, Revolutionary, Historian. That gives us a total of16 hats to try on, and to fit to our various political rivals. See how you get on.

Me, I'm **PDLT**, a Hippie Historian (who'd have thought it?); this makes me the polar opposite of an **AJRW**, an Authoritarian Reformer. (Like, for instance, Charles Clarke.) Works for me.

Existing Actually
existingactually.blogspot.com

113

Larry Teabag, on the other hand, still saw merit in the old labels of left and right. Here, he asks…

 May 2006 – Which Wing Are You?

What with so many former *left-wingers* heading rightwards, and still other right-wingers now describing themselves as 'left', it seems an open question whether these terms even have any meaning in modern Britain. Various people have been struggling to make sense of this issue recently. So in order to help, I've put together 15 easy questions, for anyone interested in determining once and for all which wing they should call home:

1. Who do you hate more?

    a) Jews.

    b) Muslims.

2. Which do you hate more?

    a) Yourself.

    b) Multiculturalism.

3. Do you think the word 'bogus' adds extra meaning to the term 'asylum-seeker'?

    a) Yes.

    b) No.

4. Do you wish we could all just get along?

    a) Yes.

    b) No.

5. What is your opinion of [*Daily Mail* columnist] Melanie Phillips?

   a) A bigoted mental-case.

   b) One of the few remaining voices of sanity.

6. Why do you hate Tony Blair?

   a) Because of his close relations with Washington.

   b) Because of his close relations with Brussels.

7. How do you view Britain's past?

   a) A repressive puritanical nightmare of Victorian values and stifling hypocrisy. Thank God you weren't there.

   (b) A proud catalogue of glorious achievement, from Shakespeare to Dunkirk, until the moment the rot set in: when Kenneth Tynan said 'fuck' on national television.

8. How do you view Britain's future?

   (a) As an egalitarian Utopia where lesbians, Muslims, and the disabled can bask together without fear in an atmosphere of mutually assured non-judgemental respect.

   (b) As a hell on earth, where armies of terrorists, hoodies and paedophiles roam the land preying on law-abiding citizens with impunity.

9. Do you think global warming is something we should be concerned about?

   (a) Yes absolutely, it's the most important issue of our generation.

   (b) No, it's a lie dreamt up by anti-globalisationists to force their agenda down everyone else's throat.

10. Do you think Dhimmification is something we should be concerned about?

(a) No, it's paranoid hateful nonsense.

(b) Yes. If we don't tackle it now we'll wake up one day soon in the Islamic Republic of Britain, to find our sisters and daughters wearing burqas and being stoned to death.

11. Do you make much of the fact that 'Nazi' is an abbreviation of 'National *Socialist*'?

(a) No, obviously not.

(b) Yes, obviously.

12. How do you view the 9/11 and 7/7 attacks?

(a) As heroic blows for freedom against the capitalist West.

(b) As exactly what we should expect from the Koranimals of the so-called 'Religion of Peace'.

13. If you were at a demonstration and you saw someone carrying the Union Flag, what would you chant?

(a) 'Burn it! Burn it! Burn it!'

(b) 'There ain't no black in the Union Jack!'

14. Have you ever used the phrase 'moral equivalence', except possibly as a joke?

(a) No.

(b) Yes.

15. What sort of hat do you wear?

    (a) Beret/bandana.

    (b) Top/bowler.

How did you do?

Mostly (a). You're left-wing. You're an anti-American anti-Semite in bed with radical Islam. The guilt you feel at being raised in a prosperous society has led you to rebel against it, and you now dedicate your life to bringing it to its knees. A demented idealist, you'd think nothing of slaughtering millions in the name of some non-existent greater good. You have no interests outside politics, and live for the day when the revolution comes. You vote RESPECT, and your blog of choice is *Class War UK* (Warning: not pleasant or work-safe).

Mostly (b). You're right-wing. Motivated entirely by hatred and selfish greed, you despise almost everything about contemporary Britain, especially the Guardian, the BBC, immigrants, gay marriage, high taxes, single mothers, the BBC, and the BBC. On the other hand, you love wars (past and present), cars, capital punishment and the free market. Call yourself 'Decent Left' if you wish, but you're fooling no-one. You vote BNP, and your blog of choice is *USS Neverdock*.

Tampon Teabag
tamponteabag.blogspot.com

It's fair to say that Charles Clarke, when he was Home Secretary, with his plans for ID cards, 90 days' detention for terrorist suspects and all-round disdain for 700 years of civil rights, didn't endear himself to political bloggers of either Left or Right. The treatment he meted out to the father of Rachel North, a survivor of the 7/7 bombings and campaigner for a public inquiry into the atrocity, merely served to confirm what many had suspected of the man they had less than respectfully dubbed 'the Safety Elephant'.

Very few bloggers are able to challenge directly the politicians that they write about every day. Rachel was given that opportunity, although not in circumstances she would have chosen herself.

 March 2006 – This is an insult

My dad, who is a parish priest and honorary canon, read my draft article on Forgiveness ('The F-word') last night, and it so happened that he was going to a clergy meeting this morning at Norwich Cathedral where the special guest was the Home Secretary Charles Clarke.

Clarke is my father's MP.

Clarke, in his speech to the assembled clergy, made much of the fact that he had spoken to the PM 'only yesterday' and the PM was at the time considering the problem of an angry Sedgefield constituent concerning the closure of a school. Clarke remarked upon this system of top executives still being MPs and responsible to their constituents, and how unusual this was compared with most parliamentary systems. You lucky people, even though I am the Home Secretary, I am still also your MP and here to help with all your little problems and enquiries, etc.

He didn't actually say 'You lucky people,' Dad said, but that was the inference. Dad was pleased that he could finally ask his MP, Charles Clarke, the question he has been keen to ask for some months. Dad waited eagerly to ask his question; he had already written to Clarke in December 2005 with his question. But Clarke had not replied.

Dad was therefore very keen to be part of what was advertised in the meeting notes as '30 minutes of reflection' after Clarke spoke. (In these meetings, '30 minutes of reflection' means '30 minutes of debate'. But it a clergy meeting, so they all 'reflect', rather than shout and argue. It's more dignified and godly, see.)

Unusually, according to Dad, on this occasion there was not a debate and questions from the floor, as is usual with these meetings at which Clarke was the special guest today – there were instead only three questions, which Clarke answered at length. The questions seemed to Dad to be pre-prepared to give Clarke an opportunity to talk about such things as prisons and police in a self-congratulatory way.

Dad was not able to ask his question – the last question finished and it was announced that there would be Eucharist in 2 minutes. Dad was very angry that 'the Eucharist was being used as a filibuster'. And still he had not had a chance to ask the question that was by now burning him up inside. It was time to break bread together; people began to leave the room.

My father tells me he at this point left his seat and strode up to Clarke, because he wanted to ask his question, and he said:

'Congratulations on fixing the meeting so that nobody can ask questions! You will have heard about Rev. Julie Nicholson who is so angry she cannot forgive the bombers who killed her daughter on July 7, well, I have a question, my daughter was feet away from the 7/7 Kings Cross bomb, and she and some other survivors have said they are not angry with the bombers, but with the Government, because there was no public inquiry. Why is there no public inquiry?'

Charles Clarke looked at my father 'in a very nasty way', and then he said to my father:

'Get away from me, I will not be insulted by you, this is an insult.'

And he stormed past, and Dad was so upset he could not share Eucharist with this man, and my father left the Cathedral in despair.

Dad has cheered up a bit now, but he was almost in tears at being so insulted by Clarke when I spoke to him; he did not think he had insulted Clarke at all.

Why is it an insult when the father of a bomb survivor, a gentle man of God, who has never caused trouble in his life, asks for a public inquiry? Why is his question not answered?

Rachel North
rachelnorthlondon.blogspot.com

The story reached the mainstream media pretty quickly. Some of the coverage was almost as vitriolic as that in Blogland – 'less welcome than terminal cock cancer' said Devil's Kitchen, a 'rancorous thug' echoed Matthew Norman in *The Independent*.

A few weeks later, after having written to Rachel's father to apologise, Clarke offered to meet both Rachel and her father.

 April 2006 – Meeting the Home Secretary

And so, the meeting between the Home Secretary, my father and me.

My father and I arrived early, at 9.45 a.m., and we sat in our suits outside Mr Clarke's offices, which were on the top floor of a former Church building in Norwich city centre. I had expected something grander, but there was the Home Secretary, the MP of Norwich South, at his desk, in a small office, clearly visible through a glass front. Mr Clarke looked up and saw us, got up from his desk and stepped outside his office, and greeted us, shaking our hands, saying *'Oh, so you are here already, do come in.'* His handshake was warm. He did not ask me for proof of identification.

And he led us inside. We sat at a small table facing him, and Mr Clarke requested that a constituency secretary be able to attend the meeting too. We agreed and we thanked Mr Clarke for his time, and especially for seeing me, which was unusual, as was his personal office's response to me, answering my questions raised on my blog.

(Nobody took notes in the meeting, which was scheduled for 10 minutes but went on for 25. I made notes as soon as I came out from which this post is drawn.)

Mr Clarke sat opposite me, with his arms crossed over his chest, resting his forearms on his tummy (which is exactly what I do, when I am thinking what to say and how I feel about saying it). He said that he wanted to say a few things first: to express his personal sympathy for what had happened to me and my family, to agree that water had passed under the bridge with regard to the Cathedral altercation ('though I still don't accept the version that was published about it'), to point out that he would always meet his constituents, to stress that he had given a very great deal of time and consideration to the matter of a public enquiry, and that he had spoken to many different people and departments during the course of the decision-making process, 'including families, whom I met after the November 1 service, and Muslims'.

I explained that I felt that I pretty much knew WHAT happened on 7 July ('though I'm sure the narrative will have some interesting nuggets'), but what I was interested in was WHY July 7 happened 'because if we can understand that, we can have a dialogue and then there are seeds of hope for the future'. I thanked him for his letter explaining the points that I'd raised on my blog, and I said I understood its confirmation that there were a number of internal inquiries going on behind closed doors, with police, intelligence services, politicians, 'but this debate is not just for police and politicians to have. It affects all of us, the whole country – and it is ordinary people like me who take the tubes and buses, not politicians'. And that was why I supported a public inquiry.

He asked about Kings Cross United (KCU). I explained that it was a group of over 100 survivors. I explained that the group was non-political, comprised of people of all ages and backgrounds with different opinions, yet we had all found a sense of unity and support in talking together. And that I had been struck that there seemed to be a common desire amongst the survivors I had met to understand the reasons for July 7, and to get something positive out of the experience, some learnings. I explained that I and some other survivors had recently had a letter from Tessa Jowell 8 months on expressing sympathy and offering a meeting, and that this had arrived after survivors had given evidence in public at the London Assembly. The London Assembly was the first time that we had been asked for our testimony or feedback as far as I knew.

Mr Clarke listened carefully as I spoke, and rocked backwards and forwards slowly (something I do when I am listening but also thinking what to say, and am little uncomfortable). He replied that he understood, and that he had survivors of dreadful tragedies come to see him before, and it was notable how people 'usually want two things, to understand why it happened and to get something positive out of it. And, we're not set up very well in this country for that to happen, for various reasons, usually legal ones and insurance ones'. He looked thoughtful. He explained that there was a great deal of desire to learn lessons from July 7, and that he was sorry that the letter from the Department for Culture, Media and Sport (DCMS) took so long to arrive, and that there had been a division of responsibilities early on, with care of the victims and the organising of the Memorial Service being done by the DCMS, and the Home Office managing other areas.

I said there was a sense of frustration when you felt you had useful things to contribute but were not able to. And that though I was not part of a political group, but just a random group of people who were on a tube train, I suppose the questions I was asking were 'political'. But I also thought this was above politics and not about blame. I said I'd consider personally moving from a public to an independent enquiry 'if things like Crevice[1] and defence of the realm stuff meant that some parts could not be shared with the public'. But I didn't see why we shouldn't be learning all we can, and discussing it together, publicly.

Mr Clarke looked thoughtful again. And then he offered to meet KCU, personally, and to come to one of our meetings, so he could listen to people's concerns and we could ask questions of him. He mentioned the media. I said KCU meetings were private and no media had ever been allowed access. And I thanked him, and said I would discuss it with the group, but I personally thought that would be fantastic.

And I do. I think it is a great result.

My father talked of how there was a lack of trust between people and authorities including the Government, how he had been reading *Exodus* in the morning's service and spoke of people's anger and alienation from Government and power, then and now. He said for a moment, in the Cathedral, he had felt something of the rage and impotence of the young men, not being listened to. There was a brief moment of discomfort when Mr Clarke quickly said that he didn't want to go over 'the incident' again. But then Mr Clarke said he agreed that there was a lack of trust between people and Government. He began to speak almost wistfully about meetings he had attended 10 years ago, set up by the Labour Lord Mayor of Norwich, Harry Watson. These meetings were an open forum when local politicians and the Bishop and local

[1] Operation Crevice was a programme of anti-terrorism surveillance and raids conducted across London in 2004.

priests talked together two or three times a year, about the issues of the day.

This was ten years ago, it must have been in the early days of the Blair administration. My father said he remembered the meetings, and he offered to talk to the Bishop about setting them up again, and Mr Clarke agreed. Or maybe he even suggested it, I can't remember.

He asked us if we had any more that we wanted to say, and I said, would he like a KCU badge? I gave him the badge, and he thanked me, and said that he could wear it if he met KCU. And I thanked him, and so did Dad, and the meeting was over. Dad and I had coffee in another converted church (medieval-wool-boom-town Norwich is stuffed full of medieval church buildings now used for other purposes, such as puppet theatres and cafés). Then we walked home.

I emailed KCU to let them know about the Home Secretary's offer to meet up with survivors. I phoned J. [Rachel's partner – Ed.], and then three friends from KCU.

And then I got out of my suit and into something more comfortable and chilled out on my parents' sofa with a cup of tea and some cheese and biscuits.

Later: I think it is good that Mr Clarke offered to meet some survivors, but the point of yesterday for me was to say that it wasn't really behind-closed-doors private meetings and narratives that were appropriate, it is about asking and answering people's questions in public. If we get the KCU meeting with Mr Clarke in the diary, that is what I will say to him: this is about more than the people who were on the train – we're just a random section of the public – this is about everybody. The questions and the answers and the debate should be opened up to all of us.

Rachel North
rachelnorthlondon.blogspot.com

The actions and policies of the Blair Government created something of a coalition of incensed bloggers from the Left, the Right and the Centre. A seemingly unnecessary and vindictive announcement from then Home Secretary Charles Clarke inspired this splenetic post from Tim Worstall. *The Times* was so impressed it printed a less sweary version the next day.

 April 2006 – Fuck him

Via The Englishman[1] we get this[2]:

> *Spending on compensation paid to those wrongly convicted of crimes is to be cut by £5m a year, Home Secretary Charles Clarke has announced.*
>
> *Those who win their appeals at the first attempt will get no compensation. Others who have spent years in prison will see any pay-outs capped.*
> *...*
>
> *A discretionary compensation scheme, introduced in 1985, which paid out £2m a year would be scrapped immediately because it had become increasingly anomalous, Mr Clarke said.*
>
> *Scrapping that scheme means people will not be allowed compensation if their cases have been quashed while going through the normal appeal process – winning at the first attempt.*
>
> *And new limitations will be placed on claimants under a statutory scheme which will remain in force which currently pays out £6m a year.*
>
> *'The changes I have announced today will create a fairer, simpler and speedier system for compensating miscarriages of justice,' Mr Clarke said.*
>
> *These changes will save more than £5m a year, which we will plough back into improving criminal justice and support for victims of crime.*

[1] www.anenglishmanscastle.com/archives/002624.html
[2] news.bbc.co.uk/1/hi/uk/4921230.stm

So let's think through what happens when someone is wrongly convicted, shall we? They lose some years of their life to the prison system. Sad but true, and there's no way we're ever going to have a justice system where this doesn't actually happen to some unfortunates at least occasionally.

What matters is what we do when it does happen.

There are a few other trivial things that happen too. They miss seeing their children grow up perhaps, lose their jobs and careers. Most will probably lose their house, whether rented or mortgaged. Some trauma, possibly, at finding the State imprisoning you for no good reason.

All in all, you could say that there's some direct damage, both economic and psychic, from such wrongful convictions.

So what does Charlie the Safety Elephant suggest? That if you've only spent, what, 20 odd months, damn near 2 years inside (the length of time it usually takes to get an appeal heard), lost perhaps your house, job, maybe even family, well, that's just the way the cookie crumbles, eh? Y'know, bad things happen, not my fault Guv?

And for what? To save 5 million a year? 5 fucking million? Out of 500 billion that he and his wastrel compadres are spending each year?

That is, 0.001% of public spending is going to be saved by not compensating those whose lives have been irretrievably fucked up by the actions of the State?

Have these people no shame?

Do you know what else costs some 5 million a year? Subsidising the snouts in the trough in Parliament. Literally[3]:

> *parliaments £5.7m annual catering subsidy*

Talk about your misplaced priorities, mate. Nope, sorry, I don't care how nice he was to Rachel [North][4] and her Dad (eventually), think nothing of whatever laws have

[3] politics.guardian.co.uk/redbox/story/0,,1093175,00.html
[4] rachelnorthlondon.blogspot.com/2006/03/charles-clarke-writes-to-my-dad-again.html

been passed about the incitement to terrorism and don't give, quite frankly, two shits about the consequences of this statement.

Charles Clarke should be hung from the nearest lamp post, assuming we can find one to bear the weight of the fat fucker, and the assembled political parties forced to watch as he tap-dances on air and happy children gambol at his feet.

If we as a society get things wrong and imprison the innocent it is our duty, as that very society, to both say sorry and to compensate them as best we can. What we offer can only ever be inadequate but to deny this moral fact, to save the price of MP's pork pies?

You fuck, Clarke, for shame.

Tim Worstall
timworstall.typepad.com

Of course, Charles was gone a few weeks later, the fall guy for the Home Office's foreign prisoner scandal and New Labour's poor showing in the local elections. His successor was political hard man John Reid. Had things just got better or worse? On the issue of the public enquiry into the bombings, the new Home Secretary was as steadfast in his refusal to hold one as his predecessor. As Holly Finch, another blogging survivor of the bombings, pointed out at a meeting with Reid, the reasons for his refusal were evaporating.

 July 2006 – Meeting the home boy

Well, the Home Secretary and the Secretary of State met with us, survivors from the bombed Piccadilly line tube, on Tuesday evening.

Dr Reid is a politician, I suspect, harbouring a severe case of short man syndrome. I can picture him, as a youth, battling with his comrades in a bulldog-like manner. Doggedly fighting until the end, stubbornly refusing to be beaten or shamed.

He has not changed much. Whether it is job, his age, or he has been unchanged since birth, I do not know. But I can say with certainly that one thing he adores is the sound of his own voice. That man can talk.

He purposely, I imagine, seemed to miss the point by a whisker; launching himself instead into wordy responses whilst ambling through topics he felt safe discussing. 'Discussing' is perhaps too balanced a term, it was more of a monologue that frustrated 'survivors' eventually felt brave enough to challenge.

There was the hint of a patronising tone, which emerged from time to time. Something that fired me up and made me more determined than ever that we should match him at his game. For a game is what it was, and what it has been from the start.

The Government do not want a public enquiry, or indeed an independent one. They will meet with us and the families of those that died, but it is lip service at its very worst.

He delivered the Government line, although it has been edited behind the scenes. They are running out of excuses fast. The last two remaining were money and resources. Lack of money is not an argument that would stand against a newborn child. So they are left with their last round of ammunition which they are spending fast. 'Resources' it is, the reasoning behind the 'no'. With Bloody Sunday (7 years and £20m) cited repeatedly as a glowing example. 'Surely', I queried, 'it is your job to do it better?' How is 'this is a bad idea because last time it went wrong' a credible reason not to forge ahead and do what's right?

I told him that I felt the Government had been on the back foot since the moment those boys blew themselves up. They had been reactive instead of proactive. All we had heard was them telling us the reasons they weren't going to have a public enquiry – where were the positive steps they were taking? 'Surely', I asked, 'the single aim of every person in this room is to do our damnedest to stop this from happening again, and make sure we learn everything we possibly can from this experience so that next time we do it better?' Sincere nodding all round to this. We should be working together, every single one of us, to uproot the seeds of this hatred, instead of playing political games. 'This Government', I said, 'has been nothing but negative and defensive whenever this subject is raised'. A pause, a purple face followed a spluttered retort: 'I am NOT being defensive!' Point proven, I think.

Then how, I wondered, can a public enquiry be wrong? 'I don't care', I told him, 'if the enquiry brings up nothing more than we already know, I don't care if it means you can turn around and say: "You see, we were right". But there is no excuse to leave a single stone unturned and this will only be done by an independent party.

'Resources,' he muttered from behind his now familiar glow. 'Muslims… Arabic speakers… ethnic minorities… takes a long time to train… it's not lack of money, it's lack of trained manpower'. He said that MI5 had more important things to do, such as preventing further attacks. 'Some questions', he said, 'just don't have answers'. MI5 has grown from 1000 staff to 2500 and is still expanding. At any one time, he said, there are tens of major terrorist investigations underway.

We have a lawyer in our midst and she was quick to interject. 'Tens?' she said. 'At any one time? In that case, could you tell me how many were involved in the case of the four bombers on 7 July?' He squirmed and would not answer the question. The point she was powerfully making is that it couldn't have been more than about 20. An inquiry would not be carried out by MI5 itself – the clue there is in the word 'independent'. Hence as many people as required could be gainfully employed in seeking the facts and that would not hamper the fight against terrorism. They would be lawyers, most probably, not members of the security services. Only 20 would be called upon to give evidence which would not, I suggest, hamper their productivity whilst it was happening. So, it seems to me, that resources has been quashed as an excuse too, so what is it now?

The question of the influence of Iraq came up and was, again, dismissed. Four terrorist attacks have been prevented in this country in the last 15 months, he told us. I asked him how many had been uncovered prior to 7 July. I was hoping for it to be less and for that to give me an opening to ask him why he thought that was. He was one step ahead, though (that is why he is Home Secretary and I am not), and didn't answer. Instead he told us that the first al Qaeda plot to be foiled in this country was in 2000 in Birmingham. He kept doing that, throwing in facts that we were bound to not know, thus tripping us up on our way. In his opinion the first war in Iraq had a greater radicalising affect than this one. 'At the time Jermaine Lindsay was four', someone helpfully pointed out. 'I doubt he was radicalised by it at that age, do you?'

On the subject of the errors he has admitted in the narrative [the Government's account of the bombings which contains several factual errors – Ed.], 'We never said it was comprehensive', he said. Oh well, that's okay then, silly me. They fully intend to communicate any further errors to us and will do their best to inform us when stories appearing in the press are untrue.

They are compiling a 'lessons learnt' report that will cover issues from before the attacks to concerns raised in their meetings with us. This is a 'dialogue', they said, that they intend to continue. When pushed, the Home Secretary would not commit to meeting us again; Tessa Jowell, however, did.

Holly Finch
hollyfinch.blogspot.com

Following stories (related elsewhere in this volume) of what John Prescott did or didn't do with his cocktail sausage, another scandal erupted over other trysts the Deputy Prime Minister had enjoyed, this time with billionaire Phillip Anschutz. The Ministry of Truth, in a forensic post, reckoned it had Prescott and the Government banged to rights over dealings concerning the Millennium Dome and the super-casino Anschutz wants to build there.

 July 2006 – Following the money…

From a series of posts on his blog – here[1], here[2] here[3] and here[4] – it looks very much as if both myself and Iain Dale have been simultaneously working on the same question – just what was John Prescott actually doing in visiting Colorado-based billionaire, Phillip Anschutz, at his home, last July.

The story so far is that Iain's definitely up on me on this one:

> *I can exclusively reveal that 2 days after John Prescott's overnight stay with Philip Anschutz John Prescott flew to Los Angeles where he was a guest at a champagne reception hosted by the Chief Executive of AEG*

[1] iaindale.blogspot.com/2006/07/coming-next-evening-of-media-whoring.html
[2] iaindale.blogspot.com/2006/07/meet-philip-anschutz-prescotts.html
[3] iaindale.blogspot.com/2006/07/exclusive-further-prescottanschutz.html
[4] iaindale.blogspot.com/2006/07/snape-ducks-newsnight-debate-with-me.html

Tim Leiwke. AEG is the company which runs the Dome and is owned by Anschutz. This man is on record in The Independent *saying that 'a casino licence is fundamental to the future of the Dome'. So if that is so, how could Prescott and Anschutz discuss the regeneration of the Greenwich Peninsula without talking about a casino licence?*

But we're pretty much even on the revelation that Anschutz, a mild-mannered businessman by day, by night turns into Stephen Green[5] on steroids.

In the past, Mr Anschutz has donated large sums of money to Colorado for Family Values, an organisation with explicit homophobic views. He is also a major patron of the Republican Party and funded 'Amendment 2', a voter-initiated ballot to overturn gay rights in the state of Colorado. He is also a major donor for the Institute for American Values, who campaign against single-parent families. Voters approved 'Amendment 2' in 1992, which changed the state's constitution to explicitly ban laws that protected gay and lesbian people from discrimination based on their sexual orientation. The approval of the amendment by voters led some activists to label Colorado as a 'hate state', and there were mass protests by LGBT campaigners outside of churches... (From Pink News[6])

I should also note that another of Anschutz's favoured causes is the Discovery Institute, who are, of course, the leading proponents of the errant and unscientific wingnuttery that is so-called 'intelligent design'.

What's bothering me about this whole story is that if there really is anything to it at all, then something about it just doesn't add up.

Put it this way: if Prescott genuinely has been playing footsie with a billionaire would-be super-casino owner then, as the usual quid pro quo in such a relationship goes, there seems to be an awful lot of quid potentially heading Anschutz's way but not a lot of pro quo on Prescott's side of the equation.

It just doesn't add up...

[5] en.wikipedia.org/wiki/Stephen_Green_(Christian_Voice)
[6] www.pinknews.co.uk/news/articles/2005-1896.html

I wrote the first part of this about 10 o'clock this evening, then took a break to watch *Newsnight*, which has confirmed what has been my line of enquiry on this. Documents obtained under FOIA (so say the Beeb – more on this later on) appear to show that Prescott took a keen interest in casinos and that OPDM was monitoring progress on a few things in relation to Anschutz's plans to place a casino/hotel complex inside the Millennium Dome, amongst other stuff.

Iain Dale was also interviewed, but only in much the same vein as Nick Robinson's line on his blog today[7] – i.e. bloggers are biased and don't have to research stories and verify the facts like us professional journalists, so we're better than them. Nyar-nyar-nee-nyar-nar! It seems the BBC has now started with much the same kind whingeing about bloggers we've getting from the dead tree press for months.

Well, *Newsnight* – let's just see you suck on this.

First, while it's nice that you managed to obtain these documents, can I ask you specifically WHEN you obtained them?

Considering that this whole story has blown up in the matter of, what, a couple of days, and that the Government is certainly not in the habit of responding to a fresh FOIA request in such a short space of time, one has to wonder quite how you managed to have just the right documents for the story at just the right time…

…unless you've either

a) known about this story for a while and sat on it, until bloggers smoked it out and forced you out into the open; or

b) your request for information has been fast-tracked by whoever dealt with this request because someone on the inside sees it as being in their interests for you to have this information.

When is a leak not a leak? When it's a conveniently timed release under the FOIA?

Second – and this is going in bold type…

[7] www.bbc.co.uk/blogs/nickrobinson/2006/07/prescott_for_du.html

Even with all the information at your disposal, you still succeeding in missing completely the single most salient and important fact in your whole report!

Look, it's simple – all you need to do is follow the money.

Anschutz's entertainments company, AEG, takes the desperately embarrassing white elephant that was the Millennium Dome off the Government's hands under a 20-year lease on what amounts to a 'pay as you go' deal.

This deal, as the report explained, entails AEG paying nothing until it has recouped its investment in various things – including an arena and the aforementioned hotel and casino complex – plus some degree of profit, following which the taxpayer will start to get its kickback (by way of what appears to be a share in the profits from the Dome over and above what the Chancellor normally takes by way of taxation and any licensing costs, if the casino licence is granted).

That's the deal between the Government, specifically the DCMS, and AEG for the Dome – and this was mentioned, albeit briefly, in the report.

The documents obtained by *Newsnight* also indicate that AEG's view of the whole project was that a casino licence would be essential to its success – bottom line, the casino is, in AEG's view, the cash cow that makes the rest of the project work. And not only that – if AEG does get the casino licence, which amounts to a licence to print money, then it will also recoup its costs much more quickly, deliver a profit and start paying on the terms of its lease, which means money paid over to the taxpayer – or rather the Government.

And who collects this cash? Well, ultimately the Treasury, of course, but the Department that signed off on the deal was the DCMS…

…who by complete coincidence are also the Department responsible for issuing casino licences.

Now everything would have been hunky dory, were it not for a bit of media-driven furore over gambling and a bit of opposition in the Commons and Lords, which resulted in the number of licences on offer for the kind of unlimited jackpot, super-casino that AEG wants to put in the Dome down to just one…

… for which there are currently eight eager bidders, all of whom want the big prize and the largest piece of the action.

Now according to *Newsnight*, all this could create the unfortunate impression that AEG has had a bit of preferential treatment on their bid – which is where they completely miss the key point in all this.

All you need to do is follow the money through the deal between the DCMS and AEG for the Dome – if AEG gets the super-casino licence it will start to generate big profits; the sooner it generates the profits, the sooner it begins to pay its contractual kickback to the taxpayer for the lease on the Dome… and unless there's a set cap on this kickback, this also means that the more profits AEG make, the more money slips quietly in the Treasury's coffers.

This is NOT about Prescott's freebies and whom he may, or may not, have been shagging while off on his jolly little junket.

It is NOT EVEN about AEG maybe getting a bit of preferential treatment and ministerial solicitude.

> *What it is about is a government that has a direct pecuniary (i.e. financial) interest in seeing AEG get the super-casino licence, and one compounded even further by the fact that it is the same Department (Culture, Media and Sport) that made the deal with AEG for the use of the Dome, that will now issue the licence for the super-casino.*

Now some may see that as a canny bit of business – that 'some' certainly will not include the seven other bidders for the same licence who, when the penny drops, are likely to notice that they're bidding against a competitor (AEG) who has a considerable advantage over them due to a deal they've already cut with the Government for use of the Millennium Dome.

What the other bidders have to offer, in strict cash terms, is whatever they pay for their licence plus whatever the Treasury rakes off in taxes, but when it comes to AEG, not only does the Treasury get the licence fee and taxes, but it also, somewhere down the line, gets a direct share in AEG's profits.

On top of which, you now have the little matter of Prescott hanging out with the owner of AEG – oh, and before I forget, it's also worth mentioning AEG's other little favour to the Government, which involves the arena it's going to build in the Dome being used for a few events at the 2012 Olympic Games, including the basketball tournament…

…and, oddly enough, Prescott just happened to take his trip out West to see Anschutz last July (2005) while, by strange coincidence, London's success in bidding for the Olympic Games was announced on 6 July 2005.

This leads me to two observations.

The first is that if you were involved in any of the seven rival bids to AEG's, then you could easily be forgiven for thinking that maybe, just maybe, the fix has gone in and the outcome of the decision on awarding the licence for the one super-casino that the Government is allowing is, shall we say, looking suspiciously like a bit of a foregone conclusion.

The second observation is simply that, with all the resources at its disposal and its 'oh, so professional' reporters and editors to rely on, it seems rather strange that no one at the Beeb appears to have noticed or seen fit to comment on the glaringly obvious pecuniary interest that the Government has in AEG's bid, even though all the information required to make the connection was in the actual report.

Simple oversight, a bad case of post-Hutton gun-shy syndrome, or maybe just playing it cute in the hope that some blogger might just make the connection… I'll let you decide.

As for Prescott – to me he looks like the fall guy as usual, because instinct suggests there are bigger fish to fry somewhere in all of this…

BTW – in relation to my comments earlier in this post about when I started to write this up – there are a number of fine, upstanding, bloggers who can, if necessary, testify to my having made the connection at the core of this piece at least a couple of hours before *Newsnight* aired, although I am happy to credit *Newsnight* with having provided the evidence that verified my thinking on this subject.

Ministry of Truth
www.ministryoftruth.org.uk

Nosemonkey sees little to hope for in another Government initiative.

 August 2006 – The politics of hope (but mostly fear)

Finally, an admission from the Government, in Ruth Kelly's speech[1] launching Britain's own Truth and Reconciliation Commission[2], the Commission on Integration and Cohesion:

> 'Muslims feel the reverberations from the Middle East. Wider global trends have an impact.'

So despite all the previous denials, foreign policy DOES affect British Muslims' attitudes? Glad we've finally got that one sorted.

There's also a nice nod to Gordon Brown's recurring desire to define what it means to be British with questions about 'who we are and what we are as a country' – and even an acknowledgement that multiculturalism may encourage 'separateness', to keep *The Daily Mail* on board. There's also a subtle adoption of one of the Tories' most controversial[3] slogans from the last General Election:

> 'We must not be censored by political correctness.'

In other words,

> 'It's not racist to talk about immigration.'[4]

The only trouble is, of course, that despite Kelly's assurances that this new Commission 'is not, and must not be, a talking shop... [but] a practical exercise', it's incredibly hard to think of anything genuinely practical this Government has done in the last few months (at least). All we seem to have had is talk and pointless shows of state strength

[1] www.timesonline.co.uk/article/0,,2-2326811,00.html
[2] en.wikipedia.org/wiki/Truth_and_Reconciliation_Commission
[3] europhobia.blogspot.com/2005/04/its-not-racist-to-impose-limits-on.html
[4] www.conservative-party.org.uk/tile.do?def=news.story.page&obj_id=121612&speeches=1

– be they endless assurances about the state of the NHS or high-profile (but ultimately proven to be mistimed and misplaced) counter-terrorism raids.

Believe me, I'd love nothing more than to be able to find something positive in politics again, but for the last few years there's been nothing about HOPE in the rhetoric of any of the parties, merely fear. Fear of the Tories, fear of terrorists, fear of Europe, fear of economic collapse, fear of immigrants. The few times our politicians have appealed to our aspirations rather than our night terrors, their promises have proved to be either empty or ill-founded, their policies soon either abandoned or altered in the face of adversity.

Even Kelly's speech, which seems to be trying to promise a brave new world of cross-cultural harmony, focuses more on the current negatives than the possible future promises. She asks about 'who we are and what we are as a country'. I'm rather worried that the answer to both may be 'distrustful wannabe-isolationists' – and that refers as much to the Don't Attack Iraq brigade as the Little Englanders...

Europhobia
europhobia.blogspot.com

Political party conference season. The interminable speeches. The back-biting. The over-analysis ('What did he mean by that?', 'What does his body language say?' and on and on...). Rafael Behr does the lot with an elegant economy.

 August 2006 – Party conference season – a preview

We need reform. And we must modernise. The goal of this modernising reform process will be renewal. Modernise, reform and renew now. Oh, and unite. We must unite. There is no alternative. Well, there is, but it is stagnation, division, decay and ultimately death. And that is a bad alternative. Not like reform. And modernisation. Which are good.

Rafael Behr
rafaelbehr.typepad.com

At the time of writing (mid-September) Tony Blair is still Prime Minister. If that has changed between now and your reading this I'd like to take the opportunity to wish Prime Minister Brown/Reid/Cameron/Beckham (delete as applicable) well.

At the end of the week that saw a so-called failed coup against Blair by Brown and the Brownites, and Blair announcing he would resign within the next 12 months, Shuggy wrote an early obituary for the Blair years.

 September 2006 – For the virtues of faithlessness

Blair's long goodbye looks finally to be drawing to a close. Yet there still remain, and will perhaps for ages yet, caves in which his shadow may still be seen. For some loyal souls[1] are keeping the faith[2]; they enjoin others to do so. Should you decline, these people will not understand your faithlessness, your lack of loyalty.

I don't understand them. Theirs is the politics of faith but with regards Blair I am both unclear about what it is they believe and why they believe it.

One facet of this belief seems to be the idea that Blair should be rewarded for his foreign policy[3]. Naturally, this would be impossible for someone who opposed the invasions of Afghanistan and Iraq, but even for someone like myself who supported both I find this inexplicable. The Left has always been obsessed with foreign policy in general, and with the Middle East and Latin America in particular. It is because it is felt that it is here that political conflicts are played out in primary colours – in a way that demands that no one can remain neutral.

The former I recognise in myself; the latter less so. Those who are insisting that Blair be rewarded for his stance against what some of us have no hesitation in calling fascism should, I believe, ask themselves the following questions. In the admittedly unlikely event that Ian Duncan Smith had been Prime Minister, should he have been rewarded

[1] hurryupharry.bloghouse.net/archives/2006/09/08/the_real_blair_backlash_begins_here.php
[2] www.keepingthefaith.org.uk
[3] normblog.typepad.com/normblog/2006/09/lowering_the_to.html

for supporting American foreign policy? Because there can be no doubt that he would have followed the same course as Blair. Or historically, were the working-class voters of Britain wrong to turn their backs on Winston Churchill in 1945? And if so, would there be a Labour tradition for them to claim to be the true heirs of?

If the answer to any of these is yes, declare yourself to belong to the Right and be done with this appeal to the legacy of British socialism and social democracy. If it is yes, it is because you believe that Blair – independently of his foreign policy – represents in some way the incarnation of these traditions.

If you believe this, you are wrong. For Blair, in the position he has taken on the twin pillars of liberty and equality, has been on the wrong side. Blair, as both his public utterances and his policies show, believes in neither. Do we have to demonstrate this? Blair has explicitly said he does not believe in greater 'equality of outcome', preferring instead the spurious notion of 'meritocracy'.

One of the key mechanisms by which British citizens are to gain this equal right to pass by on the other side is through education, education, education. Fortunately, I don't have to work in the English system but the means by which this to be achieved under New Labour has been to renew the Thatcherite war on teachers. The notion that one might possibly improve educational standards in this country by enlisting the support of people who actually work in it is dismissed as 'unreconstructed', wankerish and so, like, yesterday, man.

Instead we have a brave new world where the Thatcherite micro-management of the classroom pursued by a remorseless diet of continuous assessment has been embraced with great gusto, replete with the fear and loathing of that mythical creature, the 'trendy teacher'.

The only criticism that many of the true bearers of the Left tradition can find to make of Blair's project to turn our education system into a supermarket is that it simply doesn't go far enough. More should be done to allow people to escape the contamination of the 'bog-standard comprehensive'. Of those left behind? These are the undeserving poor. And if you, like me, should be unfortunate enough to feel it your vocation to teach such as these, understand that these new 'progressives' despise you for it.

So much, so personal – but is it really so difficult for the Blairistas to grasp that, his limited improvements notwithstanding, what has disappointed so many of us is the sheer waste of it all – the squandering of two colossal Parliamentary majorities by behaving as if to all intents and purposes the election campaign was still on? Were they never squeamish at the way in which this regime sought to ingratiate themselves to the proud and the powerful? Did they not share a sense that these Labour governments have achieved less in the way of redistribution than one might expect of a Christian Democrat administration on the Continent? One anecdote had it that, during a disagreement between Blair and Chirac over the reform of the EU, the latter remarked, 'You see, the basic problem is that whereas I am a man of the Left, you are one of the Right'. What has been said of George Bush in a different context can be applied here: just because it is Chirac saying something, it doesn't mean it isn't true.

But it is on liberty that Blair's failure has been the greatest. This is because he clearly does not believe in it. That the Freedom of Information Bill is a genuine advance in liberty, I would concede – we know this because of the negative way in which successive Labour Home Secretaries have responded to revelations made under the auspices of this Act. And there is no point in holding up the equalisation of the age of homosexual consent as an example of New Labour 'tolerance' because there is no need for tolerance of things you approve of. In contrast, wherever there is something this government disapproves of, they have never failed to attempt to circumscribe the autonomy of British subjects: as with jury trials; as with the right to protest and demonstrate; as with the right for the accused to be presumed innocent until proven guilty and to hear the evidence that the state holds against them; as with the right to live and move without being watched and recorded by the state; as with the right to express one's contempt for organised religion without the fear that in doing so one is committing a criminal offence.

Disagreement with one or any of these points on a rational basis you could cope with. What is insufferable is the notion that to do so is in some way a betrayal of the working class – who, we are reliably informed by people who, I suspect, are acquainted with these only through descriptions – are only too happy to have their liberty sold for around a fiver an hour. Because they have this – or possibly the benefit of tax credits, if they can negotiate the Byzantine world of means-testing – the dumb proles are blissfully unconcerned about issues such as religion in schools. I would like to take this opportunity to cordially invite the Blairite blogger who suggested this contemptuous and fatuous idea to me to on a guided tour of the city of Glasgow. Re-acquaint yourself with the place, y'know?

Behind this whole thing is TINA – the notion that there is no alternative. It's better than the Tories, don't you know? So Blair's illiberalism is beyond criticism because, well, he's lifted all these families out of poverty, he's done as much as he can. Leaving aside the impossibility of the Blairistas ever crediting the hard-pressed working families with lifting themselves out of poverty (which is odd, since they are obviously fans of Samuel Smiles[4]) there's a slight philosophical problem I have: even if this were so, since when are we obliged to welcome something simply because there is no alternative to it? And even within the narrow confines of what is believed to be inevitable by the Blairistas, why so little imagination? They believe 'globalisation' has forever limited the range of fiscal options open to the state. Very well – so why not advocate a smaller state that taxes less but redistributes more? Because as it is just now, the least wealthy are paying a disproportionate share of their income to the Treasury. And this might actually bring some reality to the cant spouted by the Government about 'empowering communities'. Has it never occurred to them that this would require them to do less?

It hasn't – because the extent to which the Blair regime seeks to manage the lives of British citizens knows no bounds, for it extends even unto the womb[5]. I'd like the Blairistas to consider this: as the Labour party under Blair has lurched to the Right, British politics has increasingly resembled the American situation where ever-smaller differences in economic policy have been accompanied by a partisanship that is increasingly shrill, hollow and personal. But if the Blairistas insist, I'll play the politics of personality too. Blair once said, with his usual air of exasperated righteousness, 'I mean, I can't bring up people's children for them', as if this was obviously the ideal solution. If for no other reason, I am glad this sanctimonious twerp who has never understood that he is not our President but merely the Queen's first minister is leaving office. Blairistas may accuse me of being irrational about this but to date I've yet to read an argument of theirs that could be considered rational. All I can see is the politics of blind faith. Here's Hitchens[6] on Blair's departure:

> *When I first interviewed Blair, as newly elected Labour leader in 1994, he answered my question about the role of his Christianity in his politics by saying, 'I can't stand politicians who go on about religion.' If I had to date the moment when my own misgivings*

[4] en.wikipedia.org/wiki/Samuel_Smiles

[5] modies.blogspot.com/2006/08/potentially-illiberal.html

[6] commentisfree.guardian.co.uk/christopher_hitchens/2006/09/the_hitch.html

about him began, it would be the time – starting after September 11, 2001 – when he began to emphasize his own 'faith' as a motivating factor in his moral stand.

A saving element in British politics is that such appeals are usually considered embarrassing. They may also suggest a slight tendency, on the part of those uttering them, to believe in some kind of supernatural endorsement.

So Blair's concession that he must leave office, a decision so long postponed and so disastrously protracted, represents among other things a triumph of the mundane over the permanent temptation to believe that politics is about anything else.

Quite so. And not for the first time, I find I'm chronologically ahead of Christopher Hitchens in my thinking: I cannot point to a date on which I started to have doubts about Mr Blair because I never had any faith in him in the first place.

Shuggy's Blog
modies.blogspot.com

You And Me Against The World
Activism

It's true to say that while blogging has proved the ideal inducement to people sitting on their arses, it's also provided many incentives for people to get up off them as well. If you've got a cause, blogging is the perfect medium for rallying others to it.

Coupled with other online tools (Pledgebank.com, where people pledge to perform a certain action, and WriteToThem.com, which allows you to email your MP), blogging has become a real force, if not exactly for holding Authority to account, then at least for going a long way to informing it of what it is its true bosses (that is, us) are thinking and want.

Here, amongst other articles calling for awareness of important issues, we see how a cause, a blog and a little bit of good old-fashioned pluck, can bring about real results.

Under the Serious Organised Crime and Police Act 2005 it is now illegal to protest or make any kind of political statement in Parliament Square in Westminster without prior permission gained 6 days in advance. British Blogland's very own merry prankster, Tim Ireland, saw an opportunity for some mischief. Here's the text of his invitation to a Christmas carol service with a difference.

 December 2005 – Public carol service

You are cordially invited to a public carol service in Parliament Square at 6pm on Wednesday 21 December 2005.

This inclusive service will contain both Christian and secular verse, and is expected to last no more than an hour.

Candles and song sheets will be made available, with donations going to Medical Aid for Iraqi Children[1].

Programme:

(*Introduction and welcome*)

Come All Ye Faithful

Away in a Manger

Little Drummer Boy

The Twelve Days of Christmas

Deck the Halls

Good King Wenceslas

The First Noel

[1] **www.maic.org.uk**

Joy to the World

We Wish You a Merry Christmas

Jingle Bells

Rudolph The Red-Nosed Reindeer

Santa Claus Is Comin' to Town

(*Message of thanks followed by a one-minute silence*)

Amazing Grace

God Rest Ye Merry Gentlemen

Hark! the Herald Angels Sing

Silent Night

(*The Lord's Prayer, led by Brian Haw*)

Legal Implications:

Please note that if you attend this carol service, it will classify as a spontaneous demonstration (of faith, hope, joy and/or religious tolerance) and there is a possibility that you will be cautioned or arrested under Section 132 of the Serious and Organised Crimes and Police Act 2005.

Section 132 Serious and Organised Crimes and Police Act 2005:
This draconian law was designed to evict Brian Haw[2] and stifle dissent at the heart of our democracy. On that first count, it failed[3] but on the second.... well, you're probably already aware that Maya Anne Evans was arrested and convicted under this law, merely for reading out names of soldiers killed in Iraq at London's Cenotaph[4].

[2] www.parliament-square.org.uk
[3] www.parliament-square.org.uk/PR290705.htm
[4] news.bbc.co.uk/1/hi/england/london/4507446.stm

Section 132 – Demonstrations in vicinity of Parliament[5]
Demonstrating without authorisation in designated area:
1) Any person who –
> *a) organises a demonstration in a public place in the designated area, or*
>
> *b) takes part in a demonstration in a public place in the designated area, or*
>
> *c) carries on a demonstration by himself in a public place in the designated area,*

is guilty of an offence if, when the demonstration starts, authorisation for the demonstration has not been given under section 134(2).

A formal warning usually precedes any action, but the police may arrest any person committing an offence under Section 132 of the Act and if found guilty that individual may be liable to a fine of up to £2 500 and/or a term of imprisonment of up to 51 weeks.

In this instance, the police have not been notified. They've been invited, certainly, but they have not been notified. We believe that the public has the right to gather in a public place and sing Christmas carols. The police may see things differently; we shall see. (Technically, under the act, while this may be a spontaneous demonstration of faith, hope, joy and/or religious tolerance, it still classifies as a demonstration.)

Tim Ireland
www.bloggerheads.com

---

[5] www.opsi.gov.uk/acts/acts2005/50015--l.htm

The concert went off without a hitch and a tidy £300 was raised for the charity Medical Aid for Iraqi children. Rachel North reported back.

 December 2005 – *Amazing Grace*

We did it! We protested, a loud speaker was used, a political speech was made. We sang carols, and we demonstrated our contempt for the stupid law that criminalises peaceful protest outside Parliament.

We sang carols and festive songs (and we sang them well, apart from a rubbish rendition of Little Drummer Boy with too many rum-pum-pums) and we said the Lord's Prayer, and held a minute's silence, and we sang *Amazing Grace*, which had me crying, as usual.

And my friends were there, and I made some new friends, and I was proud to be part of it. Well done[1], Tim!

And so the law[2] was broken, but no arrests were made. This is important, in a small but significant way.

BBC[3]:

> *Since the law came into force in August, several people have been arrested and other protesters have been warned off.*
>
> *Human rights lawyer Michael Schwartz, who was among the singers, said the new law was vague – as demonstrated by the lack of police officers on Wednesday.*
>
> *'Is it compatible with human rights law, which is supposed to protect freedom of expression and assembly, particularly around Parliament, which is supposed to be the mother of democracy?', he added.*

[1] 5thnovember.blogspot.com/2005/12/seriously-organised-criminal-carol.html
[2] www.opsi.gov.uk/acts/acts2005/50015--l.htm
[3] news.bbc.co.uk/1/hi/england/london/4545704.stm

A Metropolitan Police spokeswoman said: 'We treated the event as a carol service and not as a demonstration so the legislation did not come into play.'

But of course it *was* a demonstration. We came there to make a point, and we knew we risked arrest.

We were protesting against an unjust law; that was why we turned up. We pushed it, and 100–130 people assembled and demonstrated, and sang and nothing was done. Hooray. About time. A stupid law was defied, and well done to the police for treating it with soft hands. The law is an ass, so let's give it a sugar lump, and pat its flanks, and let it walk away. It's an embarrassment to enforce. What does that tell you, Mr Clarke? Mr Blair?

That this is the way that it ends, not with a bang, but with a whimper?

Independent coverage – news.independent.co.uk/uk/politics/article334675.ece

BBC Report – news.bbc.co.uk/1/hi/england/london/4545704.stm

Urban 75 report – urban75.org/photos/protest/carols-parliament.html

Listen to us on BBC Radio 4 News – www.blairwatch.co.uk/down/radio4carols.mp3

Rachel North
rachelnorthlondon.blogspot.com

What the Government gets up to with our money is a subject that seems to leave most people rather uninspired. However, once you get down to it, it doesn't take long for righteous indignation to manifest itself. Here, Wat Tyler, who has made it his life's work to expose government profligacy, explains how the Private Finance Initiative works and why we should be up in arms about it.

 January 2006 – PFI Panic

In principle the Private Finance Initiative could be a good deal for taxpayers. Instead of trying to build and maintain hospitals and schools itself, the Government gets private sector specialists to compete for the job. Not only should the price be lower, but also the risks of things like project overspend are transferred to specialist operators who are better equipped to manage them. Everybody should win by eliminating waste and inefficiency. Hurrah.

Yes, well... sadly it hasn't always worked out quite like that. For one thing, the government has used PFI principally as a tool to borrow off-balance sheet[1]. The best estimate is that PFI debt now amounts to a chunky £90bn. And the pressure to borrow covertly means they have driven through deals that would have been cheaper funded directly by the public sector.

There's also a suspicion that our commercially naive hospital trusts and education authorities have not always cut a good deal for taxpayers. It's clear that many of the early PFI deals have subsequently yielded substantial refinancing gains to the contractor/bank consortia that did them.

Of course, just like a mortgage, all of these deals commit some public sector entity – such as a hospital trust – to a stream of payments stretching many years into the future. And the sums can be big, say a quarter of a hospital's annual income for the next 25 years. If they don't pay up, they can expect the bailiffs. Whatever the spin says, this is public sector debt.

Now, finally, the Treasury seems to have woken up. Hospitals could go bust, just like

[1] burningourmoney.blogspot.com/2005/12/mired-in-debt.html

the PFI Queen Elizabeth[2] in Woolwich, whose Chief Executive says:

> *In traditional commercial terms we are insolvent – and we are not alone. We are relying on temporary cash borrowing to enable us to pay our creditors, staff and PFI partners. It reaches a point where there is no way out on your own. Somebody is going to have to come along and restore our balance sheet.*

That 'somebody', of course, is the Treasury. Time to hit the panic button.

Which is why they've just pulled the plug on the biggest PFI deal of all – the £1.2bn Barts/Royal London rebuild[3]. Well, strictly it's Commissar Hewitt who's done the deed (*'We have not ordered a review of the whole Barts and London PFI scheme. We have simply asked the local NHS to commission an independent review looking again at the proposed redevelopment'*– hmm, I see.)

Unfortunately for us taxpayers, the PFI consortium involved – Innisfree/Skanska – have met these panicky prevaricating politicos before. They evidently took the highly sensible precaution of getting themselves a contract. Which *reportedly says*[4] *if the scheme is not approved by the end of January, Skanska will be entitled to leave the project claiming £100m costs, or continue on the basis that it will be paid more.*

So that's another £100m down the drain, then.

How many MRI scanners is that?

The Docs at Barts/Royal are naturally up in arms, demanding Tony step in. Fat chance of that. Perhaps their time would be better spent sorting out the Commissar's arse and elbow problem.

Burning Our Money
burningourmoney.blogspot.com

[2] society.guardian.co.uk/privatefinance/story/0,8150,1668724,00.html
[3] www.timesonline.co.uk/article/0,,2-1987998,00.html
[4] politics.guardian.co.uk/publicservices/story/0,11032,1687434,00.html

The debate about energy – how we produce it and how we use it and what we do with the carbon dioxide created in the process – gained greater prominence than ever this year. The idea of carbon offsets were trumpeted. It's not a very good idea, said Merrick.

 April 2006 – Carbon offsets are a fraud

The Independent recently published a piece on 'How To Fly Around The World Without Costing The Earth'. They ignored the only credible answer (evolve yourself some wings) and went with the idea of using aircraft and then paying people to plant trees as carbon offsets.

A chap called Duncan Law responded. He points out that simple measuring of emissions is not enough; as aircraft emit at altitude, their impact is around three times as bad as if it were done on the ground. His most persuasive point is that carbon offsets are a nonsense because the emission is instant whereas a tree's absorption is over many years.

There are, however, many other problems too. It's impossible to say how much carbon a tree will store, so you cannot know how many trees to plant for your emissions. Beyond that, you cannot tell what your emissions are; figures on offset websites for, say, per mile driven, usually don't take into account your m.p.g. or how many passengers to divide it among. Figures for a train journey should surely be different if it's a packed rush-hour train compared with a late afternoon one with only half a dozen of you on board.

Then there's the problem of just counting the number of trees planted. Some offset projects have been buying land that's cheap, clearing existing mixed woodland trees and replacing them with their monoculture plantations.

Whilst all these things are true, they only show why offsets are clumsy and ineffective.

There is a bigger, more disturbing truth, that paying for offsets lets us think we can carry on with our unsustainable high consumption, and were we to face the facts that offsets don't really work, we would be forced to concede the reduction on emissions so urgently needed.

Corporate Watch's characteristically excellent article[1] explains:

> *Planting trees and energy efficiency are important things to do in themselves, but the trouble with linking them to offset programmes is that their positive impact is cancelled out by justifying and condoning a negative one, implying that we can consume at current rates guilt-free as long as we have the money to salve our consciences, which takes us no further forwards in reducing emissions. If anything, it takes us backwards, as corporations are able to ride on the image boost of appearing greener, whereas the truth of the matter is that they are a complete fraud.*

Not just ineffective or counterproductive but 'a complete fraud'? This is where we hit the biggest and most disturbing truth. You can't offset carbon emissions.

Burning fossil fuels adds CO_2 to the carbon cycle. Trees merely store some of it for a while before releasing it once they rot or burn. They're not an offset, merely a delaying device.

As Oliver Rackham[2] said, it's like drinking more water to keep down rising sea levels.

The wish to avoid actually changing the things we've come to rely on is understandable, but it's effectively a blindfold we're putting on to tell ourselves we're not facing what's in front of us as we walk toward the cliff edge.

The reader response to *The Independent* also featured incredulity at environmentalists wanting to ban damaging activity.

> *Do they really expect ordinary people to subscribe to the notion of...* 'punishing those who damage the environment'?

Given that 'the environment' means the single system we have for survival, I'd answer yes.

[1] www.corporatewatch.org.uk/?lid=2069
[2] en.wikipedia.org/wiki/Oliver_Rackham

And it should include mandatory measures. If I saw a line of sick babies in incubators and somebody was trying to inject poison into their oxygen supply, yes, I'd want to force them to stop.

The welfare of future generations of people and other species lies in our hands and we're poisoning their fundamental essential prerequisites for survival. If it's not right to poison people and take away their food and water today it's not right to do it to them tomorrow. We should not respect anyone's claim to a right to do so, we should be tackling them head on, and if they won't respond to appeals to their common humanity then they should certainly have their toys taken off them.

If only it were their own future they were fucking up. Again, I see the curse of our allotted three score years and ten. Were we to live for several centuries then averting the worst effects of climate change would be our top priority.

Bristling Badger
bristlingbadger.blogspot.com

A common feature of Blogland is the creation and spreading of 'memes'. A concept invented by Richard Dawkins, memes are ideas as viruses. Tell someone your idea and they are immediately infected with the virus. Daniel Davies created another. Spread the word.

 March 2006 – Thought for the day

If I started using the term 'anti-Semitic' as a general term of undifferentiated disapprobation, like 'lame' or 'gay' (as in 'God, those trainers are pretty anti-Semitic', 'The first few series of Friends were quite sharp and funny, but it got really lazy and anti-Semitic toward the end', 'I don't know; there's nothing specific about Shoreditch that I don't like - it's just a bit anti-Semitic'), how long do you think it would take to catch on? And what sort of reaction would I get in the meantime?

D- Squared Digest
d-squareddigest.blogspot.com

So, you want to help save the planet. How about starting small and cutting back on your energy consumption by insulating your house? That's what Charlie Whitaker decided to do. Getting help to do it, however, means negotiating a system seemingly designed in committee by Orwell and Kafka and then built by M.C. Escher. You have to admire Charlie's tenacity.

 June 2006 – Stuck to the back of the filing cabinet, in the basement ...

Reeling from winter's three-figure gas bill – a scale of energy expense I'm totally unfamiliar with – I've set myself the summer task of insulating my home. By accident, I'm living in an 1895 flat. It has no energy-saving features at all. (Contrast this with the fact that a properly designed house[1] – in Britain's mild climate – can well be lived in with no heating appliances extra to the lightbulbs and the hot water tank: 400mm of wall and roof insulation will take you there.)

First task: figure out how much the project will cost. Like me, you might have a vague memory of government grants being available for insulation. Finding out more should be easy. To the internet...

• Ignoring Google's ads for now, we find the National Energy Foundation[2]. It appears to be a non-profit something. Dig deep for a list of links to government sites/grants[3]...

• Top of the page: *Energy Efficiency Advice Centres*. Clicking on the link takes you to ...

• The Energy Saving Trust[4]. It too appears to be a non-profit organisation. Is it the government agency that hands out grants? Let's click on the insulation link ...

• And then let's click on the 'see if you're entitled to a grant' link ...

[1] www.passivhaus.org.uk
[2] www.nef.org.uk
[3] www.nef.org.uk/links/gov.htm
[4] www.est.org.uk/myhome/

• And apparently there are three different sources of grant. The government (in England the scheme is called 'Warm Front') energy suppliers and local authorities …

• My energy provider (nPower) doesn't seem to have any grants (discounts?) for insulation … although if I switched back to British Gas …

• There doesn't seem to be a link to 'Warm Front'. Back to Google …

• There it is – top of the list – a link to DEFRA[5]

• And I'm instructed to apply in writing to Eaga Partnership Ltd., Freepost Warm Front Team, 12054, Newcastle Upon Tyne, NE2 1BR. I wonder how many letters flop onto that doormat each month? No, wait, there's a link[6] …

So, there you have it. If it's a grant for insulation you want, disregard DEFRA, the National Energy Foundation and the Energy Saving Trust. None of those outfits does grants for insulation. Go direct to the source: a private company in Newcastle called Eaga Partnership.

Whoops: it looks as though you need to be over 60, or have a child under 16, and be in receipt of state benefits in order to qualify. It must be a different scheme I need. Back to, uh, the Energy Saving Trust. OK, so national government assistance won't be coming my way, and energy suppliers' schemes – frankly – I don't trust. That leaves my local authority. Let's go there now and see what the options are:

• A toll-free advice line operated by Creative Environmental Networks[7] in partnership with Richmond Council. Apparently I can get advice on 'Coldbuster grant applications' or the 'Energysmart discount scheme'.

• Another link to the Energy Saving Trust.

• A link to the Green Energy Centre. I think that's about renewables, not insulation.

[5] www.defra.gov.uk/ENVIRONMENT/energy/hees/index.htm
[6] www.eagagroup.com
[7] www.cen.org.uk

• And if I were someone who spent more than 10% of his or her income on energy bills (quick check ... no, not quite) I would qualify for ... the 'Stay Well, Stay Warm' advice document. Actually it's free, so I can have a copy anyway. And so can you. Here you go[8]. Useful, isn't it?

OK, so let's place a call to Creative Environmental Networks and see about these Coldbuster grants. The phone rings, is answered. Some questions. Am I over 60? Do I have children under 16? Do I receive any government benefits? No? Well, British Gas has a very good offer on loft insulation right now ...

I feel genuine disappointment. It's a bit like being 12 and queuing around the block for the cinema, but still not getting in. I'm getting the sense that's there no grant out there, but owing to the information fog, I can't be sure. And I've come across lots of offers for low-cost insulation deals – they claim to be subsidised, as if the powers that be trust builders more than they trust householders. Open book contracts, perhaps.

Update: OK, hands up. I've booked a no obligation survey from a subcontractor appointed by British Gas. They'll come and look at my loft, and we'll see. But why am I in this situation?

There are around 10 million homes in Britain with uninsulated cavity walls. A similar number have less than 100 mm of loft insulation. Government policy on improving this situation is contained in something called the Energy Efficiency Commitment[9]. The opening statement:

> *Under the Energy Efficiency Commitment (EEC), electricity and gas suppliers are required to achieve targets for the promotion of improvements in domestic energy efficiency. The EEC will contribute to the Climate Change Programme by cutting greenhouse gas emissions.*
>
> *At least 50% of energy savings must be focused on a priority group of low-income consumers in receipt of certain benefits and tax credits/ pension credit. So it is expected that the EEC will also contribute to the eradication of fuel poverty.*

[8] www.richmond.gov.uk/stay_well_stay_warm.pdf
[9] www.defra.gov.uk/environment/energy/eec/index.htm

The first thing to note is that the Government has passed the task of insulating existing housing stock to energy suppliers, who now have 'obligations' and 'targets'. How are these measured[10]?

> *In order to comply with their obligations, suppliers are required to notify Ofgem of their energy efficiency actions or 'schemes'. Ofgem will approve a scheme notification if it is satisfied that it would promote an improvement in energy efficiency. Once a supplier has completed a scheme it must notify Ofgem who will determine the actual improvement in energy efficiency to be attributed to that scheme.*

The intention is to save 130 terawatt hours between 2005 and 2008. Ofgem's assessment methodology is here[11]. Numbers are involved; however, they seem to relate to an arbitrary scoring system, rather than a measure of energy, viz:

> *Where a supplier carries out an innovative action, Ofgem will increase the improvement in energy efficiency attributable to that action by 50% where the total improvement in energy efficiency attributed to such actions in relation to the supplier's target would achieve no more than 10% of that target.*

The second thing to note about government policy on insulation is the emphasis on low-income energy consumers. This entangles the issue of energy efficiency with the issue of relative wealth. Is this helpful? Planetary physics makes no distinctions with respect to the income of the polluter: carbon fuel burned is carbon fuel burned. Wouldn't it be better to facilitate energy saving across the board – and increase benefit if necessary?

But that's where we are. Forget government information campaigns. Forget public agencies dedicated to making it easy for you to claim your subsidy. But have faith: energy suppliers will come knocking on your door any day now, demanding to inspect your loft. You just know they will. You may already have seen their leaflets. We want to sell you less gas, honest. Trust them. They know what you need.

Charlie Whitaker
www.perfect.co.uk

[10] www.ofgem.gov.uk/ofgem/shared/template2.jsp?id=1596
[11] www.ofgem.gov.uk/temp/ofgem/cache/cmsattach/10969_29004.pdf

In August, Metropolitan Police Commissioner Sir Ian Blair's observation that it was safe to leave front doors unlocked was met with peals of ironic laughter from many. Wat Tyler mounted a rebuttal against Blair's vision of Utopia.

 August 2006 – Down these mean streets

Yesterday Tyler met up with a friend who lives in Sir Ian 'Bonkers' Blair's[1] crime-free metropolis. The friend confirms that he and his neighbours do indeed routinely leave their front doors unlocked, but only because the doors have been jemmied open the previous night and the Polish locksmith hasn't yet got round to fix them.

He and his wife live in Primrose Hill, where crime is rampant, but the Met are 'too busy' to do anything about it. Well no, that's not fair: in conjunction with the People's Republic of Camden they have set up a Safer Neighbourhoods[2] policing team, boasting:

> *Safer Neighbourhoods is a truly local policing style: local people working with local police and partners to identify and tackle issues of concern in their neighbourhood... Each team has a minimum of six uniformed officers comprising one sergeant, two constables and three police community support officers, dedicated solely to the needs of one specific neighbourhood. '*

Except, of course, you can never get hold of any of them. The mean streets of Primrose Hill – home to bankers, media types, and David Milliband – are not deemed to need their full complement of police, so they've been redeployed elsewhere. The rest are doing paperwork, or skulking around well out of harm's way. But that's OK, because Blair's Met and the People's Republic reckon the crime problem is all in the mind anyway:

> *Despite recorded crime falling in Camden and the UK in general, research shows that one-third of people believe crime has risen 'a lot'.*

[1] www.thesun.co.uk/article/0,,2-2006380793,00.html
[2] safety.camden.gov.uk/ccm/content/policing-and-public-safety/community-safety/csp-subsite/neighbourhoodsafe/safer-neighbourhoods.en;jsessionid=aOn_gySArE8

Clearly people like my friend don't need policing, they need counselling. (The real facts are summarised here[3] – Primrose Hill has the fifth highest overall ward crime figures in London).

Anyway, this friend recently intervened in yet another attempted vehicle theft in his road. The young thug involved is notorious locally, and responded by threatening to burn down my friend's house, with him in it. And since then, he's attempted to assault him while out walking. The police response (after four unanswered phone calls and only because my friend had spotted a rare community policeman hunkered down outside a kebab shop) was:

> 'I see Sir. Well, there's nothing we can do. But you should get all this down in writing to us, because if... er... anyone gets hurt... we've got a record.'

Fantastic.

For most people, of course, the only option from there is to purchase a baseball bat and a Ninja sword.

But Primrose Hill is different: it's rich. So the residents have another option: private security patrols[4]. It began after one couple:

> 'came home after an evening out to be ambushed by three masked men armed with machetes and clubs. They were forced into their house in Lower Merton Rise with their two children and marched from room to room at knifepoint. They were ordered to hand over money and valuables, an experience which left the family traumatised.'

Hardly surprising, then, that residents realised they could no longer rely on the police to protect them. Instead, they clubbed together to pay for a private security firm to patrol the road.

[3] www.thisislocallondon.co.uk/news/topstories/display.var.889199.0.londons_most_dangerous_streets_revealed.php
[4] www.findarticles.com/p/articles/mi_qn4153/is_20020527/ai_n12008361

For £1000 pa each, they get regular visible patrols, and a 'meet and greet' service if they come home late:

> The guards carry no weapons and have no police-style powers, but can carry out citizens' arrests. A spokesman said: 'We have caught car thieves breaking into a vehicle and caused what we know were burglars to leave the area. If criminals see us, hopefully they will move on.'

And business is booming. Not only have other roads in Primrose Hill taken up the idea, but also, from South Kensington to Hampstead Garden Suburb, there are now hundreds of similar schemes across London alone.

The police are completely cool with it. A Yard spokesman said: '*We recognise the role security firms have to play in reassuring sections of the community*'. Clearly they see the ex-Israeli, South African, Russian, Ukrainian and British soldiers who man the patrols primarily as outreach counsellors, which saves them the bother.

Less relaxed are other local residents who are not subscribers. That's mainly because they're feeling the brunt of machete gangs displaced from the patrolled roads, although some fret about more Millibandesque issues – the editor of Wallpaper ('*the online resource for international design interiors and lifestyle*'), recently moved up to Primrose Hill from downmarket Dalston, and has been driven to some serious hand-wringing[5]:

> There has been much talk of how to prevent crime in my bijou corner of north London. Half of the residents are keen on an improved neighbourhood watch scheme and, Cameron-like, on cuddling the hoodies who have been causing the problem. The other half want to hire a private security firm to patrol the streets and keep the riff-raff away.

> The latter proposal hovers dangerously close to class apartheid: why should the residents of Camden's less photogenic corners be made to feel unwelcome by Primrose Hill residents just because they can't afford to live there?'

[5] www.guardian.co.uk/commentisfree/story/0,,1852820,00.html

Clearly the machete boys haven't visited him yet.

According to the Met's 2006 Policing Plan[6], their total projected spending in 2006–07 will be £3bn, and total police numbers will be 31,582. Given the Met area population of 7.4m, that means each of us gets £400 pa of policing (around £1000 pa per household). Those are significant sums, and you can bet the residents of Primrose Hill contribute more than their fair share of the costs. They are lucky to be able to afford private policing as well, but many, many people cannot.

The lesson should not need repeating, but let's do it anyway. Britain's current policing arrangements cost us plenty, but are totally unresponsive to the paying customers. Roll on elected sheriffs. And Met Commissioners.

Burning Our Money
burningourmoney.blogspot.com

[6] www.met.police.uk/about/documents/Police_Plan_2006.pdf

Sometimes it does a blogger good to get out of the house. Nick Barlow took this to extremes by embarking on the trek from John O'Groats to Land's End. His walk was done in the aid of the Brain Research Trust charity after his brother Simon died from a brain tumour.

At the time of writing (mid September) Nick is still yomping. By the time you read this, and with a following wind, he will have completed his epic journey and be enjoying a well-earned rest, but you can still drop a few quid in his virtual bucket here: *www.justgiving.com/nickswalk*. Nick's blogged his journey at every opportunity and this dispatch from the wilds finds him following the backbone of England.

 August 2006 – Mud, mud, inglorious mud

If anyone ever tells you that you should walk the Pennine Way because it's fun and enjoyable, here's what to do: go straight to your nearest outdoor shop (Milletts or Blacks, most likely) and buy yourself one or two walking poles – preferably aluminium ones, not carbon fibre – then go back to your friend and beat them repeatedly around the head with them until they see some sense.

Yes, I've had my Pennine Way experience over the last few days, and it's safe to say that I don't like it. It's muddy, it's damp, it goes through countryside for which 'bleak' is perhaps an overstatement and it seems to take special pleasure in avoiding anywhere interesting. For instance, there's a bit further south from here where the route takes all sorts of weird twists and turns to avoid going into Hebden Bridge. They boast that 250,000 people use it every year, but as that includes just about anyone walking around Kinder Scout, Malhamdale or Pen-Y-Ghent for an hour or two, it leaves very few people who make any sort of effort to walk the trail.

I could write a much longer post about all this, but it comes down to the difference between hikers and walkers – and the Pennine Way was designed much more as a trail for hikers than a path for walkers. Suffice to say that Wainwright[1], perhaps the

[1] en.wikipedia.org/wiki/Alfred_Wainwright

best example of a walker, hated it.

Anyway, it's not all been bad these last few days – Thursday's walk from Melrose to Jedburgh was very nice, except for contriving to lose one of my walking poles when I left it outside the Post Office in St Boswells. This wouldn't have been a problem in that I tend to only use one, and I had two, except the other one broke yesterday…

Friday was pleasant from Jedburgh to the border, following back roads that became increasingly rough and narrow until they eventually became a track up a hill, following old fencelines until I finally – without any ceremony, signs or waiting border guards – crossed back into England, where it promptly began to rain on me, making the descent into Byrness not at all pleasant. Saturday, I did follow the Pennine Way while it stuck to forest tracks through Kielder, then switched to back roads for the walk into Bellingham. One thought that did strike me is that the youth hostels I stayed in at Byrness and Bellingham (and Alston, where I am now) are set to close in the next month or so, meaning that I could well be the last End-to-End walker to pass through them – so I've made a little mark in history, perhaps.

Sunday saw me avoiding the Way again, instead taking to the back roads through Wark to get to Hadrian's Wall, and discovering a lovely little village called Simonburn on the way. It was one of those little marks on the map that could be a village, or could just be a large farm, but turned out to be an old Northumbrian village of about 10 or 12 houses around a green with an old church and a tearoom-cum-shop that served the most amazing hot roast beef sandwiches. It's the sort of place you dream about finding in the middle of a day's walk, so it is entirely possible I was hallucinating about a Pennine Brigadoon and sitting in a field eating grass – if anyone else can confirm it exists, I'd be grateful.

From there, it was along the Hadrian's Wall Path for a while towards Once Brewed, which was interesting but somewhat marred by the strong wind coming from the west that I was walking into. One bizarre thing I've discovered is that the official guide to the path suggests walking it from east to west, which means that not only do you start at Wallsend, where I thought the name would be kind of a clue as to the best way to travel, but you're also heading into the prevailing wind for the whole journey.

And then yesterday, I turned south, heading through Haltwhistle[2], which claims

[2] en.wikipedia.org/wiki/Haltwhistle

to be the centre of Britain and thus may well mark my halfway point. It might have been apt to have stopped there, but it was only 11 o'clock, and there was a nice path down the old railway line from there to Alston, where I'm now enjoying my day off, 5 weeks and 480 miles on from John O'Groats. At times, it doesn't seem that long since I left, yet at others it seems as though it was years ago, given how much I've done since leaving there. I think I've got just over 5 weeks to go, though – having done some rough calculations and barring accidents, I'm expecting to finish on Saturday 7 October. That might lead to me doing some days in the last week that are either very short or very long to make it there on schedule, but I figure that if I finish on a Saturday, then anyone who wants to come and meet me at the finish can get to Land's End and back over the weekend, meaning I should have someone there to celebrate with on the Saturday night.

What You Can Get Away With
www.nickbarlow.com/blog/

The mainstream media cottoned on to interaction in a big way this year. Members of the public were asked to send their eyewitness accounts, photographs and semi-coherent musings to news channels desperate to fill the hours. It was called 'citizen journalism' by some or, more plainly, 'getting the public to do our job for us for nothing'. Here, Web of Evil subverts the idea…

 September 2006 – Get it off your chest

[Sent to BBC News 24. Really, letters to broadcasters, magazines, etc. should be written in green crayon, but I've found that only makes a mess of your monitor.]

At last! I've found a use for the 'send us your emails' slot. Obviously none of this one will be read out on air, and I'm glad: I watch BBC news (and indeed pay for it) because I want to hear news from trained, halfway competent professionals, not just what struck Ted from Surbiton while he was sprawled on his sofa munching Doritos. If I want to hear unformed lumpen opinions from flatulent numpties I'll pop over to the pub. Please keep the news for people who have a clue what they're talking about.

Which ties in with what I'm actually mailing about – the lack of aforesaid news. 'Tony Blair might shortly exit this building.' 'We're bringing you live shots of the podium where we expect the press conference to happen in the next 5 hours.' 'We've sent our helicopter up in the hope it'll find something to film before the fuel runs out.' 'While we're waiting for that delayed press conference to begin, here's a shot of Steve, our vision mixer.'

For God's sake put this stuff on another feed, even the actual live coverage of press conferences. That's what the digital multi-channel option is for. Please don't clog the main channel with filler that doesn't count as information. There's a million things going on around the world right now, none of which are illuminated by an unwavering shot of an empty podium or Downing Street from above. The countdown to the top of the hour features images of scalding beams of NEWS swooshing into Television Centre from correspondents sequestered all over the globe, which contrasts starkly with what often ends up happening during the day: someone told me (I couldn't bear to sit through it myself) that one of the World Cup press conferences was broadcast live for one and a half hours.

News 24 is far better at delivering news at night, when there are fewer distractions, and fewer people awake to speculate at us. Right now, though, I'm watching incredulously as reporters are sent all over the country to try and reach as many people as possible who don't know the first thing about Tony Blair's intentions about staying in office. Fruitless speculation and pointless helicopter shots of Number 10 do not constitute news. Unless there are plans to change the channel's name to BBC Generally Arsing About 24, why not get on with telling us about other actual news – not just asides about the other couple of top headlines – and then let us know about Blair as soon as you actually know something? No?

I know, I know, that's not what *Sky News* does. But some of us are very glad that you're not *Sky News*. The Beeb is a different animal. The London bombings last year illustrated how it works: you'd go on to the Sky site first because they'd be first with any scrap of information they had, even if it turned out to be wildly wrong, and then you'd visit the BBC site, which would be more circumspect at first while it checked and verified, but – and this is the important bit – would then be utterly reliable on actual facts.

If it were down to me – and obviously it's not, it's all in the hands of people who can use phrases like 'delivering outcomes' in cold blood – I'd urgently recommend focusing on the whole 'facts' thing, and knock the speculation, the timewasting and the idiot emails on the head.

(I would also, while we're at it, grab by the lapels and vigorously shake the person responsible for adding the headline to the 'spinning world' graphic. 'What the hell were you thinking?' is pretty much what I'd yell. 'It's the most crass, witless, unnecessary and potentially offensive thing a news programme has done since ITV played mournful music over slow-motion footage of 9/11'. The newsreader has just told us what the headlines are. There is then no need for the words 'GAZA DEATHS', 'MASSIVE FIRE', 'SPACE TOO SHORT FOR HEADLI' or whatever to go jauntily scrolling past. I switched on a month ago to see 'LONDON BOMBS' as the main headline. 'Oh God, not again,' I thought. But it wasn't another round of incendiaries; instead, it was news about one of last year's bombers. The headline isn't just annoying, it can also be misleading. Someone's clearly very proud of it, though, and I have to accept that no one's going to change it just because it's a bad idea.)

On the plus side, the new text format is good, with the ticker far more legible in black and white and the imbecilic BREAKINGNEWSBREAKINGNEWSBREAKINGNEWS in a slightly narrower, less intrusive font. But please, especially in view of your insistence on the use of the phrase 'Breaking News' every three damn minutes (honestly, if *Sky News* told you to jump off a cliff, etc.), don't just give us reporters telling us hopefully that someone important might turn up shortly, or people talking about what they think might one day happen. You can be so much better than that.

Web of Evil
webofevil.livejournal.com/

Blood, Sweat and Beers
Work and Play

Life, as a great man* once said, is the name of the game, and I want to play the game with you. Did you know that in an average lifetime we spend around 25 years asleep and 6 months on the loo? We also spend about 20 years at work and 10 years eating. That only leaves around 15 years for the pleasures of drinking to excess, smoking, le cinéma de Bruce Willis and vigilante campaigns against paedophiles.

Let's face it, work is a hateful activity. Anybody who says they enjoy their job is a teetotal sociopath with a threadbare social life. This chapter consists of a vicious critique of the bitter ennui that is working for a living. It's tempered by a vibrant celebration of those priceless jewels of hope, joy and wonder snatched from the claws of the beast known as work-commute-sleep-work, along with other meditations on the human condition.

* Bruce Forsyth

Tokyo Times' Lee Chapman explains how the Japanese, with their famous attention to detail, do business.

 November 2005 – Toilet Techno

Not content with making the bathroom a place for the leisurely perusal of poetry[1], toilet trailblazer TOTO has produced a lavatory with a built-in music player.

As well as the now almost standard wash and dry facilities, TOTO's unusually named Apricot N5A[2] has the ability to bang out a few tunes, whilst you, erm, bang out other things. A company spokesperson explains, 'We conducted a survey in 2002 where we asked people to tell us what they wanted from a toilet. The most common response was a heated water cleaning system, which was closely followed by the desire for audio-visual functions'.

Yet don't for a minute think that this means some kind of cheap stereo with an inbuilt muzak soundtrack. Far from it. The inclusion of a memory card slot means that users can set the music to suit their needs. A couple of short and snappy pop ditties could be ideal backing for an equally brief 'business trip'. Alternatively, a 1970s prog-rock marathon would perhaps be better suited to those looking at a more prolonged visit, with the addition of volume control allowing any embarrassing splashes or splatters to be easily drowned out by a timely cymbal crash or screeching guitar solo.

With the Apricot N5A, however, the fun doesn't stop with musical accompaniment. For those whose bowels run like clockwork, the toilet seat can be set to warm up at specified times. Plus the embarrassment of frantic flushing after a particularly large and stubborn deposit should be a thing of the past, as the intelligent toilet is capable of analysing what it's dealing with, taking the appropriate action once dimensions and consistency have been accurately calculated. Yet perhaps the Apricot's biggest boon – at least for the ladies – is that the seat puts itself down automatically.

Whilst such lavish lavvies may seem a little over-the-top to some, Kuo Ue, director of the Japan Toilet Association, claims to know why such advancements have become

[1] www.tokyotimes.org/?p=703
[2] www.toto.co.jp/products/toilet/t00004/03.htm

so attractive. 'Japanese are a people who have placed great importance on hygiene since the olden days and really focused their attention on the toilet. There's even a saying that if you want to be beautiful, you should first clean your toilet.' He finishes with a slightly controversial parting shot: 'There's a tendency for toilet talk to be taboo in the West, so they haven't progressed'.

Tokyo Times
www.tokyotimes.org

The World Weary Detective, a Metropolitian Police detective in London, gives 'a view of life from the thin layer between you and the underclass'. Here's an account of the short-term thinking of senior officers that prevents street robbery from being tackled properly.

 January 2006 – Stop and search does not work

Recently published crime figures reveal that street robbery figures have risen by 11%. This is despite efforts to massage this situation away (see here[1] for more on this).

The offence of street robbery is an obsession of senior police officers, particularly in inner-city areas. For senior officers at a local level, daily robbery figures cause sleepless nights and obsessive days. No other type of offence comes close. Each force is set targets by the Home Office. These are based on a reduction in the number of offences, and on the number of crimes 'solved', or 'detected'.

The majority of senior officers in the Metropolitan Police Service have very little experience of crime investigation, and have little interest in long-term goals. Their objectives are predominately led by graphs and figures coupled with forecasts and statistics. Short-term 'solutions' are adopted in knee-jerk responses to pressure from above. There is no place for pro-active detective work with a view to providing medium- and long-term results at a local level.

[1] **worldwearydetective.blogspot.com/2005/11/day-in-life-of-robbery-report.html**

When a robbery problem is identified in a particular area, a number of uniformed officers are tasked there. Their success is measured on the associated crime reduction. Their personal work rate is assessed on the number of arrests they make, and the number of stop-and-searches they conduct. This tactic is deployed with monotonous regularity. It does not solve the inherent problem in the area concerned. Crime is displaced. It still happens, only in a different place until the police leave.

Stop-and-searches rarely lead to arrests. Small amounts of cannabis and occasionally weapons are found. These are a tiny proportion of the number of stops conducted. Any robber worth his salt is quite capable of seeing the police coming. They do not stand and wait to be searched. The power to search gives the police the power to detain for that purpose. Mere discussion does not. Such tactics have been discredited many times before, but are still used as performance indicators. Stop-and-search produces little but alienation in inner-city areas.

While the uniformed officers are searching youths who 'smell of cannabis' or are 'in an area of high robbery offences', the detectives are under pressure to detect the robberies already reported. This often means hours of viewing CCTV footage. This hardly, if ever, produces tangible results (see here[2] for more on this).

The funding expires, the extra police leave and the robbery problem returns. The confidence of the community is in doubt following excessive use of searches and the fact that the robbers are still at large. The police managers are satisfied that while the stops were happening, robbery figures in that area were down.

The police have a number of tried and tested covert policing methods. The senior management will not authorise their use because they do not provide short-term quick fixes.

Community-based policing that does not rely on confrontational use of stop-and-search enhances the relationship between police and public. This is turn will increase confidence which leads to information-sharing. By this method, the identities of the youths committing the robberies can be discovered. This can be coupled with police intelligence.

[2] worldwearydetective.blogspot.com/2006/01/watching-you-catching-you-locking-you.html

Intelligence-led pro-active detective work can then take place, targeting the priority offenders. This method will ensure that the best evidence possible is obtained and the public are protected. The muggers will actually be arrested and charged with substantive offences that are likely to result in custodial sentences. The quality of the evidence obtained should be such that a guilty plea will be offered at court, therefore saving the public money, and avoiding the stress of court appearances for victims.

The cycle can then begin again. The community will see that the robbers are being removed from the streets. The fear of capture will once again be instilled in the criminals. Making communities safer is a long-term commitment. Current tactics are failing the community, as the figures show.

World Weary Detective
worldwearydetective.blogspot.com

If you want to know what goes on inside the National Health Service, Dr Crippen's diaries are unmissable. And, like the World Weary Detective, he gives an insight on what it's like on the front line, and continually buffeted by the short-term whims of politicians, managers and bureaucracy. Infuriating, heartbreaking and darkly humorous in equal measure, the diaries make for essential reading. Here's the Good Doctor having One Of Those Weeks.

 March 2006 – The Crippen Diaries (Week 11)

A particularly bad, trying day at work. Arrived in at 7.50 a.m. feeling glum and chatted to two of my partners. We have all read the same articles in the newspaper over the weekend. The blessed Patricia [Hewitt] is now saying that the problems in the NHS are due to the doctors.

All right, she is only a politician. It is nonsense. But it is in the papers. People will believe it. It is deeply dispiriting, and our morale is already rock bottom.

++++++++++

First patient is David. Elderly man. Charming. He was a tank commander during the war. He is in atrial fibrillation, he is not maintaining his blood pressure, he keeps flipping in and out of heart failure and is being admitted for pacing in two days. When Dr Crippen was a houseman, all patients such as this were 'clerked in' by the houseman. That does not happen anymore. Nowadays, they are assessed by cardiac nurse specialist. She is much cleverer than Dr Crippen because she can do this assessment by telephone. David has had a letter saying that he should be at home by the phone this afternoon, waiting for her call. He is puzzled. 'How can she assess my cardiac status over the phone?' Beats me. I have to use a stethoscope, but then I am only a doctor.

++++++++++

Third patient in is Mary, one of the local speech therapists. She is approaching retirement. I sent her husband into hospital three weeks ago in rip-roaring heart failure. He was on CCU for 3 days but now is on the far flung corner of Dixon, one of the medical wards. He is partially sighted due to an old stroke, and is hard of hearing. The nursing care is appalling. He has developed pressure sores on his sacrum and heels and, oddly, a suppurating area above both ears which Mary thinks is caused by the oxygen mask he uses being too tight. He is losing weight because he cannot really manage to feed himself. Mary was in each day over the weekend. Uneaten food from Saturday was still on his bedside table on Sunday. Mary went to the nursing station at the end of the ward. The nurses were all eating take-away pizza. Deep-pan pizza from Pizza Hut. Mary remembers that particularly. Mary thinks her husband is dying. She is not sure which consultant he is under, and has not been able to find a doctor to talk to. The nurses over the weekend do not speak English. She tried to tell them that her husband is partially sighted but they do not understand. They show her the nursing assessment. Under 'visual problems' it says 'none'. Mary is in tears and asks what she should do. I suggest she phones the Chief Executive and makes a formal complaint.

I do not suppose that Pizza Hut pizzas carry harmful bacteria, but should they be on an acute medical ward?

++++++++++

Mavis is a hugely efficient retired social worker. Her husband has Alzheimer's disease, quite advanced now. There is a 3-year waiting list for inpatient care of Alzheimer

175

patients and he has only just gone on it. Social services offer her 2 weeks' respite care a year. She is not managing. She is on her knees. She has a bit of angina (stable) and needs full investigation but will not go for it at present.

Trouble is, she is looking after her husband really well. So when social services 'assess' her, she is classified as low need. She knows the system. She worked in it herself. 'The best thing I could do is have a heart attack, then we would be high need', she says.

She is right.

++++++++++

Thursday 16 March

Phyllis is a very valuable patient. She is 59. She is overweight. She smokes 40 cigarettes a day and has done for years. She takes no exercise. Her cholesterol is 7.2 and her BP is 168/90 despite treatment, or perhaps because she does not take the treatment that we give her. She works in the local petrol filling station. She lives alone in a small council flat and she is terrified of doctors. One could earn a fistful of Quality and Outcomes Framework[1] points from here if one did all the nagging one is encouraged to do by the blessed Patricia. We do try. Gently. But Phyllis is frightened of doctors. She does not like taking tablets and she does not really understand the significance of high cholesterol. But we do out best.

A few weeks ago she made an appointment of her own volition rather than after being chased by the practice nurse. She had developed angina. It was not easy to get the history from her. There were no abnormal physical findings apart from the raised blood pressure but, on the history, it was unstable angina. It was coming on at random, often at rest.

Patents with unstable angina need immediate hospitalisation. I arranged for an ambulance to take her in. She was both horrified and terrified.

[1] http://www.primarycarecontracting.nhs.uk/16.php

The NHS is good at this sort of emergency. She was assessed in the local hospital, had an arteriogram, and was then transferred to the regional cardiac centre for a coronary artery bypass graft (CABG).

On arrival there, someone noticed that there was a shadow on her chest x-ray which looked ominous. She had a bronchoscopy the following day and the biopsy confirmed a lung cancer. Not surprising with her history. She was asymptomatic from the lung point of view and in a back-to-front way was probably lucky that she had developed the angina as it enabled us to discover the tumour earlier than we might have done. And it is operable. All the screening investigations were normal.

There was one thing outstanding. 'I have to go to another hospital for a PAT scan.' She meant a PET scan[2]. The first hospital had made the appointment for the scan. Then she had received a phone call from the second hospital saying the scan was cancelled as they did not have the funding, since they were in a different Primary Care Trust (PCT)[3] area. Could she phone her doctor to get him to make sure that the PCT funding for the PET scan was in place, and then could she phone the hospital back to arrange another date?

Phyllis is frightened of doctors. Phyllis is frightened of lung cancer. Phyllis is frightened of operations. Phyllis is mystified by arcane three-letter acronyms and, it transpires, Phyllis is a bit frightened of using the telephone. Phyllis was in tears. Not because of the cancer. Not because of the angina. But because she was not able to cope with having to arrange a scan herself.

So we did it all for her. It took awhile but it is sorted. Whilst the receptionist was attacking the bureaucracy, I checked her blood pressure and reviewed her medication. She is on the full whack of anti-anginal, anti-hypertensive medication and the angina is controlled for the present. She still needs surgery. She asked me if they could do the operation on the lung at the same time as the CABG. She had been too frightened to ask at the hospital. Ashamed to say I was not certain. I suspect you have to go in a different way for a pneumonectomy or lobectomy so it may mean two goes. I will have to find out.

[2] http://www.petscaninfo.com
[3] http://www.nhs.uk/England/AuthoritiesTrusts/Pct/Default.aspx

She will have the PET scan in a few days and, I hope, will have the surgery. Then her angina will be sorted out. And, staggeringly, she has stopped smoking. She must be frightened.

The best and the worst of the current NHS, all in one patient. Phyllis will get all the treatment she needs. But she was left having to negotiate two hospital switchboards to try to arrange a specialised scan that she did not understand. Not the end of the world but, for someone like Phyllis, it was all too threatening. It should not happen.

NHS Blog Doctor
nhsblogdoc.blogspot.com

Here is another piece from the Good Doctor; long but vital reading. The best blogging has the power to change the way you think and see the world, and here's a fine example.

 March 2006 – Schizophrenia

There is no area of healthcare more ignored, more under-funded and more misunderstood that the care of the chronically mentally ill. And of the chronically mentally ill, the worst cared for are the schizophrenics. There was a general clear-out of British long-stay mental hospitals about 20 years ago. The 'right-on' slogan was 'care in the community'. The chronically mentally ill were thus pushed out of the cuckoos' nests on to the streets.

The government does not even pay for the cardboard boxes.

The care of schizophrenics in the UK is a disgrace. It is a matter of national shame. The majority of psychiatrists take no interest and pretend that the GPs are looking after them. The majority of GPs take no interest and pretend the psychiatrists are looking after them. The few who do try to take an interest – and it is one of Dr Crippen's areas of interest – get no support. Most of the work falls upon the community psychiatric nurses, and there are not enough of them.

It is just as bad, or worse, in the USA. In Africa it defies belief

It is usually said that the incidence of schizophrenia is 1%. This is an exaggeration, but it is still a common condition.

The disease is misunderstood and feared. Jekyll and Hyde. 'Split personalities'. Axe murderers. That's how the general public sees schizophrenics. In reality, the chronically mentally ill are no more likely to be violent or dangerous than any other section of the community. To talk of 'dangerous schizophrenics' is as relevant and as helpful as it is to talk of 'dangerous architects'.

Dr Crippen is upset and angered with the common misuse of the word. An eminent politician might say of an opponent, 'Oh yes, he is a bit schizophrenic about that'.[sic]

What is schizophrenia really about?

Schizophrenia is about Emma. Emma was a good friend. We met at school as teenagers several years before she became ill. She died recently. Her family asked me to speak at her funeral. At first they did not want me to mention her 'illness'. I could not do that. Emma herself never wanted to hide it, and would have been furious if it had been glossed over at her funeral. So this is what I said:

We meet together today to mark the sad and untimely death of Emma.

> *It is always easier at times like this to talk in terms of celebrating a life, but the problems that afflicted Emma, and her premature death just a few days before her 46th birthday, make it a bit more complicated. And, whatever else one may say, Emma's life was complicated.*
>
> *She was born in May 1959 in Cornwall. Her parents were David and Jane, both of whose families went back several generations in Cornwall. Emma was a third child, and young sister to Derrick and Peter. She was unmarried and had no children of her own, but was aunt to Derrick and Peter's children, David, Alice, Jane, Peter and Freddie.*
>
> *Emma was educated locally, first at ... primary school until she was 7 when she moved to .... Then, at the age of 11, she went to ... boarding school in ... . She stayed there until 16 to do O-levels and then she left boarding school and returned home to study for A-levels*

179

locally in Cornwall. After A-levels, she went to university in Nottingham to read for a degree in English, but only managed a year of that course before she left, once again to return home to her parents.

Her father died in 1978 and thereafter Emma mostly lived with her mother in Cornwall. In 1984 her mother developed cancer and died the following year in 1985.

So far, perhaps, an unremarkable story.

A little nomadic, the sad loss of both parents, but still nothing out of the ordinary. But there was one problem that was very much out of the ordinary.

Emma suffered from schizophrenia.

Schizophrenia is much misunderstood and frequently misrepresented by the media. It is nothing to do with 'split personalities'.

Simple schizophrenia, from which Emma suffered, has a characteristically insidious onset, usually in the late teens. It frequently manifests itself with odd and alienating behaviour. Many years may pass with the sufferer being labelled as difficult rather than as ill. It frequently runs a course of gradual but unremitting social and mental decay, and so it did with Emma.

It is a cruel illness that separates the sufferer from people.

Emma was exceptionally intelligent. She was a voracious reader. She passed 10 O-levels with excellent grades. She was on track for Oxbridge entry.

She may have been destined for great success. We shall never know.

Things started to go wrong in her late teens. For no apparent reason, she found it increasingly hard to concentrate. She began to feel that people were getting at her. She developed odd, seemingly trivial anxieties and obsessions but, trivial or not, they gradually took hold of her and began to dominate her life.

She knew something was wrong. She realised that her concentration and thought processes were becoming abnormal. So she did what she always did when there was something she did not understand. She started to read it up. She researched the problems herself and, round about the age of 18, one morning she announced to her family that she was developing schizophrenia.

No one believed her. 'Don't be so silly Emma, pull yourself together'.

Well, she did try to pull herself together, but she wasn't being silly. She was not formally diagnosed by a doctor until she was in her early 20s but it is clear in retrospect that the illness was starting when she was 16 or 17.

Her own diagnosis had been correct.

She was unable to complete higher education. She tried to work to support herself. A variety of jobs followed, initially secretarial work, then office work, then work in pubs and catering. As she deteriorated, she rarely held any of these jobs for more than a few weeks, even the menial ones such as washing-up. She became increasingly dependent upon psychiatric care, with frequent and often prolonged admissions in various hospitals in Cornwall and then Birmingham.

She saw the best and the worst of the National Health Service.

There were many cruelties to endure. Long-term unemployment. Boredom. Loneliness. Lack of interest. Loss of friends. Rejection.

Finally, thankfully, she came under the care of Professor Peter Smith, and for the first time in years, she had prolonged periods of stability during which, though unable to work, she was able to cope living in the community with some support.

Despite treatment and her own best efforts, she gradually deteriorated. In her teens, 20s and 30s she read widely. She would have completed her English studies at university had she not been ill. Reading, always a source of great pleasure now became, in addition, a refuge.

But her ability to concentrate deteriorated further. Gradually, she found she could only manage books she had read before and knew well. She was fond of the Brontës. She would read and re-read Jane Eyre, time after time.

Finally, she could no longer manage even that.

So, one of the final cruelties she had to endure was that her illness, which had already separated her from people, now separated her from books. She went to the theatre, and occasionally the opera, but often could not really follow what was going on. Even television was difficult.

So what can we find to celebrate in this sad and unfulfilled life? Can we look back with any feelings other than sadness? How can we best remember her? Emma would not wish to sweep her mental illness under the carpet. She had schizophrenia and it damaged her life beyond repair.

Her childhood and early teenage years were happy. And as she grew older, despite her illness, there were many periods of happiness, some in Birmingham, and particularly during the years in the Cornwall when she was living with her mother. She could not return to Cornwall as frequently as she would have liked but she talked of it often.

Emma may have had schizophrenia, but she was not mad.

Apart from the periods of acute and distressing illness, she retained complete insight into her condition, its outlook and prognosis.

Buried under the often sad face was an incredible sense of humour. She was able to laugh at herself and at her illness, and she frequently did. She was capable of great kindness and consideration. She thought the world of her five nephews and nieces.

With help and support from many others, some of whom are here today, she managed to live in a flat in Birmingham with considerable independence.

And there were achievements. Achievements which, in context, *were huge. She was an indulgent aunt. She was supported by, and sometimes supported others, with similar problems to her own. She nursed her mother through a prolonged and at times distressing final illness. Most of all, Emma did not give up. She fought. At times a losing battle, but she fought. Trapped inside this wretched illness, there was an intelligent, kind and witty person.*

We must remember the intelligence.

We must remember the kindness.

We must remember the flashes of wit and humour.

We must remember that Emma tried so hard and for so long.

Above all, we must remember.

+++++++++++++++++++++++++++++++

Shortly after Emma died, her family picked up her clothes and personal possessions. There was not much. The personal items would have fitted inside a carrier bag. Indeed, as is so often the case with schizophrenics, they were in a carrier bag. There was a small loose-leaf folder, and in it a poem copied out in Emma's own handwriting.

> *If there is any life when death is over,*
> *These tawny beaches will know much of me,*
> *I shall come back, as constant and as changeful*
> *As the unchanging, many-coloured sea.*
> *If life was small, if it has made me scornful,*
> *Forgive me; I shall straighten like a flame*
> *In the great calm of death, and if you want me*
> *Stand on the sea-ward dunes and call my name.*

ON THE DUNES

Sara Teasdale (1884–1933)

+++++++++++++++++++++++++++++++

So, the next time you see a tramp, or a bag-lady, remember that they are probably schizophrenics taking advantage of care in the community. And the next time you are about to describe someone's behaviour as being 'a bit schizophrenic', please don't.

Emma would have been cross.

Dr Crippen closes the article with the following:

This article has been posted not only with the permission of Emma's family, but at their request. The names and other details have been changed.

NHS Blog Doctor
nhsblogdoc.blogspot.com

Forget Jamie Oliver. John Band's a lot less infuriating. Here he is with some advice for eating on a budget. And he's offering to come round and cook your tea.

 April 2006 – Healthy eating!= bruschetta-eating

Julie Bindel has a comment piece in *The Guardian*[1] about the class snobbery that permeates the healthy eating debate, and particularly about the way that fair-trade liberals sneer at the poor for eating badly. It's nearly sensible, but it falls down on a crucial point:

> *Encouraging a healthy diet has far more to do with choice than education… Although the majority have worked out that freshly squeezed orange juice is better for their child than fizzy pop, they have neither the budget nor the time to offer it… It is time we put working-class and poor people on a par with those of us who can afford to choose. It is no good sneering at people in Scotland who*

[1] **www.guardian.co.uk/comment/story/0,,1751133,00.html**

184

*deep-fry Mars Bars if we do nothing to make healthy food more
widely available.*

The point where this falls down, just in case you missed it too, is that healthy food is
not expensive or unavailable.

I'm not basing this assertion on my middle-class experience of unlimited cash or
out-of-town Tescos. Nor am I basing it on the poor areas where I've lived, which
have generally been multicultural city centre places with lots of good local produce
shops. I'm basing this assertion on the least fresh-food-friendly local shop I've ever
seen: a miniature, bullet-proof Happy Shopper on a peripheral council estate in
Greater Manchester, with more space devoted to booze than to fruit and vegetables.

A friend lived on the estate, and we'd visit the Happy Shopper if we couldn't be
bothered with the 30-minute round trip on foot to Asda. Although the local shop
was crap, it sold pasta, it sold rice, it sold onions, it sold tomatoes, it sold peppers,
it sold a limited set of herbs and spices, it sold bacon, it sold potatoes, it sold baked
beans, it sold cheese... and so on. It sold the basic ingredients for a varied selection
of healthy meals. And it sold them for less than it sold frozen pizzas and onion rings
and chicken nuggets.

This isn't a rigorous and empirical survey, and it's possible that this particular Happy
Shopper was anomalously un-awful. Even so, I'm willing to take on this challenge:
I'd happily visit any urban area of the UK and buy, for less than £2 per person, from
a shop less than 15 minutes away, the ingredients for a healthy and quick-to-prepare
meal for four people. I'm open to persuasion if I've missed something, but I can't see
how price/availability can be the problem.

But there is clearly a problem: although poor people can afford to eat healthily,
they don't. Or more specifically, some poor people don't, even though penniless
postgrads and minimum-wage immigrants do. And this has been the case for years:
Bindel's article cites a study from 1936 that also found the poor could largely afford
to eat healthily but largely didn't.

Maybe the class issue works both ways – after all, attitudes are worth more than
money or the geography of shopping areas. Maybe there's a fundamental, deep-
seated belief among the British working class that people who choose to eat healthy
food are precisely the kind of irritating, glycaemic-index-calculating, macrobiotic

185

Chris'n'Gwyneth types that Bindel's article slates.

Maybe eating chips is an affirmation that while you might die 20 or 30 years before the Waitrose brigade, you have nothing but contempt for them. And maybe by focusing on products such as organic food that will never be affordable to the poor, and farmers' markets that single working parents will never have the time to visit, the non-stop healthy eating publicity blitz is only furthering this image.

For the next campaign, how about 'cook a risotto today; it'll only take 10 minutes, it'll only cost you a quid, it'll taste OK, and it won't turn you into an Islington arsehole. Or your money back'?

John Band
www.johnband.org/blog

The internet has created career opportunities like never before, some of which are highly bizarre. Here, Jim Bliss tells a cautionary tale of an encounter with someone whose previous job was probably hiding under a stone.

 April 2006 – Comment Spam

Almost anyone with a blog that allows reader comments will be familiar with the problem of 'Comment Spam'. This is the practice of posting a comment for no other reason than to create one or more links from your website to another one. This is not in the hope that people will follow that link, but rather to help with search-engine placement.

See, search engines rank sites using complex algorithms that take into account numerous factors. One of those factors is the number of other sites that link to them. So a website about basket-weaving, for instance, which has a thousand links to it will – all else being equal – appear higher in Google or MSN searches than one with only a hundred links to it. Given that search engines generate large amounts of traffic, and people tend to click on search results higher up the list, it makes sense from a commercial standpoint to try and maximise the number of incoming links your site has.

This is yet another example where commercial interests conflict with ethical ones. Because although it may be a small issue, it is nonetheless a dishonest practice. If the owner of a basket-weaving site spends time adding links to their site on blogs, it creates a false impression of how popular that site is. Again, a relatively minor issue in the grand scheme of things, but one that nonetheless makes the internet as a whole less reliable. A thousand people saying 'This site is great' means far more than one person (the site owner) saying it a thousand times. Yet currently search engine technology cannot distinguish between the two, so you may find yourself getting all your basket-weaving tips from a dreadful site run by a dishonest spammer rather than from the excellent one that is recommended by lots of people.

As I say: it's a dishonest, unethical practice carried out by people with no real sense of decency or fair play. Nasty scum basically. The kind of people you'd cross the road to avoid. Unsurprisingly the main purveyors of comment spam are porn sites and online casinos… neither of which I object to on principle, but both of which – in practice – tend to have a significant whiff of exploitation and unpleasantness about them.

Sometimes, however, you get comment spam that is simply perplexing. Recently, for example, I've had the same comment posted to every single one of the posts on this blog. It reads: *'Great article. I am just sad I dont know how to reply properly, though, since I want to show my appreciation like many other'.*

A very nice thing to say. The first time it appeared I approved it for publication. It sounds like someone for whom English is not a first language and who wishes to express their appreciation of your writing, but doesn't quite have the words (the singular of the word 'other' gives away the potential non-native-speaker). Soon afterwards, however, the same comment began to spring up on every blog post (including the ones that are just an image and a link). I realised, therefore, that it was comment spam and deleted them all.

What is perplexing about it, however, is the fact that the spammer doesn't include any links in the actual comment, and the web-address they provide (which links from their name – 'Bonifacious') doesn't work. Ergussumatrras dot com. There's nothing there; leastways not yet; so as comment spam it's a complete waste of time. Not only unethical and dishonest, but utterly incompetent too.

The Assassination of Richard Nixon

A while ago – on my last blog but one – I received a positive comment on one of my posts. It was clear that the commentator had not only read, but actually thought about, the post. I naturally checked out his link and found it led to a blog that he kept regularly updated. I became a reader of his site and he became a semi-regular commentator on mine… always relevant and thoughtful comments. He appeared no different from any other blogger. After a while, his blog became darker and darker. He wrote about his wife leaving him and refusing him access to his kids. He wrote about how this had a knock-on effect on his work and how he was in real danger of losing not only his family, but his job and home too. I became quite concerned for the guy and sent him a couple of emails. I saw undercurrents of suicidal tendencies begin to manifest in his writing, and emailed him again suggesting he contact the Samaritans, or – if he wasn't willing to do that – then I'd be glad to meet up with him for a chat, if he needed someone to vent at.

I received no response to my emails, and wasn't willing to discuss this publicly in the comments of his blog… I didn't know how sensible it would be given his fragile state of mind; it's very very difficult to predict how someone will interpret a chunk of plain text posted to a public website. In order to deal with serious emotional issues, it's far better to do it in person.

Then there was a shift in his outlook… he began posting hints that his situation was in danger of driving him to violence. At first I became seriously worried that he might hurt his ex-wife and genuinely considered contacting the police. Then however he started talking about 'hitting back at the powerful'. He commented on one of my blog posts – an attack on Tony Blair – stating that someone should 'try to get close to Blair and do us all a favour'. Then, on his own blog, he began discussing a plan to sneak into a banquet being held at a London hotel which a number of foreign and UK politicians would attend, and poison the food.

It was only at this point that I smelled a rat. He'd been so smart up until that point… I knew he wasn't dumb enough to post details of an assassination attempt on a public website. I still believed that this was a poor bloke who'd just gone through a hellish time; lost his family, lost his job, was in danger of missing payments on his mortgage and was genuinely at the end of his tether… the assassination thing was clearly a dark joke from the mind of someone in a dark place. A plea for help… a plea for attention from his ex. It was hard to know, but I felt very bad for the guy.

The day after the banquet had passed off without incident I logged onto his blog. The blog was no longer active. In its place was a large advertisement for the film *The Assassination of Richard Nixon*. The entire thing had been part of a viral marketing campaign to coincide with the UK release of the movie. His apparently genuine messages on my blog and on his own site had merely been lies designed to part people with their money. He had taken advantage of my concern (some would say, my gullibility) and abused my trust for personal profit. What a deeply nasty excuse for a human being. True pondscum.

Yes, the film is fantastic (Sean Penn is an amazing actor). And yes, the campaign was very clever. But you can be clever and still be pondscum. And manipulative advertising for a fantastic film is still manipulative advertising. If I ever met that blogger in a pub I'd spit in his face. Because frankly, that's what it feels like he did to me.

The Quiet Road
numero57.net

There's many a tale about bloggers getting caught out and losing their jobs or being threatened with the sack for blogging. John Band of 'Shot By Both Sides' fame gave up his popular blog last year after some oily little coward took exception to one of John's posts and anonymously complained to his boss, putting John's livelihood in jeopardy (he's recently returned, with Banditry at www.johnband.org/blog). Petite Anglaise (www.petiteanglaise.com) was less fortunate in actually being fired in July after her bosses took exception to her 'Bridget Jones in Paris' missives.

Back in March, the World Weary Detective, after an edict from on high, decided discretion was the better part of valour.

 March 2006 – This is the end

On Friday 3 March 2006, the Management Board of the Metropolitan Police Service issued the following statement to all members of staff:

> 'Recently the organisation has become aware of a series of web-logs or blogs – where authors – claiming to be police officers – have offered their views on a number of issues in a highly personalised, often controversial manner.'

This statement is followed by 'guidance' on writing blogs. In summary, this states that although 'blogging' cannot be stopped, the 'impact of expressing views and opinions that are damaging to the organisation or bring the organisation into disrepute' must be considered. Disciplinary proceedings may be considered against posters of material that may be (among other things) defamatory, offensive or otherwise inappropriate.

I have committed no crime. I have compromised no police operations. I have received no payment for anything published on this blog. All opinions expressed are my own.

It is therefore with deep regret and great sadness that I must announce that I will no longer be submitting posts to this blog. I cannot challenge New Scotland Yard. I am weary indeed and cowardice is my bedmate. The protection of my family must take precedence.

To each and every one of you – take note of what has happened here and be afraid.

World Weary Detective
worldwearydetective.blogspot.com

Un-made-up was started in May this year and collects short non-fiction stories from different writers. While the stories 'don't have to have a punchline, they don't have to be dramatic, they don't have to be funny, they don't have to make a point, they don't even have to be autobiographical…they must, of course, be true'. It's well worth a day or two of your time, whether reading or (even) writing.

Here's William's encounter with the King of the Jungle.

 May 2006 – The lion

'He's late,' says the art director, leaning on a wall outside in the Florida sunlight.

People look at watches.

'We're calling his manager's mobile,' he says, 'but there's no answer.'

People roll their eyes and snicker. 'It's a joke, man. C.P. Time'. The person we're waiting for is a hip-hop star. They are never on time. Rappers are always an hour, 2 hours late at the very least, industry standard. Coloured Persons' Time.

They've hired an industrial unit for the photo shoot, a vast warehouse on an estate somewhere in Miami. I pull back the doors to go inside out of the sun, leaving natural light for neon, and walk a few paces... before I see the lion.

He stands on all four paws on the concrete floor, unexpectedly massive. It's like someone has just yanked a string on my back and tugged at every muscle in my body. My body temperature has just dropped a whole degree (or is that the air con?). I have never been in the same room as a predator before; there aren't many species left that eat humans. This fear must come from somewhere very deep. I suspect it's something very ancient that makes me check the distance back to the door before I've even realised what I'm doing. No. It's only a few yards but it's too far to run if the lion decided to leap. Instead I look at a pile of packing cases to my right. No. The lion would chase me up them and maul me before I was a quarter of the way there.

I had known the lion was going to be there; I just hadn't imagined what it would be like to be in the same room. I remember, now, video footage I've seen of a mentally ill man who climbed into a lion enclosure being mauled, almost casually.

'Any news?' asks the photographer.

'Any time now,' says the press officer, still attempting optimism.

The lion stands, a chain around its neck. It is a magnificent animal, but it looks bored. It yawns. The teeth are enormous. Claws lurk under the soft fur of the paws.

You can see where the art director was coming from. It's a cool concept. No, really. The lion as a symbol of manhood, of African-ness, indomitability, maybe, but mostly the lion as a symbol of terror. So that the man who stands beside the lion (if he were here) would be saying, 'I am afraid of nothing.' Like an illustration of a Zulu in a Rider Haggard novel, only less racist. Or maybe not. Not that anyone ever says anything like that in situations like this. Photography is so non-verbal.

In the presence of the lion, people are acting with deliberate cool. The photographer wants to take a couple of shots of the lion without the rapper, maybe just because he's being paid a day rate and he should be doing something. The thin man who comes with the lion yanks on the lion's chain until the lion is pointing in the right direction.

I ask, 'Are you, like, a lion tamer?'

'I just come with the lion,' he says. It turns out he owns it; this is his lion. He adds, 'You don't really tame lions. You just feed them.' He explains that all you do is give a lion a heavy meal. After that it doesn't want to kill anyone for a while.

'Oh.'

The lion slumps down on the cold concrete.

'When did you feed him?' I ask.

'Look at the size of his cojones', the make-up woman gasps. Laid out, his balls are indeed large, like she says. 'Can I stroke him?' she asks.

'Sure.' She's Chinese-American maybe, pretty, with long black hair and long legs in tight trousers.

She leans forward and strokes the coarse sandy fur. 'He's so beautiful', she says.

Everyone here already knows the hip-hop star will never show in time to be photographed with the lion. By the time he gets here the meat will have been digested and the lion will be considering another course. The photoshoot will turn out to be an elaborate, expensive waste of time. The whole scene will have to be photoshopped. The afternoon passes. Every now and again, someone else new enters the warehouse, but never the hip-hop star. Each time it's the same reaction as mine. They stop; their eyes widen. They are making the calculation, 'Would I make it back to the door in time?'

The make-up girl is less easily scared, though. She looks at the lion's testicles, then turns to the wiry young man who owns the lion. 'They're amazing. Can I touch them?' she asks. She wants to tell her friends she has touched the balls of a lion.

I'm waiting for him to look appalled, to tell her no, that that would be a crazy thing to do to his lion, this beautiful predator; all he says is, 'Sure.'

She leans forward towards the lion, hand outstretched.

William Shaw
unmadeup.com

Pandemian (the blogger formerly known as 'Green Fairy') chronicles the soul-destroying drudge of working life with an admirable, yet weary, wit and stoicism. The following piece was actually handwritten on a piece of notepaper and scanned onto her blog. I've tried to reproduce it here as it was written, but for the full effect go to *www.pandemian.com/2006/06/parthian_shot.html*. The real thing will be on display in the British Museum one day, you mark my words.

 June 2006 – Parthian shot

I am on a course on **How To Be Nice**. Work's CAGEY insistence that **everyone** has been only *amuses* me further. **I** arrive **late** to a sea of earnest faces and a name badge. **I** sit at the back and am noticed by **no one**. The hours tick by. We are asked if it's EVER appropriate to call someone a **twat**. Twenty heads shake slowly, *gravely*. This would make them feel **DISEMPOWERED**, we are told. Twenty pencils scratch this down. And what is the difference between **SYMPATHY** and **EMPATHY**? Hands strain EAGERLY towards the ceiling but the teacher's eyes fix on **me**, the silent one. My definition is *rewarded* with a beatific smile and green BLOCK LETTERS on the whiteboard. **EYES** turn towards me for the **first time**. Would I like to **Share** the experience that taught me this? **I** pause. **I** feel the approval of the class CLING to my answer like a stick of *candy floss* at the end of a w i n d y pier. *NO, I* say. *KURT COBAIN* taught me. I am *lost*.

Thankfully, shortly after the previous piece was posted, Pandemian was able to escape on holiday. As you might expect, a postcard and a 'Wish you were here' weren't good enough for her.

 June 2006 – Haiku d'état

Bollocks to all this.
Off to the Caribbean;
back in a fortnight.

Tales of sunburnt woe
and holiday derring-do
may follow shortly.

13th June
Ah, Alan Bennett.
Astute human observer,
rubbish beach reading.

15th June
On the nudist beach
my pale pink ass gleams brightly
amid ochre cocks.

19th June
Paragliding. Not
for the faint of heart or loose
of bikini top.

22nd June
Through dense rainforest,
I am Jack of the jungle!
I fear only gnats.

Pandemian
www.pandemian.com

An enviable skill of some bloggers is the ability to elevate the mundane and everyday to something rich and strange. Here Rhodri Marsden wonders if Surf's list of 99 Top Stains covers all the basics.

 June 2006 – 99 Top Stains

Don't ask me about Surf washing powder, because I've been a lifelong user of Persil Automatic and Lenor, and my towels are so fluffy and my tennis shorts so white – whiter than white – and even my smile is so radiant and gleaming, that I feel absolutely no need to change my washing powder. Even, I should add, swapping one box of my existing brand for two boxes of Surf. Except they tend not to come in boxes, now, they come in sleek, aerodynamic plastic containers of liquigel, and why not, it's a free country.

Anyway, Surf now claims to shift 99 Top Stains. They've been stuck at 97 for a few years, now, but what with the onward march of science, they've finally hit 99, which seems like the kind of number that's worth basing an advertising campaign around. 'We can hear you sighing from over here,' says their website. 'I know it sounds like we're making this stuff up, but honestly Surf really does get rid of 99 stains.'

Cola, Kid's Glue, Colour Pencils, Banana Milkshake, Wine Gums, Felt Tip Pens, Coloured Chalk, Strawberry Milkshake, Summer Fruits Cordial, Ice Lolly, Orange Squash, Blackcurrant Cordial, Fizzy Orange, Fresh Deodorant, Face Powder, Fag Ash, Lip Pencil, Eye Pencil, Eye Shadow, Mouth Wash, Hair Gel, Tooth Paste, Mucus, General Dirt, Baby Pee, Bird Poo, Shaving Cream, Hair Wax, Egg Yolk, Baked Beans, Vegetable Soup, Mango Chutney, Marmalade, Broccoli Soup, Vinegar, Marmite/ Yeast Extract, Tomato Juice, Mushroom Soup, Tomato, Beetroot, Mashed Potato, Soy Sauce, Honey, Lemon Curd, Garden Peas, Carrots, Mushy Peas, Salad Dressing (fat free), Strawberry and Blackcurrant Jam, Chicken Soup, French Vinaigrette, Spinach, Strawberry and Orange Jelly, Strawberry/Red Cherry and Black Cherry/Mint/Vanilla Ice Cream, Golden Syrup, Raspberry/Blackberry/Banana/Rhubarb Yoghurts, Squirty Whipped Cream, Peaches, Rice Pudding, Orange/Apple/Grape/Grapefruit Juice, Energy Drinks, Pina Colada, Cider, Irish Coffee Liqueur, Tea, White Wine, Whisky,

Lager, Milk, Tequila Sunrise, Sherry, Alcopops, Herbal Tea, Flower Pollen, Tomato Soup, Spaghetti Rings, Tomato Ketchup, Fruit Baby food, Red Cabbage, Self-Tanning Cream, Yellow Pickle, Strawberries, Red Wine, Blood, Newspaper Print, Cappuccino, Brandy.

This could be a useful cross-referencing tool for anyone who finds themselves accidentally stained over the next few weeks. If you happen to be skateboarding on a bridlepath, hit a craggy boulder and find yourself lying with your chest in a steaming pile of horse shit, consult Surf's 99 Top Stains. Is it there? No. 'Bird Poo' it can deal with, along with 'Baby Pee', but enormous fecal deposits are not guaranteed to be shifted. To be honest, this list asks many more questions than it answers. I strongly suggest that 'Broccoli Soup' is not among Britain's 99 Top Stains – especially when 'puke' doesn't even make the list. And what's 'Wine Gums' doing on there? The last time I spilt a wine gum, it bounced harmlessly onto the floor, whereupon I picked it up, dusted it down and popped it in my mouth. And as for 'General Dirt', that's a catch-all get-out clause if ever I heard one. Surf wouldn't want to know about the things that I class as General Dirt. I'm now off to precariously balance a tray on my head, which is laden with a Tequila Sunrise, Hair Gel, Mushy Peas, Newspaper Print, French Vinagrette and Blood. Wish me luck.

Do You Come Here Often?
rhodri.livejournal.com

It was a hot, hot summer this year. Britain felt as if God, like a small sadistic boy, had got his magnifying class and was making us tiny creatures scurry and yelp in the terrifying heat. The Eyechild spotted that a traditional element of classic summers was missing.

 July 2006 – Jaspers

It's summer but... something's missing... hmm. Sun – check, beer – check, barbecues – check, Tim Henman losing at Wimbledon... yeah. Wait a minute, that's it, WASPS! I don't know about you but I've seen hardly any this year!

And where are all the wasps, anyhow? Have they been priced out of London too then? Not that I'm bothered, they were hardly key-workers in the accepted sense. In Manchester the advent of summer always brought with it the shadow of the wasp, who would be there before you at the beer garden (like Germans at the sun-loungers, yeah), and almost certainly there after, hovering drunkenly round the last quarter-inch or so of your pint of Stella. Wasps get pissed too, in all senses, especially in late summer when they're just looking for trouble, and should you get lary with them, they release a pheromone, so all their mates show up minutes later for a piece of the action. Truly, they were the bane of the sugary drink drinker's sunny afternoon, and universally disliked.

Seriously, I reckon even Noah probably planned to ditch the wasps prior to the flood and it was only after he awoke the morning after setting sail to hear two rattling away behind his blind that he realised his scheme had been thwarted. Wasps possess the apex of that blind insect instinct to find their way into your room, through any hole – no matter how small, without being able to do it in reverse, even were you to demolish the wall of your house and attempt to usher them out with a jet turbine. I assume they navigate by the moon/sun like moths, since they also have a tendency to fly directly into any lightbulb, producing a sound like someone training a dentist's drill on it. Eww, that sound. I also remember wasps flying into my bedroom, perching on the lampshade and audibly crunching away on the paper (of course, this was before I got into listening to techno at artillery volume, so a wasp would probably have to be inside my ear now before I could hear such a thing). Terrible thought.

One thing about wasps is that pretty much everyone is united in their hatred of them. This blog here[1] is like some kind of wasp genocide bulletin board:

> 'It's us against them, people. We can't let the enemy take over our homes!
>
> I'll let you know how it goes. Great stories!'

froths one contributor excitedly. Uh, ok, they are kind of annoying, I guess. Ever read Watchmen? One thing's for sure, if it turned out wasps were poised to take over

[1] www.kryogenix.org/days/2003/07/31/wasps

the world, Osama Bin Laden, George Bush and Kim Jon-Il would be united in their struggle against the striped menace quicker than you could say 'Yeehaw, let's nuke those fucken yellerjackets!'

Anyway, here's my favourite wasp anecdote (you might want to save this for Hallowe'en, mind). Are you sitting un-comfortably? Well, I'll begin:

I was back at my mum and dad's one summer whilst studying at uni. My brothers were in the two rooms next to mine. I awoke at about three in the morning hearing an all but subliminal 'WHHHUFF' sound from my brother Harry's room, punctuated by short panicky gasps of 'Shit!' coming from the lad himself.

Seconds later 'middle-bro' Dan awoke, and stomped into my brother's room.

'What THE FUCK is going on?'

He roared.

What, it transpired, had happened was that a load of wasps had chosen to nest in the roof just outside his bedroom window. Now my brother liked to keep his bedroom window open in summer (and bedroom light on), and perhaps unwisely, the presence of several thousand stinging insects just outside was not sufficient to deter him. You can perhaps guess the rest. While he slept and under cover of darkness, the wasps let themselves in and my brother had an extremely rude awakening when a wasp crawling over his face decided to sting him on the cheek. The first sight to greet his no-doubt horrified eyes when he opened them was a roiling vortex of wasps circling beneath his room's naked lightbulb. Not to be deterred he rolled out of bed, grabbed a can of Lynx and a lighter and got medieval on those wasps' tapering asses.

Yes, that 'WHHHUFF' sound was none other than a deodorant-based flame-thrower my brother had hastily fashioned. A quick glance around his bedroom door the next morning revealed a war zone, with drifts of scorched wasps lying everywhere. It was like The Wasp Factory in there, or 'Aliens Redux' where the Marines win. Those wasps fucked with the wrong guy all right. They sure got to know the true power of the Lynx effect.

The Eyechild
theeyechild.blogspot.com

They say there are eight million stories in the naked city. Tales of hope and redemption are my favourite. Here's poons with his.

 August 2006 – Anniversaries

They come around with startling regularity.

This time last year I was lying in a hospital bed, on the wrong end of a long history of alcohol abuse and with a 'heroic' quantity of paracetamol coursing through my digestive and blood system.

It was a classic cry for help scenario, and but for the grace of NHS personnel here go I. It was also a particularly cold and calculated scenario that I undertook, buying beer and tablets from many venues across town before stuffing eight or nine cans of 9% lager and approx. 98 pills down my throat before calmly walking back up the river bank to the bridge and calling an ambulance. I'd already checked that unless I lay prone at the river bank then that amount of pills would not kill me, though perhaps going for a swim at one point was bordering on the not a very good idea area of life preservation.

Lasting memories of the day include the despatcher asking me whether I was likely to be violent to the ambulance crew. I laughed and ensured them I would be more likely to pass out. I was highly embarrassed when they switched on the 'blues and twos' to ferried me to safety, and I think that was the moment I realised what a complete and utter dick I had been.

Then there was the guy who administered the dose of something that 'may make me feel a bit queasy'. He lied. I have never vomited like that before or thankfully since, and I never intend to again.

There was the conversation with the ward sister (after I had been moved from A&E) whom I told that I still had some beer in my bag. I said, 'I guess you're going to take that off me?' She said, 'Not unless you want me to'. This spun me out, so when I said 'Yes, please', and she asked me if I wanted her to destroy them, I was even more phased. I of course said 'Yes', and after a brief stay on the ward I walked out a free man, and so totally detoxicated that far too many people (many who do not know the full story until they read this) commented on how healthy I was looking.

So 12 months on, the 'beast' is tamed, totally for quite some time, and now is allowed out with a muzzle.

Over those 12 months I was again embarrassed by the concern that people showed and how happy they were that my drinking was in check. I didn't react that well to said concern – I've never been that good at that sort of stuff – but I'd like to say thank you to all those who expressed that concern, and all those who made me realise that I was loved so much. It really did help.

I no longer feel the urge to get totally pissed every night, and in some ways I'm glad I did what I did. I still feel supreme guilt at the NHS resources I wasted, the stress that I put my closest friends under, and the fact that I was so weak in spirit to just do something by myself, but one year on I have plans forming in my mind that don't involve me drinking myself to death, and that can only be a good thing. I hope.

Howlingspoons
howlingspoons.blogspot.com

Shuffling Off
Death

Death, like syphilis, incontinence and vegetarianism, is all very well unless it's happening to you. Then it's not so much fun, obviously. Here we'll explore the deepest of mysteries, examine the greatest of levellers and try not to get too down about the biggest of bummers.

To paraphrase Malcolm in Macbeth, nothing in this life becomes us like the leaving it. There seems little point in worrying about it other than to rail against the unjust deaths visited upon so many in the world today. And also, to make peace and reconciliation with the fact that we ourselves will one day, to quote more Shakespeare (Hamlet this time), shuffle off this mortal coil. (No, I'm not convincing myself either.)

In other words, this is a chapter in which we reaffirm that death is like a Cliff Richard record at Christmas: there is no escape. It's a bad business, to be sure.

Here's Ed Rooksby with a powerful – and graphic – meditation on violence and death.

 October 2005 – Violence

I had a nightmare not long ago – a particularly vivid one that has stuck in the back of my mind ever since. Like most people (I assume), I find that most nightmares are memorable – I can recall the images, events or 'story-line' of quite a few I've had in the last 20 years or so. However, it is mostly the case that the actual horror of the nightmare – the feeling of unease or terror associated with the images/events of the dream – dissipates quite soon after waking up, so one can recall the details of a nightmare without re-experiencing the unpleasantry. Sometimes, in fact, nightmares become quite comical in retrospect – quite the reverse of the original experience. This one, however, is different. It is still (at least mildly) upsetting and unnerving.

I was in Iraq. I was standing on a dusty road with yellowy-brown sand on either side stretching off into the distance. In front of me was a scattering of metallic and mechanical wreckage across the road, blocking my way. Behind the wreckage, the road was cratered and scorched and a spiral of black smoke trailed into the sky. There were a small number of corpses and half-dead men sprawled across the wreckage and on the road. I got closer to the wreckage and found out that in fact these men were alive. They were grotesque. They were stinking, bloated, swollen, green and rotten – and they were still moving around. One of them was horribly burned – his skin was a black, cracked and flaking mess (like the surface of a badly burned piece of toast). Two of them sat on top of a piece of wreckage that was now a burned-out car and seemed to be drinking something and talking. Another, with the top of his skull sliced off, was walking towards me. I remember thinking (and this was the horror) that none of them deserved this – all had been in the wrong place at the wrong time. They were the cannon fodder of other people's warfare. They had been turned into stinking corpses for reasons that could never be justified to them. They had all died thinking 'Why me?' and they continued to ask the same question

205

endlessly in death. I woke up feeling sick.

I remember that in my dream these men had been the victims of a coalition airstrike. But really that wasn't the point (if we can talk about the point of a nightmare) – they could easily have been the victims of an insurgent bomb.

The images from this dream, together with a real associated feeling of horror, come back to me from time to time. They come back to me when I read about Fallujah, or when I read about recent operations in Tel Afar. They come back to me when I hear that civilians have been murdered in a market-place or mosque bombing. They come back to me when I hear that US or British troops have been killed. They come back to me when I read some twisted, gung-ho blog or media person cheerleading for coalition operations. They come back to me when I read some cheering for death from some on the Left.

There is a romanticising of violence at play here. There is also a terrible rejection (even mockery) of ethical considerations in the name of 'realism'. In relation to the former, in some accounts of what's going on in Iraq, the bombings and the shootings are spoken of in terms that obscure the real effects of violence. The excitement, the explosive booms, the flash of fire from machine gun muzzles, the heroics, the rush, the changes in the balance of power between opposing forces, the tactics and the strategy are discussed animatedly and with relish. This is a little boy's version of warfare – it's how we experienced violence as 8-year-olds in the school field playing soldiers with our friends. In these games there was no death – not really. If 'shot' you would simply clutch your hands to your chest dramatically, groan and quickly fall to the ground. You would get up again 2 minutes later. There was no blasting off of limbs, no faces sheared off by shrapnel, no evisceration, no guts spilling onto the ground, no screaming, no crying, no begging for your life, no panic, no terror, no bits of another man's brains on your boots, no pissing and shitting yourself, no vomit, no bloated bodies, no putrifaction, no maggots. Cheer for that.

In relation to the latter, I have seen people claim – pro and anti-war – that one cannot condemn the mass killing of civilians out of hand. You cannot say, it seems, that there is something wrong with the sight of a market-place strewn with the twisted corpses of children. Indeed, to appeal to 'right' and 'wrong' here is regarded as hopelessly naive – to call the deliberate mass murder of civilians 'bad' is, more than that, something to be mocked. We see it in pro-war responses to the death toll indicated by *The Lancet* report and we see it in the arguments of the most hardline supporters of the insurgency. All ethical or moral considerations in terms of violence and human suffering are jettisoned – or at least relegated to some secondary and pretty insignificant order of understanding. What matters is Objective A, or Objective B – everyone along the way is just cannon fodder. Pile up the corpses. There's nothing we can say about it.

I have seen it claimed that one cannot understand violent acts (or any other) in terms of human decisions or choice. The sole causal factor here is history – social and political circumstances. People do not choose to bomb a market place full of civilians (oddly, this line of reasoning is seldom applied to generals or presidents). Of course people are made by their social circumstances, their history, their political and economic environment. Put anyone in conditions of desperation or sustained oppression and they will act very differently. Beat a good-natured dog and eventually it will snarl and bite. People will fight back with the tools and means at their disposal too. But to say that human actions can be wholly understood in these terms is wrong. Put your finger on the detonator to a remote bomb. Do you really have no choice in the matter? Is there no small room for human agency? Would everyone, given the right conditions, push the button? Do you have no choice when you cross the road? Do you have no choice when you don't punch that old lady in the street and nick her handbag? Structures and environments shape and limit our thoughts and actions – but within those limits there is a certain room for manoeuvre, a certain space for bounded autonomy. Not everyone has the same boundaries, or the same experiences or the opportunities, or the same choices. But nothing is somehow structurally determined. There is no predestination. I am no fatalist.

These approaches are blind to the suffering of real human beings. There is a picture, which you may have seen, of a young Haitian man dying in the street. He was murdered by UN gangsters for protesting about the UN/US installed government in his country. When you look at the picture it could, at first, be a picture of a sleepy or drunken man lying in the gutter. We see his head and shoulders. He looks groggy, confused. Then you see the blood flowing down his arms. Then you see that the man has no lower jaw – just a bloody gap where his mouth should be. It is shocking. What gets me, I think, is not the blood and the gore. It's the look in the man's eyes – he looks confused and he looks scared and he looks desperate. 'Why me?' he seems to be thinking. There is a good chance that the man is quite conscious that his jaw has been shot off and it is quite possible that the man knows that he is about to bleed to death. He knows that his life is over, that all he could have been and all he could have done has now been taken from him. He has nothing. He is horribly alone. He was in the wrong place at the wrong time and now he is going to die. It is a terrible picture.

There is another picture I saw, recently, that has the same kind of effect. I was watching a programme about gangs in South Africa. There was a brutal gang leader – called 'Staggy', I think – who was abducted by a vigilante gang, beaten, doused in petrol and set alight. He burned to death surrounded by a cheering crowd. The programme showed a photograph taken by someone in the crowd. He was a horrid man – he was a murdering racketeer and gangster – but even so, this picture is sickening. Again it is not the physical horror of the photo that shocks – it is the look on the man's face. The photo shows the victim on fire: flames lick up from the man's legs, his face is blackened, and he is staring into the camera – his eyes are quite brilliantly white and his pupils bright blue. They shine out at you from the blackening face. There is a look of incomprehension in the man's eyes.

Anytime someone dies, it is a someone. When we forget this, when real individual human beings become cannon fodder for someone's foreign policy or someone's theory, when we sweep the panic and the horror and the fucking waste under the carpet, we are de-humanising ourselves.

International Rooksbyism
introoksbyism.blogspot.com

Lee Chapman has lived in Tokyo since 1998 and his blog, Tokyo Times, offers an English perspective of Japanese society. Here, he tells of an even darker aspect of Japan's notorious suicide rates.

 October 2005 – Ghoulish Gifts

For the past several years, annual suicides in Japan have exceeded the 30,000 mark[1]. A frighteningly high figure and one that the authorities are painfully aware of, but at the same time appear unable to reduce.

Now whilst not all of these unfortunate souls choose Aokigahara forest (or

[1] www.tokyotimes.org/?p=452

'Sea of Trees') as the place to end their lives, a disturbingly large number do – usually somewhere between 50 and 100 people each year. The forest itself perhaps unexpectedly located at the foot of Japan's most identifiable icon: the famous and fabulously beautiful Mount Fuji.

Whether this closeness to Fuji has any bearing on its 'popularity' isn't clear, but the forest's dense nature makes it ideal for those who really don't want to be found. Providing the perfect location for them to fade away in a private and decidedly quiet manner.

This infamous aspect of Aokigahara means that recovery teams are regularly dispatched to comb the area for bodies, hoping to identify those that they find to allow any next of kin an element of closure. According to *Spa!* magazine, however, other, more unsavoury types might be getting there before them: grisly scavengers scouring the forest, hoping to find credit cards, valuables and cold hard cash.

Yet not content with such hearsay, a reporter from the magazine claims to have taken it upon himself to explore the area, supposedly returning with a bounty that included several credit cards, a few valid rail passes, and perhaps more surprisingly, some commemorative coins.

This relatively easy- (if ghoulish-) sounding path to prosperity is, however, countered somewhat by Ryo Kurihara, the author of a book related to Aokigahara. Kurihara-san claims such spoils aren't so easy to come by, and a successful trip involves considerably more than just turning up and aimlessly ambling around:

> *I've used a handheld GPS, transceivers, goods employing the latest scientific technology and loads of people helping me and managed to find 40 bodies in the forest. However, the largest amount of cash I've ever found on one has been 90,000 yen [£450]. I've also found some driver's licences, but most of them have been ruined by being exposed to the elements for so long, and it'd be risky to try and sell those ones that aren't damaged. I've also found cards and other forms of ID.*

Not an insubstantial haul by any means, but hardly worth the considerable effort and cost. Plus lugging around such a large number of bodies could slow down proceedings considerably, creating all kinds of logistical problems. Yet despite Kurihara's obvious experience in this area, rumours amongst locals tell of passing truck drivers stopping on their way through, boosting their salaries with a few festering finds. A practice that, if true, is a decidedly macabre take on the old maxim, 'first come, first served'.

Tokyo Times
www.tokyotimes.org

In November 2005 George Best hung up his boots. To say he was a complex character leaves little room for dazzling, perplexing, infuriating and a thousand other adjectives. Militant Moderate Ken Owen, while acknowledging Best's faults, wrote of the man's talent with some fine, sincere lyricism.

 November 2005 – Where we hope to Keep safe from pain

> *'But then, what have you in common with the child of five whose photograph your mother keeps on the mantelpiece? Nothing, except that you happen to be the same person.'*
>
> *George Orwell, The Lion and the Unicorn*

To see the images of a young George Best across all the newspapers this morning was a moving experience. Moving because the only George Best I ever saw in my lifetime was the alcoholic Best; the congenial, warm man who couldn't escape from his genius on a football field. The man who appeared on TV most weeks looking world-weary and heavy, a far cry from the trendy, superlative athlete that I will, ultimately, remember him as.

Best's was not a life beyond reproach – drunkenness, wife-beating, time spent in jail. But what redeeming features he had! When you placed a football at his feet, he was nothing short of an artist. People may sneer at football, but at its best, sportsmen can do what Michelangelo, Picasso, Van Gogh never could – sheer artistry. Moments that for their grace and beauty will live in the mind for a long time; in a romanticised world, even forever. Yet they are only possible through improvisation and inspiration, for the opportunity to create them is only available in an instant.

For all the hard work that Best put in on the training ground, it was his natural gifts that made him so special. When you gave him a moving ball, an opponent out to cut him in half, and a fraction of a chance at goal, he could seize that chance, move through a space that wasn't there, and leave a collective audience of thousands gasping in awe. The fleeting nature of such artistry can never obscure its brilliance.

> *'I even found it difficult to watch myself playing on TV because I couldn't identify with the person on the screen. I couldn't get to grips with it. It was as if it was all happening to someone else.'*

When you look at a juxtaposition of Georgie then and now[1], you can't help but feel that it was happening to someone else. Yet for all the tabloid circus that surrounded him the rest of his life, it will be what he did when his boots were laced that will be the abiding memory of Best. For that is the wider power of sport. When we rest from work and focus on something so seemingly inconsequential, we project on to our heroes what we want to see. Normally, when the gap between man and myth seems so large, there is almost a sense of betrayal. Why do we feel let down when Wayne Rooney shows his petulance? Because we feel that a man of such talent shouldn't waste it so stupidly.

Best gets forgiven, for all the sense that we were watching a man who never achieved quite what he could have done. Of course, his flaws were half the fun. Would we really want him to have been soccer's Steve Davis? More to the point, if he had been Steve Davis, he would never have been so great. I am firmly of the belief that if you find a man doing what he enjoys and is good at, you get a true insight into his personality. A boring Best would have taken away his flair.

Of course, it is the fact that the team gives us a wider sense of identity that gives the sport so much power. That is why we write our dreams on to our heroes; why the minutiae of a win, loss or draw has such a powerful emotional impact. The team becomes a surrogate for the community; the star players become our friends and family. That is why Best's death has been so heavily covered by the news – although we never met him, we all felt as if we knew the man. No matter that we couldn't. How could we not know a man who we could see at all times and in all places? When George Best had a ball at his feet, he made us all happy. Through the wonder of TV, he can continue to make us happy for a long time to come. It is a testament to his

[1] hurryupharry.bloghouse.net/archives/2005/11/25/george_best_1946_2005.php

skill and his charm that it is the myth, not the man, who will be remembered.

George, I hope that you rest in peace.

Militant Moderate
kenowen.blogspot.com

With no disrespect to Ken, however, there were many, including me, for whom Best's talents were totally eclipsed by his terrible failings. My partner used to work in Chelsea and saw Best often – he was invariably sitting outside a pub on the King's Road with a pint in his hand. Her job? She worked in a women's refuge clearing up the carnage the likes of Best created. Jamie Kenny showed the kind of anger that some of the more lachrymose obituaries studiously avoided.

 November 2005 – Stick a fork in him

He's done[1].

> *'Former football star George Best has died in hospital at the age of 59.'*

Son Calum, 24, who had kept an all-night vigil at Best's bedside, said: 'Not only have I lost my Dad but we've all lost a wonderful man.'

Poor Bestie. Poor, sad, Bestie. Fuck him. He ended 30 years of living like a swine by dying like a fool. True, he could be a witty fellow, as Gordon Burn[2] illustrates:

> *It seems remarkable, given his career of drunk-driving, philandering and domestic violence, and his multiple addictions to alcohol, gambling and sex, that Best only went to prison once. That happened in 1984 when, after failing to appear in court on a drunk-driving*

[1] news.bbc.co.uk/1/hi/uk/4380332.stm
[2] football.guardian.co.uk/comment/story/0,9753,1650475,00.html

charge and resisting arrest after the police cornered him in a girlfriend's flat, he served 2 months. But it's an exchange that took place in the canteen at Southwark crown court before sentencing that has entered Best lore. His friends and defence team were staring into the bottom of their coffee cups, with nothing to say. Then George glanced across at them with a smile. 'Well, I suppose that's the knighthood fucked', he said.

But there's also the case for the prosecution:

Between the accounts of how she had been given black eyes and broken arms and had her hair hacked off in the night by her drunken husband, Alex Best's book, Always Alex, *is a litany of tabloid-funded trips to faraway places with George. A beating and a payday. Another love rat scandal, another BestEnders episode sold to the pops.*

Now wit implies self-awareness. So what's to be said about a man who didn't just choose to be a wife-beating drunk but to be a professional wife-beating drunk?

I suppose this is all going to be excused because of his being a working-class hero. Well fuck that too. John Prescott's an inarticulate oaf because he's working class. Cherie Blair's greedy and superstitious because she's working class. George Best became a professional wife-beating drunk because he comes from the working classes. And we all know what they're like, don't we?

I'm a football fan, but fuck the football too. It meant nothing from the moment he first raised his hand to his wife. If he could have avoided living like a swine by staying in Belfast and working at Tesco's, then he should have done that. One footballer isn't much of a loss. There's always another one out there.

Blood & Treasure
bloodandtreasure.typepad.com

While George Best and other public figures who died in the last 12 months were fêted with acres of news coverage, many, many more slipped away unremarked upon and unmourned. Robert Sharp

meditates on those who suffer and die away from the spotlight.

 December 2005 – Encountering the 'Submerged'

Last Monday I had cause to be working in Glasgow, in a theatre just south of the Clyde. At the end of the day, I planned to take a train back to the city centre. I arrived at the station 10 minutes after someone had committed suicide, jumping onto the tracks. The police and ambulance had arrived moments before me, and had not yet been able to remove the body. He lay there, lifeless and nameless like a mannequin. All last week I searched all the news media for an account of what happened, but there was nothing.

With no chance of a train, the tube was a better option, and I was soon in the city centre once more. Just outside Queen Street station, I met a man with a red face and no teeth selling the *Big Issue* magazine. The magazine was giving away some free postcards, so I bought his last copy. I had intended to send a postcard to some friends I had stayed with over the weekend, but they turned out to be a promotional pack for Amnesty International, who are running a campaign of awareness of domestic violence. Did you know that on average a woman is assaulted 35 times before she seeks help from outside authorities, and that every day two women are killed by a current or former partner?

Not for the first time, a doctor friend was telling me today about the evidence of domestic abuse she sees in hospital. She told me stories of young women who conceal pregnancies from violent partners or disapproving parents. Others manage to live for months without even realising they are pregnant. They arrive in the hospital with pains, and despite not menstruating and the appearance of a huge, baby-shaped lump in their abdomen, they insist that they cannot be pregnant. They only have to wait a month before unwelcome contractions prove them wrong.

Surely the biological facts of the matter are so obvious as to be unmistakable? Apparently not, said my friend. For social or religious reasons, some live in denial, scared to admit even to themselves a fact that would bring shame upon them. Others have a more clinical mind-block, a psychological refusal to see the truth in a manner similar to anorexia.

I think these are relevant digressions, because they are all examples of someone so far removed from our own daily lives, that they could be living in another country. And yet we all live in the same country. Men so sad they will jump in front of a train; men without teeth or a roof over their heads; women suffering and dying in silence, unnoticed; and girls so ill-educated that they do not understand what will happen if they have unprotected sex. I am reminded of a passage in Fergal Keane's book *A Stranger's Eye* (2000), in which he talks of the 'submerged' people, those whose lives are so far removed from the rest of the country that they seem to no longer understand us, nor we them:

> *For a few weeks in a Leeds courtroom, the story of her life and death illuminated a parallel universe in which young men, women and children lived not so much on the wrong side of the tracks, but far below the surface of the nation.* Submerged. *The majority did not end up killing or engaging in senseless violence, nor could they in any sense be said to inhabit the same moral universe as those who* murdered Angela Pearce.

> *But they did live in a submerged world. It was there all around us, in every city in the country, a world of unexplained departures and missed connections, a great, quiet tragedy that went stalking down the generations. When it spilled onto our front pages – a child dead from neglect or cruelty, a frightening drug statistic – we took notice, we were shocked. But the waves always closed over and the underwater silence resumed.*

Robert Sharp
www.robertsharp.co.uk

Oscar Wildebeest commits a minor heresy by refusing to mourn the death of one of London's most famous icons.

 December 2005 – Hold on tight, it's the end of the road

So, the Routemaster has finally been withdrawn from service across London[1].

Naturally, there has been predictable outpouring of grief and complaint for the loss of this admittedly finely designed feature of London transport. The Routemaster has become an iconic figure of London (and therefore Britain, since the two are synonymous in much of the world outside the UK). Sturdy, distinctive, long-lasting, attractive and convenient,

[1] www.bbc.co.uk/london/content/articles/2005/09/05/routemaster_book_feature.shtml

they are adored by many Londoners, by even more people outside London, and by the transport-obsessed nutcases of which this country has a frighteningly large number.

But, let's be honest: they were horrid beasts. The seats were always narrow, the upholstery threadbare. The wooden floors were filthy and unattractive. They were impossible to disembark from with any elegance, and coming down from the top floor was an exercise in injury defiance. The windows were grimy, and they were freezing in winter. The shuddering as they sped up or slowed down made my teeth rattle in my gums. There was no room to put any of your luggage (that little hole at the front was never adequate for anything bigger than a rucksack – and who would want to leave his rucksack there, in these times?). And I, for one, could never see the bloody number of the bus until it was on top of me, so dim were the lights behind the display.

From street level they were splendid to look at, and the hop-on, hop-off feature was enormously handy (as long as you were reasonably able-bodied, which seems to rule out 50% of bus passengers in my experience). And of course it was nice to have a conductor who didn't hide behind a glass screen. But anyone who thinks having a conductor on board adds an extra element of public order enforcement is still living in the 1950s. Indeed, many of today's Vicky Pollards see the conductor as an extra incentive to create trouble, an extra target to wind up, safe in the knowledge that the worse he or she can do is throw them off the bus, in which case they just wait for the next one and the whole mess starts all over again.

We may not think much of the bendy buses. The two-decker Routemaster replacements may lose in charm what they gain in safety and cleanliness. But there's going to come a time pretty soon when mourning the loss of the Routemaster is going to be like mourning the loss of the penny farthing. Clinging to such symbolic representations of our 'heritage' merely typifies the juvenile sentimentalism that typifies much of so-called Middle England. London is a modern city, a fast, thriving city – aesthetic joys can still be found everywhere in the city's architecture. We don't need to get there in antiquated splendour. Heavens, we're not complaining that the Tube isn't steam-driven any more, are we?

We've come to the last stop, folks. Are you just going to sit there and cry, or are you going to get off and move on?

Gnus of the World
gnusoftheworld.blogspot.com

On the 25th anniversary of the murder of John Lennon, Chris Dillow had some harsh words to say about Lennon's impact on British politics, specifically on the left wing.

 December 2005 – John Lennon and the decline of the Left

Since Thursday's emote-fest – a supplement in *The Times* for Chrisssakes – I've been trying to articulate why exactly I dislike John Lennon. It's not that his acclaim is out of proportion to his merit – this is true of most famous people. It's that he's a pivotal figure in the decline of the Left, the decline from empiricism to emotivism.

Think of the iconic pre-'60s liberal-left personalities: Marx, Lenin, the Webbs, Russell, Beveridge, Orwell or most of the 1945–51 government.

What these otherwise disparate figures had in common was a commitment to rational inquiry and empiricism. Be it Marx toiling away in the British Museum, Orwell's dossing down in Paris and Wigan, the Webbs' poring over blue books or Stafford Cripps working himself to death, all thought the task of the Left – be it reformist or revolutionary – was founded upon thorough hard work and intellectual endeavour.

Contrast this with the left of the late 1960s, the excrescence of which we've seen this year at Live8 and in anti-war demos. To them, a few slogans and a display of self-righteousness seem sufficient. Rather than try to understand the world, they think it sufficient that the rest of us understand their pain, their sincerity.

In this decline, John Lennon was a pivotal figure, because he offered the illusion that slogans could change the world: 'Power to the people,' 'All we are saying is give peace a chance,' and – most contemptibly fatuous of all – 'All you need is love'.

Revolution, then, ceased to be a matter of hard work and asceticism, and became an opportunity for easy self-expression, for empty gestures like the bed-in, to demonstrate the clarity and superiority of one's moral vision.

The English middle-class need little enough prompting as it is to demonstrate their smugness. John Lennon gave them even more. And it's the empty-headed emoting Lennonists who are too dominant in the meeja and politics today.

Of course, this picture's a simplification. The pre-1960s Left had a big helping of self-righteousness: Churchill said of Cripps, 'There, but for the grace of God, goes God'. And they had way too much faith in rationality and empiricism. But none of them thought self-righteousness was sufficient, in the way that much of the post-1960s Left did, and still does. And in this decline, John Lennon, maybe partly inadvertently, played a role.

Stumbling and Mumbling
stumblingandmumbling.typepad.com

In January thousands of people lined the Thames to watch a lost whale swim up and down. The cynical side of me wonders how many went home afterwards and joined Greenpeace. Here's a short but thoughtful piece from Gary Barnfield who deserves an entry for his title alone.

 January 2006 – Whale meat again

For 24 hours the tale of a whale was unfolding in the River Thames, culminating in the unfortunate animal's death in shallow waters. (Maybe they're not as smart as some folks claim.) It was a media circus[1], and the spectacle brought Londoners together, albeit momentarily, to watch the rescue efforts. It was David Blaine[2] without the heckling.

I was reminded of the Béla Tarr[3] movie *Werckmeister harmóniák* (2000). Here a whale coming to town is interpreted as a portent of doom. Who's to say that this visit won't be seen in the same way?

The Loneliest Jukebox
loneliestjukebox.blogspot.com

[1] news.bbc.co.uk/1/hi/england/london/4636278.stm
[2] www.amazon.co.uk/exec/obidos/ASIN/B0000D1F0E/qid=1137925167/sr=2-2/ref=sr_2_
11_2/wwwemalonenet-21/026-6073000-1105210
[3] www.imdb.com/name/nm0850601/

The World Weary Detective relates a tale of another victim of the Blind Eye.

 February 2006 – Mary Mary quite contrary

Mary met Keith in her early 20s. Mary had had a few boyfriends before Kevin, but nothing serious. Kevin was popular with Mary's family. He played golf, liked a pint, and followed the football. He worked hard in a local factory, and doted on Mary.

It wasn't long before the couple were engaged. They married in the local church. Mary's father gave away his only daughter. Her four brothers looked on with pride. Kevin was a good catch. They were sure he would look after their little sister.

Mary was a slight woman. She was easily dominated, and was a nervous individual when she met Kevin. Kevin did a good job of building up her confidence. He bought her nice clothes, and offered her compliments on her appearance. He came home with presents, and took her to good restaurants. She came out of her shell with Kevin. Her family and friends all noticed she seemed to glow in his presence.

Kevin and Mary lived in a small house near to the rest of her family. Kevin was the dominant one. Mary accepted her place in marriage was to keep home and look after her husband.

This wasn't good enough for Kevin. Kevin was trapped by Mary. He hadn't asked to end up like this. Little things about her started to irritate him. She let herself go after she had caught him. If she wasn't interested in looking after herself, why should he be?

Kevin went to work each day and brooded. It got worse and worse each time he came home. He would go to the pub, or bring cans home and sit in front of the TV. The compliments stopped. Any love Kevin ever had for his wife evaporated. She didn't make the effort. She brought it all on herself. It was her fault.

Kevin began to pick fault with everything Mary did. The already nervous woman became a timid wreck. She couldn't go to her family – they would think she had failed and agree with Kevin that it was her fault, wouldn't they? Her friends had all drifted away. Kevin didn't like them.

Mary injured herself in the kitchen one day. Something happened. Mary ended up having treatment for 'mental health issues'. Kevin stood by his wife. Nobody else would take her, would they? She was damaged goods. It was all her fault.

Kevin's verbal torments turned to physical violence. He would beat Mary daily more or less. He always hit her about the body so her injuries wouldn't show. Mary finally managed to tell her family. The brothers had a 'word' with Kevin. He sobbed in apology, and swore it wouldn't happen again. He loved her! Mary went back to Kevin. Marriage is for life, after all.

He left her alone for a week or two. She did something, burnt his dinner or forgot to iron his shirts or something. It was no good. She was asking for it. After all that had happened! The beatings started again.

Mary went out one morning after Kevin had gone to work. She walked to the local tube station and stood on the northbound platform among the commuters. She watched a couple of trains pass. Nobody noticed Mary. Nobody noticed the stooped figure with the empty eyes. Everyone that was there took notice of Mary when she threw herself under the next train. Everyone noticed Mary. Death noticed Mary and took her away.

World Weary Detective
worldwearydetective.blogspot.com

Rafael Behr notes a tragic collision of two of humanity's abiding passions – a thirst for knowledge and high-powered weaponry. There is one unanswered question that calls to another passion: how did it taste?

 May 2006 – It's a metaphor for something, but I don't know what

On 26 April the world's first known grizzly bear/polar bear hybrid was discovered in the wilds of Canada. How did anyone get close enough to tell it was a grizzly–polar cross?

They shot it dead, of course.

Rafael Behr
rafaelbehr.typepad.com

Why ban potentially lethal guns but not potentially lethal margarine? It's all to do with the fun-to-killing ratio, explains John Band.

 August 2006 – It's morally right that people should die for my amusement

The BBC website has a reasonably sensible, if not impartial, article by a sports shooter[1] about guns – specifically, on how they're fun and basically safe, except for the very rare occasions when evil people get hold of them and go massacring.

Unsurprisingly, the 'Have Your Say' comments are full of the usual suspects saying things like '*aha, you said "except sometimes". How dare you expect even one innocent person to die for your fun?*' This argument is generally hard to refute without sounding callous, but it's wrong.

If something provides sufficient net quantities of fun, it is easy to see that we do rate it as worth the death of one or several innocent people. How's that? Easy. Such beneficial-only-because-fun activities that kill the innocent and non-consenting as funfairs, fast cars, aviation, skateboarding, allowing men out at night, swimming pools and serving margarine to kids are both legal and socially acceptable.

Hence, society (here meaning 'everyone who is capable of even the most basic level of moral debate') agrees that if enough fun is provided, the deaths-for-fun trade-off is acceptable. The only moral question left is over the necessary fun-to-killing ratio.

That isn't quite true, philosophically speaking – there's also a question over agent-related morality. We can accept a certain level of deaths as a consequence of where we set fun levels (we know some people will have aeroplanes crash into their houses as an inevitable consequence of mass aviation), but we can't deliberately kill a whole bunch of people for our amusement (hence popular revulsion at *Running Man*-style sci-fi concepts). This is a side debate with no relevance to gun policy, however.

Returning to the main point, the only reason to justify a government-imposed ban on guns would be that they're not fun enough to outweigh the harm they cause. At this point, things like guns being less dangerous than swimming pools[2] might come

[1] news.bbc.co.uk/1/hi/magazine/5231062.stm
[2] timlambert.org/2001/07/levittpoolsvsguns/

into play (and quite possibly be refuted by the fact that they're also less fun). Either way, at least we'd be dealing with a debate rather than a witless moral panic.

John Band
www.thesharpener.net

August saw the departure of a much-loved classic. As A Dodo writes this touching obituary.

 August 2006 – Albert Camus' *The Outsider* 1942–2006

Albert Camus' novel *The Outsider* (L'étranger in the original French) died today. Or maybe yesterday. The world-famous absurdist novel, about a man who shoots an Arab for no reason and then refuses to feel guilty for what he has done, was wounded in a fatal explosion of irony at the weekend when it was revealed that the book was at the heart of President George Bush's summer reading.

The Outsider was born in 1942 to a union of absurdist philosophy and the retired goalkeeper of the University of Algiers second XI. A precocious child, by the late 1940s it was already to be seen hanging around with the likes of Jack Kerouac, its habit of wearing black polo-neck sweaters and chain-smoking Gauloises cigarettes, along with its habitual cry of 'Je suis l'étranger, daddio' making it easy to spot on its trips outside the smoke-filled interiors of bebop jazz clubs.

Tiring of its dim surroundings, *The Outsider* soon found itself migrating to university campuses across the globe. It came to Britain in the 1950s where it soon became famed among duffel-coated male students as the key to French philosophy, to the coolness of alienation and to copping off with female students. With its influence ever-increasing, by the late 1960s *The Outsider* was to be found at the head of protests and sit-ins across the globe, from the riot-torn streets of Paris to the slightly disordered desks of the Pinner College Upper VIth Form Geography Class.

As both it and its friends drifted into middle age, *The Outsider* began to abandon its radical past, eventually being persuaded to appear on A-level syllabuses, where it was to confuse generations of teenagers. Despite this it was occasionally to be found, looking a little tattered, hanging around in coffee bars with would-be intellectuals, a cigarette dangling from its lips, still trying to impress young women.

Albert Camus' *The Outsider* will be buried in a student flat, beneath several posters of Che Guevara, some Leonard Cohen CDs and a rucksack full of dirty washing due to be taken back to mum next weekend. Anyone who does not cry will be hanged.

As A Dodo
asadodo.blogspot.com

John Brissenden remembers a friend killed on September 11, 2001 and takes stock of the War Against Terror as fought so far.

 September 2006 – War Against Terror? I'll take me chances.

I have a picture of Sarah Ali from London. She and I were workmates and friends in our early 20s. She was the life and soul of the party – as a Muslim, Sarah probably didn't let on to mum and dad quite how much she enjoyed a knees-up after work. We hadn't been in touch for years, until I saw her picture plastered all over the front page of *The Sun* shortly after 9/11. She was killed in the World Trade Center as she was preparing for a marketing conference. She was 35, recently married. Had she lived, she would have been 40 this year, probably with young children. But she didn't live. She was either vaporised, suffocated, crushed, burnt to death or just jumped to escape being incinerated.

When I read the report, I called *The Sun*'s reporter, and he agreed to forward a letter of condolence to her parents. Seeing Sarah's beautiful face staring out from the paper hit me like the proverbial ton of bricks. But as a parent myself, I could guess at the hell Sarah's mum and dad had entered. The deep sadness that September 11 had thrown over us all (anyone remember that?) hardened into a visceral grief for Sarah, her family, and the countless others killed or affected by the attacks. How could we make sure nothing like that ever happened again?

Another 2996 souls are confirmed[1] dead or missing as a consequence of the attacks

[1] en.wikipedia.org/wiki/September_11,_2001_attacks

in New York City, Washington, DC and Pennsylvania on 11 September, 2001. According to today's Independent[2], the ensuing so-called War Against Terror has claimed anything from 62 000–180 000 lives and counting, and the United States alone has spent $437bn (£254bn) on TWAT.

Never mind the arguments about imperialism, a 'clash of civilisations', spreading freedom, standing up to fascism or any of the other self-regarding nonsense that we bloggers spew out day after day. Just do the sums and tell me that the endless bloodlust since 2001 in any way makes up for Sarah's murder. In the UK, the risk of winding up among the 52 killed by the explosions on 7 July 2005 is dwarfed by the risk of being one of the 35 000 killed every year on British roads. Similarly, the risk in living or working in Manhattan is infinitesimal compared to being at the sharp end of our depleted-uranium Armageddon in Afghanistan, Iraq, Lebanon and – once November's midterms are out the way – Iran. I'll take my chances with good police work against lunatic bombers any day, if this is the alternative.

Konichiwa Bitches
brisso99.typepad.com

[2] news.independent.co.uk/world/politics/article1433404.ece

Mr Eugenides marks the passing of a True Aussie Hero.

 September 2006 – At least a croc didn't get him

The World's Greatest Australian is dead [1]:

> A DOCTOR has told of the desperate efforts to save Australian icon Steve Irwin after the Crocodile Hunter was struck in the chest by a stingray barb today.
>
> Irwin, 44, died this morning after being fatally injured while filming a nature documentary off Queensland. The news has shocked the nation and prompted a rush of tributes from politicians and the public alike.

And I thought the crazy bastard would never die. Still, at least he went doing what he loved – enraging dangerous animals by repeatedly poking them. Most of us will lie undiscovered under a pile of beer cans for 3 days. At least I will.

Mr Eugenides
mreugenides.blogspot.com

[1] www.news.com.au/story/0,23599,20349888-2,00.html

Running, Jumping and Standing Still
Sport

Physical and sporting activity is to many bloggers as sexual intercourse is to the human species: sweaty and exciting; but – while vital to our survival – a lot of us aren't getting very much. That said, there's many a blogger out there who can talk the talk if not necessarily walk the walk or jog the jog.

Amongst the major sporting events of the year, the FIFA World Cup was a stand-out. What went wrong for England, cried the nation. Was it the team's strikeforce that consisted of two who were injured, a slip of a lad who'd never set foot in the Premiership, and a daddy-long legs who had to invent a robotic dance in order to endear himself to the fans? Was it the overpaid manager who was unable to give the same shafting to the opposition teams as he'd lent his lady acquaintances? Some of the articles here will try to lay bare the heart of the conundrum.

So, adjust your box, grab your half-time orange, change your tyres and scrum down. New balls please.

Mr Angry calls for radical reform of the Winter Olympics.

 February 2006 – Winter Olympics my ass!

I noticed that the 2006 Winter Olympics are now well underway in Italy. I'm not a huge fan, however I must admit I've glanced at the TV in the last couple of days to see the events going on in Sestriere, Turin and the like.

There is something utterly compelling about watching some smug French twat on skis almost throw himself off the edge of a mountain at 80 mph.

Go on.

Fall, you bastard!

However, this level of pulse-racing excitement is not true of all the events in Italy. Oh no.

Have you actually seen the curling? The British team were doing OK last time I looked, but this has to be the most ridiculous 'sport' imaginable. Essentially one guy throws a big kettle down the ice and a couple of others frantically sweep up ahead of it (in much the way I tidy up if I'm entertaining a lady friend whose arrival is imminent). How someone deserves to win an Olympic medal for that I'll never know.

More to the point, surely the title 'Winter' is misleading? Did you know that Britain's most popular winter sport is football? Second is rugby. I don't see either of these on the timetable in Italy. If you have time to do the research (I can't be arsed) I think you'll also find there are more people playing darts, pool and skittles this winter than you'll find chucking kettles around at the local ice rink.

Perhaps the 'Snow and Ice' Olympics would be better? And if it is going to be just snow and ice events, what about the events we had at school, those that we competed in religiously each break-time in our youth? I give you, the 'Alternative Winter Olympics':

1. The longest skid on your feet

Each competitor must run at full speed (in full school uniform) to the allotted marker, at which point the skid must commence; the skid ends when something other than your feet hits the ground, you come to a halt either due to lack of momentum, or are hit by a competitor of Event 2, below.

2. Furthest/most accurate snowball throw

Each competitor must launch a snowball, without rocks hidden inside (ice may be allowed), either the furthest distance, or with the most accuracy. Extra points given for hitting a moving target (see events above and below).

3. Fastest hill descent on a plastic bag

The forerunner to today's Luge event, competitors must propel themselves from the top of a hill at maximum velocity on a plastic bag (use of the 10p reusable variety is acceptable; using the big council refuse sacks is not). Again, be aware of competitors of Event 2. Points given for speed, distance and spectators 'clipped'.

4. Biggest human snowball

Deep powder isn't just for snowboarders. Another hill game this one. Each competitor must roll down the hill whilst gathering as much snow as possible on the way down. A tip: put your money on the fat kid.

I'd watch those if they were hosted by Sue Barker. Maybe we could be a bit creative in the events too; if the Summer Olympics can introduce synchronised swimming and beach volley ball, perhaps nude (female) snowboarding or 'snow burial' (the bullied kids out there will tell you all about it) could be incorporated in the next Winter Games?

In the meantime I'll console myself watching spandex-clad skiers in the hope of seeing one fly off-piste like a fucking dart.

I am livid
www.iamlivid.com

Golf club membership fees as an indicator of economic growth? Yes indeed, says our man in Tokyo, Lee Chapman.

 March 2006 – Golfing Gauge

Thursday saw the Nikkei close at its highest level in over 5 years, indicating that after numerous false starts the Japanese economy is now fairly racing down the road to recovery. But along with the Nikkei and rising land prices proving that Japan's battered economy is on the mend, another reliable gauge is rather surprisingly golf – or more accurately the sport's fluctuating club membership fees.

Whilst the game of golf itself is no different in Japan, the leisurely sport has had a few tweaks here and there, giving it a very different feel – both physically and financially. To begin with, playing 18 holes from start to finish is simply not possible, as regardless of what time you tee-off, it's nine holes followed by lunch and a few drinks. Then with a heavy stomach and a considerably lighter head, it's out on the course again to finish off the round. Yet any club choice or shot confusion brought about by lunchtime excesses will be gently eased by the wise words of your 'caddie-san', a middle-aged lady wearing unusual headgear who will clean your balls, wipe your shaft, and offer words of advice and encouragement during your trials and tribulations. All for a modest fee of course.

However, it's the aforementioned membership fees that really separate the Japanese game from its international cousins, and as mentioned prior to the digression, they are a good indicator of economic health. Mirroring the rise of land prices, the average membership cost of around 300 courses in the east of the country used to be 2.7 million yen (£13,000), but since November that has jumped considerably to a rather more hefty 3.5 million (£17,000).

These prices, though, are at the cheaper end of things, and it's at the middle- and high-ranking clubs that a bigger increase has taken place, with retiring baby boomers causing costs to more than double from their post-bubble lows. The Tokyo Yomiuri Country Club is a prime example of this trend, as after membership bottomed out at a not exactly insubstantial 18 million yen (£87,000) in 2003, it now stands at a mind-boggling 43 million (£210,000).

Yet even such figures pale into insignificance when compared with the Koganei

Country Club. This most exclusive of courses in western Tokyo is the leading barometer when it comes to the overall market, and during the bubble its membership soared to a truly astronomical 450 million yen (£2m), not surprisingly making it the most expensive club in Japan. Now whilst times have obviously changed, ensconcing oneself in the plush Koganei clubhouse will still currently cost a cool 65 million yen (£317,000). A figure that despite its almost otherworldly qualities looks set to continue rising, with analysts keeping a close eye on its movements.

Whilst almost everyone else looks on in open-mouthed disbelief.

Tokyo Times
www.tokyotimes.org

Hammers fan, Iain Dale, files an emotional report after the 2006 FA Cup.

 May 2006 – My FA Cup emotional roller coaster

I am in a bit of an emotional state as I type this. First, let me say it was an absolute privilege to have attended one of the greatest FA Cup Finals in history. There were three winners in this game. Liverpool, West Ham and football itself. I spent most of the game on the verge of tears and could quite easily howl my eyes out now. I don't know how it appeared on TV but West Ham were superb for most of the game and were only outplayed by one player: Steven Gerrard. If he hadn't been in the Liverpool team the result today would have been very different.

My team did its supporters proud and I salute every single one of them. It was a team performance and I can't think of a single player who had a bad game. Despite conceding three goals you can't fault either Shaka Hislop or the defence. Carl Fletcher and Nigel Reo-Coker were outstanding in midfield and Yossi Benayoun was a constant problem for the Liverpool defenders. Even Lionel Scaloni had a great game, even if it was from his clearance that Gerrard equalised in the 90th minute. I think when Steven Gerrard scored that third goal we all knew the writing was on the wall. Somehow the crowd's mood changed. But even then we nearly won it in the last minute of extra time. We hit the post and if Marlon Harewood hadn't been crippled he would have undoubtedly scored the rebound. It's the same old story of having to take your chances when they present themselves.

I cannot describe how I feel at the moment. I don't actually feel as if we lost the game. And to be honest, if we had won the penalty shoot-out I am not sure I would have felt we had won it 'properly'. That's why everyone came out of that game on top. And next season we're in Europe. Who would have thought it back in August. I remember the first 45 minutes of our opening home game against Blackburn and thinking we would be facing a relegation fight. Far from it. Top Ten finish. FA Cup finalists. Qualified for Europe. And Alan Pardew must surely be the Manager of the Year. So, no more football until the World Cup (some of you will be relieved to hear). And tonight? For someone who doesn't drink, I think I am going to get very, very drunk...

Iain Dale's Diary
iaindale.blogspot.com

Lucy, continuing her Spinster's Quest, thinks she's hit upon a masterplan. Where better to find a man than at the...

 June 2006 – Football

A friend received a letter from her young niece recently, saying 'Dear Auntie Sarah, Granny bought us goldfish on Saturday. I've called mine Sissy, Holly's called hers Holly and Luke's called his Frank Lampard.'

It demonstrated one of the fundamental differences between men and women. Football.

For men, football is religion. For women, if it is on their list of favourite things at all, it is at the bottom, wedged somewhere between 'pork crackling' and 'wearing hats'.

It has been professed (by cynical friends) that looking for love in a bar where football is on will lead to disaster, as men will be drunk and only interested in the game. However there is a proven formula. A big game + a big screen = lots of predominantly straight men.

BUT I do need a meticulous strategy. If I stand timidly in a corner behind someone who's 6'4" I will not find love.

I must:

1) Thoroughly scope the venue.

I have chosen a cavernous pub in the West End. Male friend comes here sometimes. It has a mezzanine level. He likes to stand there looking down on the flock of girls in low cut-tops, like Jesus but not so brotherly. He calls this booby heaven. This vantage point will be good for scoping.

2) Select subject and approach.

I shall pretend I've lost a friend. I will walk around scanning the room for my 'female friend', thus getting me up close to my subject. Then I will stand near him looking neither desperate nor alarming but quietly concerned for the whereabouts of my friend.

3) Follow up with a good opening line of conversation.

My Dad maintains that you should always start a letter or tricky conversation with something the other person wants to hear. So, 'You're the best looking person in here, can I chat to you till my friend comes back from the loo?', or 'Are you in a band?' seem promising.

I dress in what is known as 'school teacher chic'. It is a lot like 'prim secretary' but the shoes aren't so nice, since I expect to get beer on them.

I queue and pay. The bar is heaving. The smell of lager, cigarettes and man-sweat is divine. I feel like a woman. Men part so I can get to the bar. They say hello and smile. I buy a classy Hoegaarden. Not the best choice as I had some rather spicy sausages for dinner and the gas is making me burpy.

On the way up to booby heaven, I fall in love. He is a cherub. He has curly hair framing his face. He is slightly chubby. We do one of those meet-head-on-which-side-shall-we-move-to dances. He smiles. I could make it my life's mission to keep that smile on his face.

I stay near Cherub Man, looking slightly timid and concerned for my friend's whereabouts.

Suddenly a big fat bloke in an England vest joins me. He looks like the curry-smelling man who once sat next to me (and largely on me) during an 8-hour coach journey to Glasgow. He has one tooth at the front where most people have two. I think he says,

'You're too pretty to be on your own.'

They're my bloody tactics!

I smile because the convent taught me to be nice to everyone. Then I think he says something about Wayne Rooney.

'I've got legs like Wayne Rooney', I say. I'm not really sure why. It was just the first thing that came into my head.

It's also sadly true.

A little bit of his spit lands on me as he laughs.

'So has my ex-wife,' he says

'Bollocks', I think.

The match starts. It's quite good. How can they run so much?

I realise that one day in Heaven the angels were playing in God's garage where He had been working on his Perfect Man Creation. The naughty angels dropped the Perfect Man Creation and down he fell to Earth where he became known as Ashley Cole. In my mind we are childhood sweethearts, parted at the moment so I can concentrate on my acting, waitressing and blogging careers and he on his football. He is only helping the pretty one from Girls Aloud as a publicity stunt to draw attention away from the facts that she is violent and can't sing a note. We will be in

Tuscany together soon, with my cute younger brother, Lennon.

Suddenly my head is in Big Fat Bloke's armpit. Someone has scored. I must concentrate.

I get quite good at the 'upward punch in the air' when a player does something well. My favourite is the 'Polish waitress without a boyfriend' sulk, when someone misses a pass.

This is fun.

Half time and Big Fat Bloke goes to the loo. I try not to picture it.

Cherub Man smiles at me. I check behind. No, definitely at me.

'Where's your boyfriend?'

'Um, he's not my boyfriend, he's my minder. I call him the Beast II'

He laughs!

'No, I don't have a boyfriend and I've only just met him.'

'I can't believe you don't have a boyfriend.'

This cavernous pub in the West End is actually heaven.

'Well, I'm phenomenally funny and clever so I tend to intimidate most men.'

He laughs!! I beg myself not to speak again because I know I will cock it up. I'm trying desperately hard not to belch. I look at the screen and the half time commentators. Must not look too keen.

'Would you like a drink?'

It's the spinster's first conquest. She shoots, she scores.

'Yes please oh thank you, I think a white wine though, this beer makes me burp.'

I'm quickly introduced to his best friend's brother standing next to him. Beast II returns. The match starts again. We become a little dysfunctional family, sulking, punching and groaning. The boys score again. This time I land in Cherub Man's armpit.

I love football.

The match ends. Cherub Man says he has to go back to work for an hour or so. He asks me if I would like to meet up with him and some friends later. I say that I wish I could but I can't.

He says, 'I'm moving to Australia next week so I'm quite busy, but I'd really like to see you again before I go.'

'Oh wow! That's great! How exciting, Australia's an amazing place.'

Bloody Australia. Everyone's bloody well moving there.

I look at him. I wish he were staying. I give him my number. I say goodbye. I won't see him before he goes. It would be pointless. I desperately pray that he hates it and comes home in a fortnight.

The Beast II gives me bestial hug goodbye. The pressure causes me to release a long, satisfying, hour-long held-in burp. Bliss. I think I feel the cavern floor shake slightly.

'Good Girl!' he says with pride. 'You even sound like my ex-wife now.'

I leave the pub feeling a little discombobulated.

I think I might buy a goldfish and call him Ashley Cole.

Perhaps I should get him a friend called Lucy.

A Spinster's Quest
www.spinstersquest.com

The Blithering Bunny gives Venus Williams both barrels over her calls for equal pay between male and female tennis players.

 June 2006 – Venus as a downtrodden black girl

Venus Williams has a self-worth problem[1]. It's not enough being a vastly rich and successful sports champion. She's slightly undervalued, financially speaking, during the month of June, and this makes her feel like a sad teenage girl with spots. Hide the kiddies' art set! She's going to start cutting herself with Stanley knives any moment now!

What she means is that she is paid very slightly less than the men are at Wimbledon (which, actually, is not true; she's paid very slightly less than the very top men are, but much more than the majority of the men).

So the decision of the All England Lawn Tennis Club yet again to treat women as lesser players than men – undeserving of the same amount of prize money – has a particular sting.

And this, apparently, is an outrage against equality. It makes women into 'second-class citizens'. In a full-length ~~rant~~ article for *The Times*, she says she's

> 'disappointed that the home of tennis is sending a message to women across the world that we are inferior'.

That bottle of painkillers is looking particularly good to her right now. But wait, there's historical analysis as well:

> 'How can it be that Wimbledon finds itself on the wrong side of history? How can the words "Wimbledon" and "inequality" be allowed to coexist?'

Now, surely even Venus Williams isn't stupid enough to think that Wimbledon is on the 'wrong side of history'?. The gulags, the 'final solution', the Spanish Inquisition, and Wimbledon... doesn't really ring true, does it? You'd have to be some sort of modern

[1] www.timesonline.co.uk/article/0,,1072-2243249,00.html

humanities graduate from an American liberal arts college to believe what is precisely the opposite of the truth (that Wimbledon is in fact one of the symbols of civilization). No doubt that's who really wrote the article. Or else it was Billy Jean King.

Imagine! Imagine hitting balls across a net once every 2 days for a couple of weeks and only being paid £625 000 for it, rather than £650 000! The amount of outrage that Williams (or her ghostwriter) manages to squeeze out of this fact makes your petty concerns look rather, well, petty. From the way she writes you'd think she'd been sacked from her job, was losing her house, and has cancer caused by petroleum companies putting petrol fumes down her chimney at night. But no, her concerns are more lofty, she's concerned with the diminishment of the job as role model that she and all those other noble female tennis players like the gentlewomen Anna Kournikova, Mary Pierce, and Maria Sharapova perform (who else is going to teach young ladies how to continually shriek like madwomen and complain about decisions that go against them?).

I believe that athletes – especially female athletes in the world's leading sport for women – should serve as role models.

Personally, I like to think that I'm a role model for aspiring snarky bloggers. But do I get paid as much as Instapundit? No. No, I get paid nothing at all for doing this. Clearly something has gone wrong in the wonderfully fair system that Williams envisages, and she can start improving matters by sending some of the vast hoards of money that tennis players have been mistakenly receiving through some oversight to me straight away.

The idiocy in this sort of plea is that becoming filthy rich by playing tennis hardly fits the bill for equality. If we took Williams' pretend concerns seriously then we should start taking more money off the tennis players and giving it to the poor (a bad idea, of course, but why does her argument only apply to her and Federer?). She only makes this much money in the first place because of free markets. Take that away and let the state hand out the salaries and she's be back where tennis players were only a few decades ago — amateurs. AMATEURS, you stupid jock! How much did The Newk get paid for winning Wimbledon in 1967? Williams says:

> *'I'm disappointed not for myself but for all of my fellow women players who have struggled so hard to get here and who, just like the men, give their all on the courts of SW19. I'm disappointed for the great legends*

*of the game, such as Billie Jean King, Martina Navratilova and Chris
Evert, who have never stopped fighting for equality.'*

For most of this century tennis players made nothing at all by struggling so hard to get
to Wimbledon and winning it. So rather than give even more money to such prime
modern athletes as Lindsay Davenport, they should start docking their pay and right
some wrongs by sending some cheques out to Ellsworth Vines, Budge Patty and Cilly
Aussem, and the estates of Joshua Pim, Blanche Bingley Hillyard and Reggie Doherty.

So Williams only makes so much money in the first place because of the market and
the comparative advantage and the freedom of private organizations like Wimbledon
to set the prize money as they see fit. If that means women don't always get paid quite
the same as the men in the occasional event, then so be it. That's the price she has to
pay for getting so much money in the first place. Or rather, that's not a price she has
to pay, because she's making so much more money than she otherwise would. You
wouldn't hear Williams complaining if they paid women more money on the basis
that they get more TV viewers; no, that would just be free markets in action.

In fact, Williams' claims are pretty offensive, because the presumption implicit in
her article is that the less you're paid, the more you're entitled to feel like a worthless
piece of shit. But most of us get paid enormously less than Williams does. There are
even plenty of people at work who get paid much more than I do. So by her logic,
everyone except Rupert Murdoch and the guy who made Crazy Frog should be
eyeing up the ceiling joists for points of support.

But hang on – Venus deserves her money, because she's the best!

Maybe that's why I feel so strongly that Wimbledon's stance devalues the principle
of meritocracy…

Actually, there are thousands of people in the world who can beat Venus easily at
tennis. If you resort to the meritocracy angle you could argue that paying women
at all for most sports is not meritocratic. And she can't perform surgery, she isn't
qualified to audit your books, she probably can't fix a car engine, or write computer
software, or play the harpsichord. She isn't as good at analytic philosophy as I am.
And she's probably not as good at gardening as Mrs Bunny is. Yet she gets paid more
than 99.9% of people who have ever existed, most of whom are better than her at
lots of things. The only way anything resembling a coherent meritocracy can be run

is to let a free market operate. If you do well out of it, it's best to keep your gob shut when it comes to equality.

Blithering Bunny
www.blitheringbunny.com

June saw the World Cup and its attendant frenzy back in Europe: the retina-scorching action, the drone of pedantic commentators, the wreckage of so many over-inflated expectations dashed on the rocks of reality, and the inevitable booze-induced chair throwing. Here, Harry Hutton celebrates the England fan.

 June 2006 – World Cup diary

The World Cup is always a magical time for me. It takes me back to my childhood, standing on the terraces at Wigan with my old Dad, eatin' pies.

I never found out what we were doing there. I hated football, and my father was mostly into elephant polo. Nor did he ever give me any of his pies. I remember when I was eight he said to me, 'You're basically just an arsehole.'

Apparently, a lot of black Britons are supporting African teams in this tournament. A couple of World Cups ago I was in Rafah in the Gaza Strip, and the Palestinians were all cheering for Tunisia and Morocco, and dusty places generally. Yet Europeans don't seem to be afflicted by this kind of ethnic solidarity. At any rate, when Sweden score I don't think, 'Yes! Another victory for the whites!'

If anything, it slightly annoys me when they win. They think they are so great with their social spending. 'Ve are not haffing the beggars in Sveeden'. As far as I'm concerned, they can get stuffed.

Oh to be in England, now that football's there, to drive around beeping my car horn like a cunt, and taunt my idiot countrymen in German. 'Ha! Ha! One-nil, Englisher dumbkopfs'. The expression of hatred on their dim, resentful faces is one of the things that make life worth living.

Most of them are too thick even to insult me properly, although sometimes they'll come back with, 'Two World Wars and one World Cup'; which I always counter with 'Three World Cups and one economic miracle,' and then Deutschland Uber Alles or the Horst Wessel song. During Italia '90 I got in three different fights. It's always a magical time for me.

Chase me, ladies, I'm in the cavalry
chasemeladies.blogspot.com

The tournament's final will be remembered for Zinedine Zidane's sending off. Here, Daniel Davies eulogises a football player, for once, being ruled by his head rather than his heart.

 July 2006 – It was a wonderful headbutt

In the world of football, I suppose, Zinedine Zidane's legacy will always be controversial, forever tainted by his moment of madness in the World Cup Final. In the world of headbutting, however, he has secured a place in the gallery of immortals.

Oh, it was a great headbutt. Connoisseurs of the noble art of the headbutt[1] have very few opportunities to see a genuinely world-class practitioner in action; it is a banned tactic in the Ultimate Fighting Championship[2] these days. And Jimmy Nail isn't on the telly as much as he used to be. But Zidane's was a classic.

He just did everything right. There are many elements to the perfect headbutt, of which Zidane's size and strength were perhaps the least important. I was much more impressed with his technique, which was practically flawless. I am sure that Materazzi would agree with this assessment; perhaps for the first time in his life, he was left flying through the air and falling over because of actually being hit. I suppose the football fans will be less than pleased with the example that Zinedine set, but a young headbutter really could do no better than to emulate him in every detail.

[1] en.wikipedia.org/wiki/Testa
[2] en.wikipedia.org/wiki/Ultimate_Fighting_Championship

Surprise is always an important part of the butt. Unlike a punch, the headbutt is set into motion without any big wind-up or chambering action. It's initiated simply by making the decision not to stop walking toward someone, with the final snap of the head simply ensuring that the targeting is right (as you can see in this clip[3], the power is all coming from his legs and waist). This is probably why Materazzi flew so far; he wasn't ready for it at all, and the impact of more or less the entire body weight of a big man is always going to send someone flying.

Zidane also showed a characteristic intelligence and subtlety by planting the butt in the chest, rather than following the more conventional 'Glasgow Kiss' and butting head-to-head. Head-to-head butting is always a bit of a lottery, as the attacker is bound to suffer some damage himself, and you can never tell when someone has an unusually hard skull. Also, the conventional head-to-head butt is more suited to a situation where one is standing still, because it requires precise aiming (the idea is to make contact between one's own hairline and the bridge of the adversary's nose). As Zizou knew, his best bet given the distance he had to close was to select the large flat target of the chest and rely on sheer power rather than careful placement.

It was a headbutt not just for our age but for all time. Up there with the photographer who butted Jay Kay. It perhaps lacked the sheer destructive power of Duncan Ferguson in his pomp, but that can hardly be considered a criticism.

Perhaps nothing became Zidane's sublime career quite so much as the manner of his leaving it. The headbutt is perhaps the last vestige of the true Corinthian spirit in an increasingly sordid sporting world. Nobody gets rich from headbutts (even Mike Tyson started losing money when he began to rely on them). They are not even appreciated by sports fans, other than a small group of cognoscenti, so Zidane will probably never get the praise he deserves for 'punching with the big knuckle' in his last professional match. It was a truly selfless gesture on his part. And I maintain that the motivation is far less likely to have been anything Materazzi said, and far more likely to be the simple joy of the nod, the crack of skull on sternum and the slow, arching trajectory of a falling Italian striker. This world is truly not worthy of your genius, Zizou.

Daniel Davies
commentisfree.guardian.co.uk/daniel_davies/

[3] www.maj.com/gallery/JpegMasterJesse/Gifs/zidane.gif

Speaking of heads and hearts, in the aftermath of the tournament, Donald noted that if only football pundits would allow themselves to be ruled by the former rather than the latter, they might get it right more of the time.

 July 2006 – Thumbing the World Cup

A moderately successful World Cup on Betfair got me thinking about pundits and probabilities. Or, if you prefer, technocrats and managerialists. As any decent gambler will tell you, heuristics beat opinions. Thankfully, there aren't many of those about, or I'd never have bagged Switzerland at 4:5 to win a two-horse race between two teams with inseparable form.

But pundits, especially the telegenic breed you get on the Beeb and ('shudder') ITV, rarely use heuristic arguments[1]. Their trade is aphorism, cliché, blind prediction, ludicrous optimism and often erroneous morsels of common knowledge. Here are some I bottled during the last 4 weeks:

Pundit (P): England are a tournament team. They improve as the competition progresses.

Evidence for building the heuristic (H): England haven't eliminated a proper side from the knockout stages of any World Cup since 1966. They will lose to the first decent team they meet after the group stage.

P: Germany can't win. This is the poorest German side since, erm, the last time they reached the World Cup Final.

H: Hosts always do better than their form. Germans always do better than their form.

P: Having sailed through the group playing the best attacking football in the tournament, Germany can now go on and win it.

[1] en.wikipedia.org/wiki/Heuristic_argument

H: Germany haven't beaten a major footballing nation, in competition or friendly matches, anywhere, in 90 or 120 minutes, since 2001.

P: Italy can't win. Not a vintage side, match-fixing, Totti unfit, Del Piero past his best, no pace.

H: Italy haven't lost any World Cup match on European soil since 1974. They haven't been eliminated from any World Cup anywhere in 90 minutes since 1986.

P: Brazil will stroll it: Magic Quartet, blah, blah, blah.

H: Teams rarely retain the trophy, and certainly not with the same team that won the previous time. Italy tried it in 1986, Argentina in 1990, France in 2002. All failed. Plus the obvious: South American teams, bar 1958, never win in Europe.

P: This is England's Golden Generation. They will beat Portugal comfortably.

H: In four tournaments, England have reached three quarter-finals. In four tournaments Portugal have reached a final and two semis. This wasn't reflected in the respective prices, and hence value.

P: Argentina have the youth, skill, organization and talent to win the tournament.

H: Leaving aside playing at home (everyone bar the English knows that doesn't count), Argentina have never been past the quarter-finals without Maradona.

Of course, some of this was constructed with the benefit of hindsight (as heuristics must be). Some won't apply next time a World Cup comes around (it will be in Africa, for example, though intriguingly in a European time-zone). And maybe I've only thought this through in this way because I had cash at stake. In which case, despite all the well-grounded objections, perhaps demand-revealing referendums[2] really are the closest to ideal government we can hope to get.

The Sharpener
www.thesharpener.net

[2] **www.thesharpener.net/2006/05/03/dumps-and-deliberations/**

The Flying Rodent asks you to join him the bunker.

 August 2006 – War on Terror Getting You Down?

It's a drag, all this Warring Against Terror. During every ill-defined, murderous, morally dubious annexation of foreign oil, it's only natural that we should lose heart every now and then.

The eternal questions, 'Was it right to invade Iraq?', 'Was it right to bomb the almighty fuck out of all those Arabs?' and 'Jesus Christ, is that a brown guy with a backpack? Somebody call the firearms unit!'.

It's good to know that in these times of uncertainty there are 'just' wars, causes we can all truly believe in. Ladies and gentlemen, you are invited to tie a yellow ribbon round whatever you think most appropriate, hoist the flag and show your support for the troops bravely fighting in Venezuela's principled and righteous War on Golf[1].

> *The mayor of Venezuela's capital Caracas says he plans to expropriate two exclusive golf courses and use the land for homes for the city's poor... Mayor Juan Barreto has said playing golf on lavish courses within sight of the city's slums is 'shameful'...*
>
> *... Mr Barreto had ordered the 'forced acquisition' of the golf courses, city attorney Juan Manuel Vadell told the Associated Press... The golf courses... are in the city's most affluent suburbs, home to millionaires, foreign diplomats and celebrities, and are seen by some as a haven for the rich... Mr Barreto has said 5000 people could be housed in the space taken up by a single golf course.*

Now, don't get me wrong here – I couldn't give a damn about the suffering poor of Venezuelan slums, but I am deeply enthusiastic about anything that annoys golfers.

If, like me, you are rendered apoplectic by the sight of Pringle jumpers, now is our time. If ever a sub-group of society merited dehumanisation, persecution and the deprivation of their assets, it's golfers.

[1] news.bbc.co.uk/1/hi/world/americas/5297246.stm

I know whereof I speak – I hail from a part of Scotland where golfers outnumber normal human beings three-to-one, and hundreds of infernal 9- and 18-hole courses blot the landscape.

After all, we invented the accursed sport. A major tournament here is treated like the descent of Zeus and the celestial cohort from Mount Olympus, rather than a verminous infestation of tweedy dorks.

I remember the exact moment I was alerted to the full horror of golf. It was during whichever Ryder Cup it was that the American team decided to show up in full desert camo gear because the USAF had just blasted the fuck out of some tinpot Third World country or other, and proceeded to 'Hoo-ah!' their way around the course like the short, sharp shower of arseholes they were.

So, *hermanos,* let us take up arms and declare justified war upon golf and golfers. There is no need for murder, assuming they agree to come quietly.

Victimisation on grounds of religion, ethnicity or wealth is a dreadful crime against humanity.

But I say to you, extremism in pursuit of men who believe that pink jumpers and tartan trousers are acceptable attire is no vice.

Fore!

Between the Hammer and the Anvil
flyingrodent.blogspot.com

Mr Eugenides on the furore over Artur Boruc making the sign of the cross at an Old Firm football match. Our correspondent has a particular insight into what went on that many other commentators didn't.

 August 2006 – Football and sectarianism

There's a minor flap north of the border about this[1] (*Update*: pretty major, actually – the BBC briefly bumped it up to first item on the front page of their website):

> The Catholic Church has criticised Scottish prosecutors for cautioning the Celtic goalkeeper for crossing himself during a match against Rangers. Artur Boruc was cautioned for a breach of the peace over the incident at an Old Firm match at Ibrox in February.
>
> Peter Kearney, spokesman for the Catholic Church, said the move to caution Boruc was 'regrettable'. 'It's a worrying and alarming development, especially since the sign of the cross is globally accepted as a gesture of religious reverence', he said.
>
> 'It's also very common in international football and was commonplace throughout the World Cup. It is extremely regrettable that Scotland seems to have made itself one of the few countries in the world where this simply religious gesture is considered an offence'.
>
> Nationalist leader Alex Salmond also criticised the decision to caution the player. 'The procurator fiscal has taken leave of their senses. I will be demanding an explanation for this,' he said. He said the 'ludicrous' move is the type of action that brought the law and legal system into disrepute.

This is obviously a sensitive topic, but both Mr Kearney and Mr Salmond are talking shit, for reasons I will explain shortly.

For those unaware of the particular context of the 'Old Firm' game during which this

[1] news.bbc.co.uk/1/hi/uk/5288184.stm

incident took place, this[2] is a useful summary. Rangers and Celtic are traditionally associated with Glasgow's Protestant and Catholic communities respectively and, as Scotland's two most successful football clubs, the rivalry between them is intense, to put it mildly, and while in this secular age the religious tensions in the city are not what they were, there is undoubtedly a strong sectarian undercurrent in the clashes, which don't require much provocation to bring to the surface.

Rangers fans have recently been in trouble for singing 'The Billy Boys'[3], a song which can be heard at many football grounds in Scotland and England, but which in its Ibrox rendition contains the line 'Up to our knees in Fenian blood', which is generally taken as an anti-Catholic reference. For their part, the away supporters who follow Celtic on their travels do a charming line in pro-IRA ditties[4].

This incident took place in the second half of last season's third Old Firm derby at Rangers' Ibrox Park (with four league meetings and two domestic cup competitions, the two clubs can meet as often as six times a year). Celtic led 1-0 at the break, a result that, coupled with their very healthy lead in the league, would basically put their rivals out of the running for another year. As such, it was a disgruntled Rangers crowd that 'welcomed' Celtic onto the pitch for the second half, and a visiting team in celebratory mood.

This context helps explain what happened next. Artur Boruc, the Celtic goalkeeper, trotted towards his goal in front of the massed ranks of Rangers fans, who gave him hearty abuse as fans do. Boruc smiled, walked into his goal facing the fans, looked up at the crowd and slowly and deliberately crossed himself while still grinning at them. He then followed this up with a 'wanker' gesture to the supporters. Only then did he turn and concern himself with the imminent business at hand of winning a football match.

(Update: I should state for the sake of balance that I am informed by my Celtic-supporting friends that he performs 'a similar' ritual before each game at Celtic Park too, although I rather doubt that the obscene hand gesture forms part of the routine on those occasions.)

I'm able to describe the incident because, unlike Peter Kearney of the Catholic

[2] en.wikipedia.org/wiki/Old_Firm
[3] news.bbc.co.uk/sport1/hi/football/teams/r/rangers/5064472.stm
[4] scotlandonsunday.scotsman.com/sport.cfm?id=684352006

Church, and Alex Salmond of the SNP, I was present at the match and saw it – at fairly close hand. While I can be accused of bias, therefore – there are very few neutrals at a Rangers–Celtic game, and I wasn't one – I am not speaking from the position of ignorance inhabited by those two gentlemen, Mr Salmond in particular. I am trying to describe the incident, and my reaction to it, as honestly as I can.

Listening to Alex Salmond, and reading the initial reports on the BBC and elsewhere, you would think that Boruc had been cautioned for a private expression of faith. This is not the case. Had he blessed himself as he came on the pitch, as footballers round the world do, or had done so in his goal as the second half kicked off, as also occasionally happens, I would totally and unconditionally have defended his right to do so. Any police involvement would of course have been monstrous. But that is not what happened.

(*Update*: The BBC report has since been updated[5] to make reference to the 'other gestures' which Boruc made, and Jack McConnell has suggested rather acidly that politicians should think before they open their mouths, the breathtaking hypocrisy of which we will set aside for the time being.)

If you're reading this and shaking your head in disbelief, or disgust, that someone cannot make the sign of the Cross without its being interpreted as a provocation, I don't wholly disagree. There is still a great deal of intolerance in Scottish society as a whole, and there's no doubt that the ecumenicalism of some Rangers fans leaves a great deal to be desired. On the other hand, the manager of Rangers, and at least half the first team, are Roman Catholics, but this makes not the slightest difference to their standing among the fans. And as BBC Scotland has pointed out this lunchtime, the former Rangers captain Lorenzo Amoruso, an Italian Catholic, habitually crossed himself before matches without adverse comment (in Amo's case it was his shoddy passing, slapdash marking and habit of putting free kicks into the Clyde that riled the fans).

There is plenty of precedent for footballers to get in trouble for inflammatory gestures at Old Firm games. In 1987, four players were hauled up in court on breach of the peace charges, including the England no. 2 goalkeeper Chris Woods, and Rangers and England international defender Graham Roberts, who had stood in that same goal and conducted the Ibrox choir in the rendition of the Orange anthem '*The Sash My Father Wore*'[6] during a tempestuous Old Firm game. A decade later,

[5] news.bbc.co.uk/1/hi/scotland/5292656.stm
[6] en.wikipedia.org/wiki/The_Sash

another famous Englishman, Paul Gascoigne, incurred the beaks' wrath by miming the playing of a flute, a reference to the loyalist flute band tradition. (In the almighty row that broke out after that incident, Gazza was disciplined internally by Rangers and no further action was taken, but the hostile reaction, including a couple of verbal death threats, ensured the message got through even to this most cerebrally challenged of footballers that he had crossed an important line.)

Is conducting the crowd in song at a football match, or playing an imaginary musical instrument, a criminal offence? Should it even be worthy of comment? In the general run of things, of course not. Supporters give opposition players a great deal of abuse, but cry foul whenever there is the slightest reaction. This is clearly a double standard. But there is a duty on players, wherever they ply their trade, to be responsible when on the field: and in the white-hot atmosphere of a Rangers–Celtic game, this is doubly true. Context is all.

Many will feel that getting the police involved in this incident is giving the green light to bigots to try and stop players from honestly expressing their faith, and that would indeed be a terribly negative consequence. But this game needs, as I've argued, to be seen as the sporting manifestation of a wider issue; the Old Firm game is an astonishingly high-intensity clash, and its effects can be felt in terms of sporadic disorder throughout the West of Scotland for many hours after a game; anecdotal evidence[7] suggests that violence and stabbings experience a 'spike' on Old Firm weekends.

Boruc's actions need to be seen in this context. A police caution was, in my opinion, an excessive reaction to what is, or should be, a harmless gesture; neither Strathclyde's finest, nor the fans who reported the incident, emerge from this sorry affair in a very positive light. But let us be clear about this; the BBC report is inaccurate, the comments of Alex Salmond ignorant in the extreme, and those who've described this as a footballer being 'cautioned for being Christian' are, in my view, missing the bigger picture, as I've tried to argue. The player was not simply 'exercising his human rights'; he was trying to provoke the crowd, and must take his share of responsibility. In Glasgow, such provocation can have terrible consequences. It is not, unfortunately, just a football match.

Mr Eugenides
mreugenides.blogspot.com

[7] scotlandonsunday.scotsman.com/index.cfm?id=943692002

So that's it for another year. We leave things in September in order to get the book to the printers before the calendar year runs out. Who knows what the rest of the year might have brought us all? I hope the new prime minister/alien invasion/asteroid strike/Second Coming (delete as applicable) didn't prove too traumatic for you.

I hope you've enjoyed what you've read here. If you're hungry for more, check out Tim Worstall's weekly Brit-blog Roundup (timworstall.typepad.com), which collects the best of each week's blogging. Britblog.com, a directory of British blogs, is worth a browse, as is the Wikablog collection at www.wikablog.com.

If you've never blogged before and fancy giving it a go, your first stop should be Blogger (www.blogger.com), where you can have your own blog up and running within minutes. It's free and easy to set up. Some bloggers use Typepad (www.typepad.com), which hosts blogs for a monthly fee and offers more options than Blogger. If you're technically minded a WordPress (wordpress.org) blog on rented webspace has even more flexibility but there are costs and fiddling involved.

All you need then is a dash of original writing with halfway competent grammar and syntax ('which,' as George Orwell said, 'are of no importance so long as one makes one's meaning clear') and you're on your way. Post articles regularly and get involved in the discussions in your comments section. Blog anonymously or pseudonymously if you find that makes you feel less inhibited about writing. Most importantly: ENJOY YOURSELF.

Add a visitor counter – SiteMeter (sitemeter.com) is one of the most popular ones – and a few links to some of your favourite bloggers. They'll come and have a look, and if they like what you're doing they'll link to you in return. Blogging is, after all, a peer-reviewed medium and quality will out. If you're good, people will find you.

You never know, you might make The Blog Digest 2008.